Cyberpunk in a Transnational Context

Cyberpunk in a Transnational Context

Special Issue Editor

Takayuki Tatsumi

MDPI • Basel • Beijing • Wuhan • Barcelona • Belgrade

MDPI

Special Issue Editor
Takayuki Tatsumi
Keio University
Japan

Editorial Office
MDPI
St. Alban-Anlage 66
4052 Basel, Switzerland

This is a reprint of articles from the Special Issue published online in the open access journal *Arts* (ISSN 2076-0752) from 2018 to 2019 (available at: https://www.mdpi.com/journal/arts/special_issues/cyberpunk)

For citation purposes, cite each article independently as indicated on the article page online and as indicated below:

LastName, A.A.; LastName, B.B.; LastName, C.C. Article Title. *Journal Name* **Year**, *Article Number*, *Page Range*.

ISBN 978-3-03921-421-1 (Pbk)
ISBN 978-3-03921–422-8 (PDF)

Cover image courtesy of ni_ka: "Hikari" (Light).

Contents

About the Special Issue Editor vii

Preface to "Cyberpunk in a Transnational Context" ix

Takayuki Tatsumi
The Future of Cyberpunk Criticism: Introduction to Transpacific Cyberpunk
Reprinted from: *Arts* **2019**, *8*, 40, doi:10.3390/arts8010040 1

Mike Mosher
Some Aspects of California Cyberpunk
Reprinted from: *Arts* **2018**, 7, 54, doi:10.3390/arts7040054 4

Frenchy Lunning
Cyberpunk Redux: Dérives in the Rich Sightof Post-Anthropocentric Visuality
Reprinted from: *Arts* **2018**, 7, 38, doi:10.3390/arts7030038 16

Lidia Merás
European Cyberpunk Cinema
Reprinted from: *Arts* **2018**, 7, 45, doi:10.3390/arts7030045 29

Elana Gomel
Recycled Dystopias: Cyberpunk and the End of History
Reprinted from: *Arts* **2018**, 7, 31, doi:10.3390/arts7030031 46

Martin de la Iglesia
Has *Akira* Always Been a Cyberpunk Comic?
Reprinted from: *Arts* **2018**, 7, 32, doi:10.3390/arts7030032 54

Denis Taillandier
New Spaces for Old Motifs? The Virtual Worlds of Japanese Cyberpunk
Reprinted from: *Arts* **2018**, 7, 60, doi:10.3390/arts7040060 67

Janine Tobeck and Donald Jellerson
Caring about the Past, Present, and Future in William Gibson's *Pattern Recognition* and Guerrilla
Games' *Horizon: Zero Dawn*
Reprinted from: *Arts* **2018**, 7, 53, doi:10.3390/arts7040053 82

Takayuki Tatsumi
Transpacific Cyberpunk: Transgeneric Interactions between Prose, Cinema, and Manga
Reprinted from: *Arts* **2018**, 7, 9, doi:10.3390/arts7010009 100

About the Special Issue Editor

Takayuki Tatsumi has taught American Literature and Critical Theory at Keio University, Tokyo, since 1989. He served as President of The American Literature Society of Japan (2014–2017) and of The Poe Society of Japan (2009–), and as Vice President of the Melville Society of Japan (2012–). He is currently a member of the Editorial Board of PARADOXA, *Mark Twain Studies*, and the *Journal of Transnational American Studies*. His book *Full Metal Apache: Transactions between Cyberpunk Japan and Avant-Pop America* (Duke UP, 2006) won the 2010 IAFA (International Association for the Fantastic in the Arts) Distinguished Scholarship Award. Co-editor of the "New Japanese Fiction" issue of *Review of Contemporary Fiction* (Summer 2002), *Robot Ghosts, Wired Dreams* (U of Minnesota P, 2007), the special "Three Asias—Japan, S. Korea, China" issue of PARADOXA (No. 22, 2010) and *The Routledge Companion to Transnational American Studies* (Routledge, 2019), he has also published a variety of essays in *PMLA, Critique, Extrapolation, American Book Review, Mechademia, The Oxford Research Encyclopedia of Literature,* and elsewhere on subjects ranging from the American Renaissance to post-cyberpunk fiction and film. His recent collaborations include *The Cambridge History of Postmodern Literature (2016) and The Liverpool Companion to World Science Fiction Film* (2014). His recent monographs include: *Young Americans in Literature: The Post-Romantic Turn in the Age of Poe, Hawthorne and Melville* (Sairyusha, 2018).

Preface to "Cyberpunk in a Transnational Context"

Since the inception of cyberpunk in the early 1980s, which coincided with the dawn of the Internet and the rise of computer hackers, the movement, with William Gibson as super star and Bruce Sterling as theoretical chairman, has consistently created a tremendous impact on today's literature and culture, ranging from manga and anime to cinema. William Gibson's 1980s Cyberspace Trilogy (*Neuromancer* [1984], *Count Zero* [1986], and *Mona Lisa Overdrive* [1988]), which explored the frontier of cyberspace—another name for the Internet coined by the same author—was followed by his 1990s "Bridge Trilogy" (*Virtual Light* [1993], *Idoru* [1996], and *All Tomorrow's Parties* [1999]) featuring a virtual idol Rei Toei, without whom no AI Beauty (such as Hatsune Miku) could have been created. However, here we should reconsider the extraterritorial status of Gibson, who immigrated from South Carolina to Toronto, Canada, to evade the draft. Being a typical outsider, Gibson put special emphasis on the Lo-Tek spirit of a countercultural tribe in the post-apocalyptic near-future, and replace the keyword "steampunk" with "post-apocalypse". This was to be shared by the punk kids that Otomo describes in Akira and the human weapons distinguished director Shinya Tsukamoto represents in his *TETSUO* trilogy (1989–2010), one of the major inheritors of the Japanese Apache created by Komatsu Sakyo, a founding father of Japanese science fiction, in his first novel *Nippon Apacchi-zoku* (The *Japanese Apache* [1964]) as I detailed in *Full Metal Apache* (Duke UP, 2006). A further descendant of cyberpunk could well be easily noticed in Neil Blomkamp's South African post-cyberpunk film, *District 9* (2009), in which the natives of Johannesburg and the miserable aliens lost in space turn out to have the Lo-Tek spirit in common.

Yes, cyberpunk is a literary and (sub-)cultural subgenre not so much celebrating the growth of high-technology as the neo-extraterritorial spirit of Lo-Tek tribes born out of postmodern streets. What matters now is that, in this context, cyberpunk has started gaining new significance, not only in today's arts of representation, but also in international/transnational politics. The present collection of essays showcases a diversity of cyberpunk possibilities ranging from Cool Japan, Dystopian narrative down to the postmodern extraterritorial and Anthropocene.

Takayuki Tatsumi
Special Issue Editor

arts

MDPI

Editorial

The Future of Cyberpunk Criticism: Introduction to Transpacific Cyberpunk

Takayuki Tatsumi

Department of English, Keio University, Tokyo 108-8345, Japan; CXQ04644@nifty.com

Received: 19 March 2019; Accepted: 21 March 2019; Published: 25 March 2019

The genesis of cyberpunk criticism could well be dated to March 1987, when Stephen P. Brown inaugurated the first cyberpunk journal *Science Fiction Eye* together with his friend Daniel J. Steffan, with Paul DiFilippo, Elizabeth Hand, and myself as contributing editors. Of course, it is the impact of William Gibson's multiple-award-winning *Neuromancer* in 1984, featuring the anti-hero Case's adventures in what Gibson himself called "cyberspace," that aroused popular interest in the new style of speculative fiction. This surge of interest led Gibson's friend, writer Bruce Sterling, the editor of the legendary critical fanzine *Cheap Truth*, to serve as unofficial chairman of the brand-new movement. Thus, on 31 August 1985, the first cyberpunk panel took place at NASFiC (The North American Science Fiction Convention) in Austin, Texas, featuring writers in Sterling's circle: John Shirley, Lewis Shiner, Pat Cadigan, Greg Bear, and Rudy Rucker. As I was studying American literature at the graduate school of Cornell University during the mid-1980s, I was fortunate enough to witness this historical moment. After the panel, Sterling said, "Our time has come!" Thus, from the spring of 1986, I decided to conduct a series of interviews with cyberpunk writers, part of which are now easily available in Patrick A. Smith's edited *Conversations with William Gibson* (University Press of Mississippi 2014).

However, without Brown's plan in 1987 of publishing the new journal *Science Fiction Eye* focusing on cyberpunk criticism, my early interviews and articles could not have been published in their original form. It was in May 1986 at Disclave'86, the annual local science fiction convention held in the Washington D.C. area, that I could have my first interview with Gibson and come to know his close friend Steve Brown, who wanted me to get involved in his new project. Since then, Brown taught me everything he could about science fiction journalism. What is more, he provided me with whatever he found intriguing and necessary in this field. He sent me a copy of Jeanne Gomoll's monumental symposium on "Women in Science Fiction", featured in a fanzine called *Khatru* #3 and #4. It is true that the cyberpunk writer community is sometimes called another boys' club, with the exceptions of Pat Cadigan and Ellen Datlow, the legendary editor of the *OMNI* magazine who was nicknamed "the queen of cyberpunk." Nevertheless, Brown's editorship also opened up a heated discussion among feminist speculative fiction writers and critics such as Connie Willis, Pat Murphy, Karen Joy Fowler, Lucy Sussex, and Mari Kotani. Thus, the cyberpunk movement very naturally initiated me into the rise of cyborg feminism, as presaged by the proto-feminist and proto-cyberpunk writer James Tiptree, Jr in the 1970s, and firmly established by distinguished historian of science Donna Haraway of the University of California, Santa Cruz in the 1980s. At that point, I did not anticipate that Haraway's astonishing article "The Cyborg Manifesto" (1985) was to be admired in the 1990s as part of the canon of Cultural Studies. This article was first translated into Japanese by Mari Kotani and included in my edited book *Cyborg Feminism* (Treville 1991), along with the major African American speculative fictionist Samuel Delany's critique of Haraway, together with feminist heroic fantasy writer Jessica Amanda Salmonson's essay on Anne McCaffery's *The Ship Who Sang* (1969).

Thus, cyberpunk refreshed not only the science fiction criticism that had been cultivated by Anglo-American academic journals such as *Extrapolation*, *Foundation*, and *Science Fiction Studies*, but also critical theory as such in the wake of Franco-American structuralism, semiotics, and deconstruction, championed by Roland Barthes, Tzvetan Todorov, Michel Foucault, Paul de Man, and others. This is the reason why my friend Larry McCaffery of San Diego State University, the guru of Avant-Pop, included in his splendidly edited *Storming the Reality Studio: A Casebook of Cyberpunk and Postmodern Science Fiction* (Duke University Press 1991) not only hardcore cyberpunks but also postmodern theoreticians such as Jacques Derrida, Fredric Jameson, Jean Baudrillard, Arthur Kroker, Darko Suvin, and others. This casebook well deserves the name of the first academic collection of cyberpunk criticism that paved the way for critical theory to come in the age of the digital humanities.

In retrospect, since its inception in the early 1980s, which coincided with the dawn of the internet and the rise of computer hackers, the cyberpunk movement has had a tremendous impact on today's globalist literature and culture, ranging from manga and anime through to cinema. Bruce Sterling did not conceal his fascination with Japanese pop, such as the synthpop of Sandii and Sunsets. It is well known that William Gibson's 1980s Cyberspace Trilogy (*Neuromancer* [1984], *Count Zero* [1986], and *Mona Lisa Overdrive* [1988]), which explored the frontier of cyberspace, another name for the internet coined by the very author, was influenced not only by the punk rock of Lou Reed but also by the techno-pop of Yellow Magic Orchestra. Gibson's 1990s Bridge Trilogy (*Virtual Light* [1993], *Idoru* [1996], and *All Tomorrow's Parties* [1999]) featured a virtual idol, Rei Toei, who coincided with her real-life Japanese counterpart Kyoko Date, a 3D CG virtual girl developed by Hori Productions and without whom no AI Beauty, such as Hatsune Miku, could have been created in the heyday of Cool Japan here in the 21st century. While 1960s North American writers owed much to the counterculture developed on the West Coast, 1980s cyberpunks are more deeply indebted to transpacific negotiations.

By the same token, however, we should not neglect their extraterritorial status. While Bruce Sterling incorporated his childhood experience in India into his fiction and started to go back and forth between Texas and Europe since the 2000s, Gibson migrated in the mid-1970s from South Carolina to Toronto, Canada to evade the draft. Being a typical expatriate, Gibson put special emphasis upon the Lo-Tek (outlaw technologist) spirit of a post-countercultural tribe, which was to be shared by the punk kids Otomo describes in *Akira* and the human weapons that director Shinya Tsukamoto represents in his *TETSUO* trilogy (1989–2010). Tsukamoto, in turn, is one of the major inheritors of the "Japanese Apache" aesthetic created by Komatsu Sakyo, a Founding Father of Japanese science fiction in his first novel *Nippon Apacchi-zoku* (*The Japanese Apache* [1964]), as I detailed in *Full Metal Apache* (Duke UP 2006). A further descendant of cyberpunk could be found in Neil Blomkamp's South African post-cyberpunk film *District 9* (2009), in which the natives of Johannesburg and the miserable aliens lost in space turn out to have the Lo-Tek spirit in common.

Indeed, cyberpunk is not only a literary and (sub-)cultural subgenre optimistically celebrating the growth of high-technology, but it also embodies the neo-extraterritorial spirit of Lo-Tek tribes born out of the postmodern street. What matters now is that in this context, cyberpunk started gaining new significance not only in contemporary arts of representation but also in international/transnational critical theory.

As the guest editor of the special issue of *Arts* journal featuring "Cyberpunk in a Transnational Context," I feel very pleased to be able to present here a number of illuminating essays written by international authors who share my own interest in the future of critical theory.

Mike Mosher's (2018) "Some Aspects of Californian Cyberpunk" vividly reminds us of the influence of West Coast counterculture on cyberpunks, with special emphasis on 1960s theoretical gurus such as Timothy Leary and Marshall McLuhan, who explored the frontiers of inner space as well as the global village. Frenchy Lunning's (2018) "Cyberpunk Redux: Dérives in the Rich Sight of Post-Anthropocentric Visuality" examines how the heritage of Ridley Scott's techno-noir film *Blade Runner* (1982) that preceded Gibson's *Neuromancer* (1984) keeps revolutionizing the art of visuality, even in the age of the Anthropocene. If you read Lunning's essay along with Lidia Meras's (2018) "European Cyberpunk Cinema," which closely analyzes major European cyberpunkish dystopian films *Renaissance* (2006) and *Metropia* (2009) and Elana Gomel's (2018) "Recycled Distopias: Cyberpunk and the End of History," your understanding of the cinematic and post-utopian possibility of cyberpunk will become more comprehensive. For a cutting-edge critique of cyberpunk manga, let me recommend

Martin de la Iglesia's (2018) "Has *Akira* Always Been a Cyberpunk Comic?" which radically redefines the status of *Akira* (1982–1993) as trans-generic, paying attention to the genre consciousness of the contemporary readers of its Euro-American editions. Next, Denis Taillandier's (2018) "New Spaces for Old Motifs? The Virtual Worlds of Japanese Cyberpunk" interprets the significance of Japanese hardcore cyberpunk novels such as Goro Masaki's *Venus City* (1995) and Hirotaka Tobi's *Grandes Vacances* (2002; translated as *The Thousand Year Beach*, 2018) and *Ragged Girl* (2006), paying special attention to how the authors created their virtual landscape in a Japanese way. For a full discussion of William Gibson's works, please read Janine Tobek and Donald Jellerson's (2018) "Caring About the Past, Present, and Future in William Gibson's Pattern Recognition and Guerilla Games' Horizon: Zero Dawn" along with my own "Transpacific Cyberpunk: Transgeneric Interactions between Prose, Cinema, and Manga" (Tatsumi 2018). The former reconsiders the first novel of Gibson's new trilogy in the 21st century not as realistic but as participatory, and redefines its aesthetics with today's video game culture by renovating Walter Benjamin's philosophy. The latter relocates Gibson's essence not in cyberspace but in a junkyard, making the most of his post-Dada/Surrealistic aesthetics and "Lo-Tek" way of life, as is clear in the 1990s "Bridge" trilogy.

To sum up, this collection, which itself transgresses the boundaries between the literary and the visual, will undoubtedly provide you with the most concise introduction to cyberpunk criticism in the 21st century.

Funding: This research received no external funding.

Conflicts of Interest: The author declares no conflict of interest.

References

De la Iglesia, Martin. 2018. Has *Akira* Always Been a Cyberpunk Comic? *Arts* 7: 32. [CrossRef]

Gomel, Elana. 2018. Recycled Dystopias: Cyberpunk and the End of History. *Arts* 7: 31. [CrossRef]

Lunning, Frenchy. 2018. Cyberpunk Redux: Dérives in the Rich Sight of Post-Anthropocentric Visuality. *Arts* 7: 38. [CrossRef]

Merás, Lidia. 2018. European Cyberpunk Cinema. *Arts* 7: 45. [CrossRef]

Mosher, Mike. 2018. Some Aspects of California Cyberpunk. *Arts* 7: 54. [CrossRef]

Taillandier, Denis. 2018. New Spaces for Old Motifs? The Virtual Worlds of Japanese Cyberpunk. *Arts* 7: 60. [CrossRef]

Tatsumi, Takayuki. 2018. Transpacific Cyberpunk: Transgeneric Interactions between Prose, Cinema, and Manga. *Arts* 7: 9. [CrossRef]

Tobeck, Janine, and Donald Jellerson. 2018. Caring about the Past, Present, and Future in William Gibson's *Pattern Recognition* and Guerrilla Games' *Horizon: Zero Dawn*. *Arts* 7: 53. [CrossRef]

arts

MDPI

Article

Some Aspects of California Cyberpunk

Mike Mosher

Art/Communication Multimedia, Saginaw Valley State University, Michigan, MI 48710, USA; mosher@svsu.edu

Received: 23 July 2018; Accepted: 18 September 2018; Published: 27 September 2018

Abstract: This paper explores the rise and fall of Cyberpunk influences in California's Silicon Valley and San Francisco Bay area circa 1988–93, in prevalent technologies, industry, by artists and in enthusiastic magazines thriving there. Attentive to the Cyberpunk novelists, an animating spirituality of the time also looks to Timothy Leary and Marshall McLuhan.

Keywords: cyberpunk; YLEM artists using science and technology; SCAN; virtual reality; HyperCard; *MONDO 2000*; Timothy Leary; *bOING bOING*; Marshall McLuhan

1. Introduction

Cyberpunk is a literary genre. Yet to some of us in a certain time and place, twenty-five or thirty years ago in Silicon Valley, northern California, it is most recalled as a moment as full of characteristic constellations of sights and sounds and tropes and topics and toys and tools and conversations, sometimes consciously looking to Cyberpunk fiction for its validation.

Simultaneity of experience and representations is a hallmark of Postmodernism (William Gibson in the Economist, 4 December 2003: "The future is already here—it's just not evenly distributed".) (Mortensen 2018). To pull in a metaphor from media design, a popular late-1980s style of magazine illustration and videos called Blendo made use of video, still photography, animation and hand drawing, for digital compositing tools allowed their coordination; this might also serve to represent the eclectic style and content of the lifestyle Cyberpunk moment, its contradictory polished clarity and evocative ambiguities.

2. The Cyberpunk Moment

In his sixth INTERZONE column "Cyberpunk in the 1990s", Bruce Sterling recalled "Cyberpunk", before it acquired its handy label and its sinister rep, was a generous, open-handed effort, very street-level and anarchic, with a do-it-yourself attitude, an ethos it shared with garage- band 70s punk music" (Sterling 1998). The Cyberpunk moment incorporated some Punk cynicism, some Hippie psychedelia, and multiple workshops of digital media tools, low-end and high-end, garage tech and university or government labs. What follows is an overview of some art, some tech, and some Cyberpunk journalism that nourished, excited and inspired us at that time and place.

In *Cyberpunk and Visual Culture* (2018), Graham Murphy and Lars Schmeink build on Frederic Jameson's assertion that Cyberpunk was not only "the supreme literary expression . . . of late capitalism itself" to designate it as late capitalism's supreme visual expression (Murphy and Schmeink 2018). After a period of purposeful urban Punk grimness in the 1970s and into the 1980s, the end of the decade saw a technocratic sunniness in the Cyberpunk constellation of cultural phenomena out of Silicon Valley and the San Francisco Bay area. Cyberpunk as lifestyle, and constellation of exciting possibilities, blossomed in the late 1980s and early 1990s, a time of optimism (despite the 1987 US stock market "correction") and money flowing around Silicon Valley. San Francisco money was multiplied through investors on Palo Alto's Sand Hill Road.

Aspects of California lifestyle Cyberpunk include a PostModernist eclecticism in style and content, beyond the dystopian fictions; the desktop computer seen as a tool of personal and political liberation, and creative medium; technology as where the action is, its innovations the driver of nearly all culture. Despite industry contractions (in videogames in 1985, in multimedia in 1990), there was optimism, and there was money around, with established companies expanding and others starting up. Less optimistic were Dennis Hayes' nonfiction *Behind the Silicon Curtain: The Seductions of Work in a Lonely Era* (1989), which exposed the inequities, human and environmental costs of the Valley's boom, while a neo-Luddite critic of the zeitgeist was put forth by Mark Slouka, *War of the Worlds: Cyberspace and the High-Tech Assault on Reality* (1995).

Despite the limitations of squealing 2400 baud modems, we were all Cyberpunks then.

3. Artists with Computers

While Cyberpunk science fiction was being written, its accoutrements were being carried into the public consciousness by games, education, and especially artists. Enthusiastic books on cyberculture recognize roboticists Survival Research Laboratories and Chico McMurtie, body-modifier Stelarc, innovators in well-equipped garages or laboratories (Dery 1996). Perhaps there are no exact boundaries between cyberculture and cyberpunk. Yet one might first recognize how the games industry and the boom and bust of the mid-1980s developed and dispersed (i.e., from Atari to Apple and Electronic Arts) a lot of ad hoc practitioners that might better be called Cyberpunk. The launch of the Apple Macintosh in 1984, packaged with 800K disks of its software MacPaint, its 72 dots per inch aesthetic of visible pixel was loosed upon the world. A video image was translated into a mysterious, mediated black-pepper image, and this aesthetic flowered in Michael Green's *Zen and the Art of the Macintosh* (Green 1986). This author first created instructional graphics 1984–1985 on a Sony SMC-70, then in 1986 on a PC using Lumena and a Radio Shack 3000 with EGA card. The Amiga had a good interface to video cassette recorders and rudimentary video editing capabilities; San Francisco artist Eleanor Kent used it to create rug-weaving templates.[1] MTV, still primarily music videos, even had a short-lived, dense montage-magazine in 1989 called Buzz, which featured short portentous narrations by Timothy Leary and William S. Burroughs. In two works on CD-ROM for Windows and Macintosh, published by Ion of Los Angeles, CA, San Francisco audio artists The Residents designed an interactive album Gingerbread Man, with nine original songs and an interactive narrative with grotesques in 3D graphic environment. "The Cyber Rave Experience HEADCANDY", a CD-ROM with five original musical works by Brian Eno, provided prismatic glasses to enjoy the "ever-changing kaleidoscope of shapes and colors".

Cyberculture theorists, such as Donna J. Haraway and Allucquere Roseanne Stone were notable in academia. In the visual and hypertextual arts, Cyberpunk was perhaps more feminist than the overall cyberculture. The role of female computer-enabled artists, most on desktop PCs, Macs and Amigas, and the organizations in which they flourished, are underappreciated in the creation of Cyberpunk culture.[2] Named from the Greek concept of "exploding mass from which the universe emerged", YLEM[3] was an organization put together by intelligent, educated mid-life women to bring artists and scientist-engineers together in conversation, in the manner of the nineteenth-century Chautauqua assemblies. Artist Trudy Myrrh Reagan of Palo Alto, a 1950s Stanford graduate married to a SLAC (Stanford Linear Accelerator) researcher, was the driving force, accompanied by Amiga-enabled weaver Eleanor Kent and mutimedia artist Beverly Reiser. Exploratorium curator Larry Shaw hosted presentations and exhibitions of tech work, usually created on small desktop computers, such as the Macintosh, Amiga, or PC, and the organization published a bimonthly newsletter. Its 1991 directory

---

[1] Apple, including my electronic user documentation group, gave much attention to new tools and networking research taking place at the MIT Media Lab. (Brand 1987) enthusiastically promoted the story of Nicholas Negroponte's innovative laboratory. But science fiction comics writer Link Yaco worked at the Media Lab in the 1980s and said in private conversation to this author that many of its demos of software (not yet functional) to corporate funders—including Apple—were purely illusory, "smoke and mirrors".

[2] One book that began their belated appreciation was (Flanagan and Booth 2002). (Malloy 2003) was another.

[3] http://www.ylem.org. Accessed on 5 May 2018.

listed 262 paid members, mostly in California but including the rest of the United States, Canada and Japan.[4] Hypertext and multimedia CD-ROMs, as well as other forms of interactivity, desktop video and animation, computer-aided performance, fractals, robotics and scientific imagery were all presented at its forums and newsletter. A 1991 YLEM excursion to NASA Ames Research Center were given a demonstration by Scott Fisher of his telepresence research.

On the east coast of the US, the Philadelphia-based Small Computers in the Arts Network (SCAN 1991) began in 1980. Its 1991 Conference at the University of the Arts in Philadelphia had presentations on computers in music, VR, digital photography, desktop publishing and educational computer labs. Its Robotics panel included presentations on motion tracking, outdoor art installation, computer-aided manufacturing (CAM), and Tim Anderson of Massachusetts Institute of Technology's experiments with robots creating paintings (as if the demand for paintings so outstrips supply.)

Cyberpunk as a literary genre had been discussed and argued—forged and tempered—in specialized SF zines like *Science Fiction Eye*, though I only became aware of it when I began to work at Apple in 1987, for those members of my department who were not fanboys and aficionados were, like the Administrative Assistant, published science fiction writers; I was given Bruce Sterling's *Mirrorshades: The Cyberpunk Anthology* as beach reading on my first vacation. Apple's simple app (or "stack") builder HyperCard (1987) was loosely inspired by Ted Nelson's vision since the 1960s of a global, networked hypermedia "Xanadu".[5] Linked documents, with a metaphor of navigation through a network, engaged artists, poets, fiction and non-fiction writers, excited about creative and pedagogical uses of that network.

Virtual Reality was the three-dimensional realization of that possible network. Just preceding the Cyberpunk moment, the October 1987 issue of Scientific American magazine (Peled 1987) "The next revolution in computers" predicted social transformation through increased power, networks and advanced interface devices for handwriting recognition, eye trackers, voice communication and a wired glove manipulating an avatar hand upon the screen with evident dexterity, pictured on the cover. In 1988 Jaron Lanier, principal in VPL Research, demonstrated his Virtual Reality system, with Eyephones and Data Glove, at the ACM SIGGRAPH Conference, the special interest group in graphics of the Association of Computing Machinery. It featured an art show as well. Lanier delivered an influential demonstration of virtual reality was delivered at SIGGRAPH 1998. The first panel of its 1989 conference in Boston, chaired by Coco Conn of Homer and Associates, included Lanier, Margaret Minsky of University of North Carolina and MIT Media Lab, Scott Fisher of NASA Ames Research Center and Allison Druin of Tell Tale Technologies (Beach 1989). The SIGGRAPH 1990 conference featured a Special Session: Hip, Hype and Hope—The Three Faces of Virtual Worlds that began "Virtual world systems are the focus of the media, grist for the TV mill, and everyone's pick as the big idea of the '90s . . . Is virtual worlds technology really that important?" (Beach 1990) Soon Brenda Laurel, Theatre PhD with Atari, Apple, NASA Ames Research Lab and then Paul Allen's Interval Research on her vita, created a resonant virtual environment "Placeholder" for the Banff Art Centre in Canada. Char Davies, at Toronto 3D software developer SoftImage, created immersive abstract environments. Virtual reality was a great interest of the greater Cyberpunk community, as a realization of the state of personal fusion with networked machines predicted in science fiction only a short time before.

Artists had long been intrigued by programmable systems, like the "Telematic" work of Roy Ascott in the UK or Sonia Sheridan's work in Chicago. The Inter-Society for the Electronic Arts (ISEA) grew out

---

4   YLEM Artists Using Science and Technology (1991). This author exhibited HyperCard fiction kiosk "Hucklefine" at one 1990 YLEM gathering at the Palace of Fine Arts, San Francisco and performed HyperCard-aided performance "Christopher Cumulonimbus" there in 1992, contributed several newsletter articles and graphics, and served on YLEM Advisory Board.
5   (Nelson 1987). Apocryphal corporate lore says that when HyperCard inventor Bill Atkinson asked Apple CEO John Sculley to include HyperCard with each Macintosh computer sold, he agreed in anticipation that the increased demand for storage memory would stimulate the sale of Apple hard disks.

of the First International Symposium on Electronic Art (FISEA) held in Utrecht, Holland. Subsequent symposia were held in Goningen, Holland; in Sydney, Australia, then Minneapolis, MN. The fourth, in 1993, at the Minneapolis College of Art and Design, where board member Roman Verostko, inventor of a computerized abstract drawing generator, attracted more desktop computer-using American artists. Hirano Saburo of Japan demonstrated "Nervous Nest" installation of synthesizers, sensors, loudspeakers and computer running agents reactive to movement or ambient sound, creating an audio environment reminiscent of woodland insects. Judith Kerman demonstrated hypertext poetry in Eastgate Systems' Storyspace, while and Anita J. Stoner created a multimedia poem structured upon the metaphor of a pinball game.[6]

4. *MONDO 2000* Shapes Perception

Perhaps the most authoritative, or well-funded and therefore big, glossy, worldly and ubiquitous, was MONDO 2000. That its animating traits diffused into the wider culture testifies to its success. I will talk about them in context of a scene, events and creative conversations and cultural creations, largely in northern California. The entire corpus of *MONDO* and its predecessors High Frontiers and Reality Hackers (as well as friendly rival *bOING bOING*) deserves a much closer reading than this author will give them here. Its entire corpus should be unpacked as time capsules of memes, technologies and hardware or software products, the hippest musics, and quirky individuals, I shall ignore most tech articles and music coverage, to note its neo-psychedelic spirit, and its dialogues between old Leary and Cyberpunk novelists.

There were many small zines and papers in late 1970s/early 1980s Punk era San Francisco, including *Waterdrinkers, Nancy, Revolutionary Wanker*, and *Search and Destroy*. The publishers of the latter began REseach Publications, glossier and more professionally designed, with issues featuring Burroughs and Ballard. The publishing project of editors R.U. Sirius (Ken Goffman) and St. Jude (Jude Milhon), and "Domineditrix" publisher Queen Mu (Allison Kennedy) began in 1986 as the oversized post-Punk tabloid *High Frontiers*, then was incorporated into a second publication, the glossier *Reality Hackers*. Here we will review the contents of one exemplary, and pivotal, issue.

Issue #7 of *Reality Hackers*, still cheery, optimistic, eclectic and drug-friendly, bore the new name MONDO 2000. This was a sophisticated magazine for an in-crowd, in the tradition of the *New Yorker* and *SPY* magazine, but out of the San Francisco/Berkeley/Silicon Valley metropolis. The first thing noticeable about examination of *MONDO* #7 is its impressive weight, 160 glossy pages, color covers but black and white text, photos and graphics within. Yet this is the watershed issue, the moment when Cyberpunk is at its most inclusive, embracing garage-tech and psychedelic advocates.

The cover of *MONDO 2000* Fall #7 (1989; again, really Reality Hackers #7) lists "Cyberpunks, Todd Rundgren (pictured, looking at an earlier Reality Hackers issue), Tim Leary, William Gibson, Max Headroom, Virusgate, Future Media". Inside front cover says CYBERPUNK Issue, featuring Rudy Rucker, Vernor Vinge, Gibson, Bruce Sterling and John Shirley. The cover logo done on the Mac II with Electronic Arts' Studio 8 by Brummbär, formerly of Germany and adept on the Amiga 2000 as well, each letter in the name its own iconic representation. The "M" is urban neon, the "O" is the planetary globe, "N" is a lubricious devil's horn encircled by a halo, "D" is digital circuitry, and the last "O" is the Ouroboros snake biting its own tail.

There is a sparkle to the glossy magazine, like the airbrush gleams on the leather bodysuit and mirrorshades worn by Cherry Poptart. She's Larry Welz's big-eyed shapely blonde hero of adventures published by Last Gasp and now, in *MONDO*, friend of Ellie Dee in Cyberland, a new comic cyberpunkess. One peruses the cheery clamor of the marketplace, small garage tech as mail order products. In the exuberance of a Renaissance Faire, the Homebrew Computer Club or Jim Warren's annual West Coast Computer Fair there proceed numerous ads for UFO Detector, ELF Generator,

---

6   From informational handouts distributed at FISEA '93.

Multi-Wave Oscillator "for direct stimulation of any part of the body with the high frequency high voltage Tesla Coil output", an Orgone Energy Blanket from Super Science of Dayton, and a catalog of books from Borderland Sciences. One is reminded of the Star Wars cantina, many planets' species shoulder to shoulder, as the magazine commits to be "the leading edge in hyperculture ... the latest in human/technological interactive mutational forms as they happen" (Sirius 1989, p. 11).

"Quark of the Decade" by Timothy Leary begins with the back-scratching assertion "On my screen, Bill Gibson is the MVPP (Most Valuable Performing Philosopher) of the decade as a prelude to "High Tech High Life: William Gibson and Timothy Leary in Conversation" they talk fondly about Burroughs, Pynchon (whose LSD use Leary notes), Sterling, and the characters in Gibson's Neuromancer. Leary asks if Gibson would describe cyberspace as the matrix of all the hallucinations; Gibson replies "Yeah, it's a consensual hallucination that these people have created. It's like, with this equipment, you can agree to share the same hallucinations. In effect, they're creating a world. It's not really a place, it's not really space. It's notional space". (Leary 1970, p. 61) Rudy Rucker is interviewed, followed by "Rudy Rucker on What Is Cyberpunk", where he praises Punk as fast and dense, Cyber (mathematics) progressing from Infinity's quantum mechanics and LSD to Information, driven by computers into a time of fast, dense, info-rich Cyberpunk SF. (p. 78.) Vernor Vinge (p. 114), and John Shirley (p. 88) are interviewed, and Bruce Sterling tells Jude Milhon, "What Shirley said about writing—science fiction especially—is that it's a mirror you can edit". (p. 100). In a thoughtful "PARTING SHOT: Have We Missed the Revolution?" Lee Felsenstein, organizer of the Community Memory Project, an early computer network in Berkeley ponders. "Let's develop a little punk computing, folks!" (p. 153). This dialectic, of technology as media of community or class-defining commodity, persists to this day.

Two years later, in MONDO #4 (Sirius 1992), Larry McCaffrey interviews Kathy Acker, Durk Pearson and Sandy Shaw, Life Extension advocates, talk about neurotransmitters, aphrodisiacs and Beta Carotene. In *MONDO* #5, Larry McCaffery and Duncan Bock talk with Mark Leyner (a sort of pop-punk style analogous to bouncy New Wave rock music, also out of New York), absurd connections of surrealism, a dense and funny stream often peppered with product names and celebrity tropes (Leyner 1990, 1995). "Maybe I'm the first Cyberpunk writer who's not a science fiction writer". (McCaffrey and Bock 1991, p. 49) Issue #6 has a review of Beyond Cyberpunk HyperCard stack by Gareth Branwyn, Mark Frauenfelder and Peter Sugarman, noting its contributors Bruce Sterling, Richard Kadrey and others. In *MONDO* #13, Rudy Rucker contributes "15 Tech Notes Towards a Cyberpunk Novel", (Rucker 1994, p. 52) while Douglas Cooper hopes to return to "proto-hypertext" novel Hopscotch by Julio Cortazar for inspiration for new literary forms. Bruce Sterling cynically reviews (Sterling 1994) Arthur Kroker's *Data Trash: The Theory of the Virtual Class*, a political scientist's optimistic description of exactly the kind of over-educated, plugged-in *MONDO* reader.

Another Cyberpunk organ of the time—still publishing in online form[7] is bOING bOING "Mutating Simian Brains Since 1988", out of Colorado, then Los Angeles. Black and white, desktop published, enlivened by editor Mark Frauenfelder's cartoon graphics. Comics were reviewed, as were zines. Books reviewed (Frauenfelder 1991, pp. 36–42) included the nonfiction *Cyberpunk: Outlaws and Hackers on the Computer Frontier* by Katie Hafner and John Markoff. Rudy Rucker books *Transreal!* and *All the Visions* are reviewed, as are zines and comic books. bOING bOING Issue 9 features Rucker and Bruce Sterling, and is dedicated to recently deceased MAD publisher William Gaines; there was an appreciation of humorist Roger Price in #7 (Frauenfelder 1991). There is in issue #9 a tame (OK, lame) but affectionate parody "Mondo Mondo" with "R.U. Delerious". Might not an appropriate label for Cyberpunk humor be "Jest Propulsion Laboratory" ... ? bOING bOING published a nascent genre of cyberpulp fiction by Paul Di Filippo, Gareth Branwyn and others, and the magazines' mix of provocative, alarming science and political information, and tomfoolery echoed nineteenth-century old west California, the era of Mark Twain, Bret Harte and Ambrose Bierce. Warren Hinckle's *War*

---

7   https://boingboing.net. Accessed on 5 May 2018.

News, a short-lived San Francisco tabloid published during the Gulf War in 1991, had similar heated rhetoric and snide asides sparkling in its journalism.

5. *Cigarette Boy* and the Limits of Cyberpunk

All of this artistic ferment circled around and interpenetrated the writings. If Gibson's foundational trilogy comprises Cyberpunk's *Huckleberry Finn* then *Cigarette Boy* (Darick Chamberlin's Site for Cigarette Boy 2018) by Darick (1991) is its *Finnegans Wake*. I was immediately reminded of the Language Poets active in the Bay Area the decade before . . . but Chamberlin's is machine language. It spatters out a programming code or technical transmission bursts, including printer instructions, bracketed and entered as if by a nerd Burroughs or Ballard. The book is printed in all caps, a sternly horizontal monospaced font, words often separated by colons. Its colons suggest coding syntax, its brackets recall formatting tags inserted in SML or HTML to shape the document. Its punctuation, repetitive use of colons like a punch press, is fatiguing, breaking its sentences into baby steps.

The book is like the essential operating manual for a piece of equipment or complicated software suite. The cover of *Cigarette Boy*, designed by the author, bears a high-contrast black and white image of an astronaut-like high-altitude test pilot in flight suit and aviator sunglasses, framed in black and yellow warning stripes atop faint technical drawings in the background. The flyboy's glove graces the back cover. The book is spiral bound with a black plastic spiral spine, like a convenient documentation for a product's end users, and published in 1000 copies. Like the self-erasing poem "Agrippa (A Book of the Dead)" by William Gibson, illuminated by Dennis Ashbaugh and published on encrypted diskette in 1992,[8] *Cigarette Boy* is a well-designed fetishization of a book; the cyberpunk narrative as the jewel-encrusted tortoise on the floor the aesthete Jean des Esseintes' library in Joris-Karl Huysmans' 1884 *Against Nature* (Huysmans 1969).

There are shiny words, references more buried than Mark Leyner's,[9] but they bubble amid data seemingly disorganized, like dropped or randomized files. In the 1970s Laurence Miller, guitarist-songwriter in Michigan band Sproton Layer and a middle-period version of Destroy All Monsters, published psychedelic poetry reminiscent of Chamberlin, in a self-published zine called *EMPOOL* (Miller and Yaco 1976, 1978). Chamberlin's is a linear paper book as syntactically ambitious as any of its pre-World Wide Web era of hypertext literature.

[INTERCUT EXTRACT CODED AS "B103": START PRINT OF B103: "HERE IN THE BIOMA HUSH FIELDS OF THE MERCURIAL DUSTER, NOTE THE ZOLO NOON RIGGERS VIAT VOTARIES OF THE ASTIN GETH: UPGRADE FUTURES ON THE 65-ELEVENTIES: STRICT SENTRIES: THICK STATIONS: GOLD DIODA SONDES AT LEAST 50% REDUNDANT: FANATIC: EGYPTIC: THAT'S PROTONILECODA . . . " STOP ON CALL VIAT STOP/STOP]: NOW "START": DEREPRODUUX LUX "D" ON A GO RAVE OF GODELLA AUTOMATICA: SHOOT "GODELLA GEDANKEN": SHOOT 'ADENINE': 'CYTOSINE': 'GUANINE': 'THYMINE': ADD: 'INFRANINE': 'ZOLONINE': 'NOVASINE': [CUE SHOOTS CONTROLS: TRIPLE HELIX CONTROLS CRUSHED VIA THE EXPEDITION FRACAS: THE SO-CALLED "INFRACAS"]. [10]

It as if James Joyce were now an assembler at Apple's manufacturing plant in Cork, Ireland. Gareth Branwyn praises *Cigarette Boy*'s pseudo-AI search results, "a horrific mass of jargon, ephemera,

---

8 Gibson, William, http://www.williamgibsonbooks.com/source/agrippa.asp. The poem, running on a 1992 Macintosh from its $3\frac{1}{2}$" disk, is at https://www.youtube.com/watch?v=41kZovcyHrU. Accessed on 15 July 2018.

9 "And you put a very flammable substance down the front of my trousers and I tried to represent words with frantic gestures & your relatives guessed Under the Volcano, The Carpetbaggers, Black Macho and the Myth of the Superwoman, naked and Fiery Forms, No Time for Sergeants, and The Three Faces of Eve". "Bedtime Story for My Wife" (Leyner 1995).

10 (Darick 1991) "presented as a proposal to The Mackert Corporation", <Rogue/Drogue>, edition of 1000 copies, © 1991 Darick Chamberlin. Excerpt of p. 16.

and frustratingly tiny fragments of useful information". what Cocteau called his own earlier experiments "machines for the generation of meaning". Interviewed by Branwyn, Chamberlin cited inspiration in being "daily barraged by bureaucratic forms, unintelligible receipts, obscure techtalk and other exotic language ecologies that we don't understand" (Branwyn 1992). Perhaps we have evolved in the past quarter century in a *Cigarette Boy*-beckoned post-meaning. Artist-theorist Hito Steyerl has written appreciatively of "Spamsoc" (a coinage like the "Ingsoc" of Orwell's 1984), the online broken neo-English spawn of, in Hal Foster's description, "bots and avatars, translation programs and heartache scams" (Hal 2018).

Into the 1990s artists worked on low-end virtual worlds, and *Garage Virtual Reality: The Affordable Way to Explore Virtual Worlds* claimed to be "Perfect for PC, Macintosh, a & Amiga Users!" (Linda 1994). Yet the decline of hegemonic Cyberpunk might be marked by three phenomena: the failure to fully address VR and sexuality in "Lawnmower Man"; attention by mass (read: mainstream, square and unhip) press; and by the misguided efforts at relevancy by Punk rocker Billy Idol. By the mid-1990s, Cyberpunk in-this-world seemed tired, spent, passé.

If the 1990s were to be less sexist, more inclusive—Brenda Laurel guided a girl-empowering games company Purple Moon—then its visionary movies should have reflected that ideal. While effective demonstrations of future human-machine interfaces appeared in "Johnny Mnemonic" (1995, based on a Gibson story), Brett Leonard's problematic "Lawnmower Man" (1991) was a high-water mark of Hollywood Cyberpunk cinema, a memorable visualization of virtual reality (and especially its teledildonic trope), yet where philosophical imagination came to its cramped end. Set somewhere in Silicon Valley, it featured a memorable Frankenstein's Monster of a villain, and visualized the concept of teledildonics (then a hotly debated topic on the WELL, the Whole Earth 'Lectronic Link) (Dery 1996) immersive virtual sex to the movie-going public. In as sexist story turn, a vibrant, sex-positive woman's mind is destroyed by the intensity of virtual sexual experience with Jobe, the mentally challenged lawn care worker enhanced by a researcher's guided virtual reality sessions. In *Electronic Eros: Bodies and Desire in the Postindustrial Age* (1996), Claudia Springer laments Jobe's exaggerated and violent hyper-masculinity, contextualized by Mark Dery's observation in *MONDO* #5 that "Man-machine miscegenation—robo-copulation, by any other name—may seem a seductive alternative to the vile body, locus of a postmodern power struggle involving AIDS, abortion rights, fetal tissue, genetic engineering, and nanotechnology" (Dery 1991). Rather than the miserable "Lawnmower Man 2: Beyond Cyberspace" how many other viewers would have rather relished sequels about the woman's continued adventures, erotic and otherwise, after her transcendental/carnal virtual knowledge? Lamentably, Brett Leonard missed his opportunity to visualize techno-feminist experience as a realm of progress and fulfillment.

Mass media took a dim but intrigued view of Cyberpunk, older and more conservative neighbors wondering how these new kids were getting all the action and buzz. In a 1991 Newsweek story on Cyberpunk, reviewer Michael Rogers is amazed how *MONDO's*, "first three issues roamed across cyber-lifestyle, with articles that ranged from artificial sex via computer to how to legally purchase drugs that make you smarter". A sidebar glossary for Brave New Words defines Cyberspace, Virtual Reality, Teledildonics, Hackers, Crackers and Smart Drugs". Paul Saffo of the Institute for the Future in Menlo Park predicted its effect would be felt decades later by teenagers who become engineers who encounter it now. "By 2000, magazines will be obsolete. We'll be the last magazine". asserts Sirius, while Mu is proud nearly half its readership (unlike the preponderantly male tech industry) are women (Rogers 1991). Traditionally, recognition in the mainstream TIME magazine was a signal that a fad or cultural strain was pretty much over, no longer hip and cutting edge. TIME magazine ran a cover story on Cyberpunk in its 8 February 1993 issue (Anonymous 1993).

Another sign of the end of Cyberpunk was Billy Idol's well-intentioned but late-to-the-party mid-1993 album Cyberpunk, on Chrysalis Records. His street credibility from London 1977 singing with band Generation X might have shattered with popularity and heavy rotation on MTV in the early 1980s, but he was a video-friendly image of Punk: sneer, spiky hair, boots, black leather garb and jingly metal accessories. In the "Adam in Chains" video[11] he sports dreadlocks like Jaron Lanier, swings a Vase pendulum like Ai Weiwei's 1995 performance drop of a Han dynasty vase.[12] In its video, blond, shirtless, longhaired, he resembles Iggy Pop, the video begins with a spoken word section "in 3D audio" by Timothy Leary, evocative of his "You can be anything you want this time around" spoken word album for the short-lived boutique label Douglas. Leary interviews Idol on ABC-TV's In Concert, and gushes that Idol has "uncanny laser-like vision of what's happening next"[13] singing "No Religion" where he leaves out Lou Reed's lyric "When I'm rushing on my run/Then I feel like Jesus' son" and instead repeats Patti Smith's "Jesus died for somebody's sins but not mine". As the WELL (Whole Earth 'Lectronic Link) was lauded—by Howard Rheingold (1993) and others—as "the digital community", perhaps in hopes of Cyberpunk community Idol published his WELL email address, and readily conversed online with fans until he soon gained an inbox full of too many of them.

6. Spiritual Ancestors

Proceeding from Billy Idol's "No Religion" to moldering issues of MONDO, I shall still trace a spiritual element in Cyberpunk.

Returning to tech artwork, in an interactive display at ISEA that addressed religion with technology, Greg Garvey programmed a Macintosh into "The Automatic Confession Machine: A Catholic Turing Test". The user presses the AMEN key to start, then follows the usual procedures of Confession in the Catholic church, but each step entered with mouse commands or keyboard typing, or delivered, onscreen. For Penance, "The priest will total your sins and calculate your penance running the expert priest software system utilizing the most advanced neural net algorithms", reminding the user to practice the Hail Mary and Our Father prayers. Inspired by Alan Turing's 1950 essay "Computer Memory and Intelligence", "the work challenges the sinner in the confessional to decide whether or not a priest or a computer programmed to act like a priest is hearing the confession". Menus include the seven deadly sins and the Ten Commandments. Garvey intended the piece to contrast the "two mutually exclusive belief systems" of Artificial Intelligence and Catholic dogma, contemplate technology's potential encroachment on the realm of the personal and spiritual. He called for the Vatican to consider whether "software/hardware separately or together can or should be ordained and thereby given the imprimatur of the Church and fully vested in the spiritual power of the priesthood". A proposed Papal Bull towards that end might further the Church's membership, funding through credit cards, influence and distribution of Sacraments in "The New Marketplace of Faith". A mobile Personal Pocket Penance Assistant, "for the busy sinner on the go", was also proposed, effortlessly reciting 200 Hail Marys or Our Fathers "necessary for salvation and reduced time in Purgatory". The artist's biography lists him a President and CEO of the (all capitals) DIGITAL RELIGIOUS AND ELECTRONICS CORPORATION (DREC) and teaching in the Department of Design Art, Concordia University, Montreal.[14]

Yet the spiritual element in *MONDO* was essentially psychedelia. Many of its practitioners may have hoped that networked technologies (especially VR) would bring the ecstasy and *agape* they had known from psychedelic drugs, prevalent among high school[15] and college students about twenty years before. Psychedelia provided a metaphor of ecstatic universal connectedness. That may be why Timothy Leary, then in his mid-sixties, was ubiquitous in MONDO 2000. "The Seven Tongues of God", Leary's 1964 lecture at psychological conference session sponsored by the Board of Theological

---

11 (Billy Idol, "Adam in Chains" 1993). The video for another song on the Cyberpunk album, "Shock to the System" was directed by Brett Leonard, and is discussed in (Foster 2005).
12 https://www.guggenheim/org/arts-curriculum/topic/ai-weiwei. Accessed on 5 May 2018.
13 https://archive.org/details/Timothy_Leary_Archives_007.dv. Accessed on 5 May 2018.
14 Informational hand out by Greg Garvey, A user's guide to: The Automatic Confession Machine Version 2.1, Montreal.
15 Author's recollection, though research at the University of Michigan Institute of Social Research, published as (University of Michigan Institute of Social Research 1983), shows a figure of only 4.7% of the Class of 1975 had used hallucinogens within past thirty days http://monitoringthefuture.org/pubs/monographs/mtf-vol1_1983.pdf, p. 160. Accessed on 15 July 2018.

Education, Lutheran Church in America, recounts experiments upon divinity students (Leary 1970, p. 13), proceeding (as his capitalized sub-chapter headings form a precis) "LSD Can Produce a Religious High", (p. 16) then asserts "Drugs Are the Religion of the People—The Only Hope is Dope". (p. 37) His book *The Politics of Ecstasy* contains sections "LSD Turns You on to God" (p. 7) cites an LSD study where "90 per cent of the subjects claimed 'a greater awareness of God or a higher power'", and "over two-thirds of a sample of sixty-seven ministers, monks and rabbis reported the deepest spiritual experience of their lives". The final pages of the book command "Start Your Own Religion", (p. 299) "Write Your Own Bible" and "Write Your Own Ten Commandments". (p. 300) "The ... psychedelic celebration was based on the life of Christ, and we used the Catholic missal as the manual for it. But each one of these great myths is based on a psychedelic experience, a death-rebirth experience ... We hope that the Christian will be particularly turned on by our Catholic LSD mass, because it will renew for him the metaphor with for most of us has become rather routine and tired". (p. 239) In his 1966 Playboy magazine interview Leary states "Psychedelic drugs are the medium of the young ... A fifteen-year-old is going to use a new form of energy to have fun, to intensify sensation, to make love, for curiosity, for personal growth". (pp. 102–3) This author was fifteen and attentive when rhetoric by Leary, and others, was published. It stuck in the mind of Cyberpunk writers, publishers and celebrants.

The spirituality that infused both optimistic and pessimistic tendencies in Lifestyle Cyberpunk is nostalgic psychedelia. About Ignatius of Loyola's Spiritual Exercises, novelist Italo Calvino wrote: "Certainly Catholicism of the Counter-Reformation possessed a fundamental vehicle, in its ability to use visual communication through the emotional stimuli of sacred art, the believer was supposed grasp the meaning of the verbal teachings of the Church ... The believer is called upon personally to paint frescoes crowded with figures on the walls of his mind, starting out from the stimuli that his visual imagination succeeds in extracting from a theological proposition or a laconic verse from the gospels" (Calvino 1985). That is to say, from a virtual reality. In an evocation of the Baroque, *MONDO* Issue #10 has a robed cover girl derived from Catholic martyr St. Lucy, a pair of round eyeballs not on a plate but rolling in her hand like a pair of dice.

The early days of World Wide Web seemed to dissipate the Cyberpunk moment, democratize and mid-Americanize what was once elite and coastal. Following a short-lived *ACCESS* magazine of "Music · Cyberculture · Style" from San Diego, *WIRED* magazine appeared in 1994, and after the first year or so settled down into an eminently readable, but more predictable, format. It might have called itself "Popular Cyberspace", in a fine 20th c. tradition of techie newsmagazines, then aimed at an audience of smart, inquisitive, mechanically adept boys (today's hacker ethic is less gendered, at least since the aforementioned YLEM, ISEA and SIGGRAPH artists). *WIRED* declared early on that it was dedicated to evangelizing the World Wide Web, and by riding the tsunami of new participation upon it, *MONDO*'s fringe science and culture was tamed, brought indoors, popularized. *WIRED* spread all manifestations of cyberculture with enthusiasm, borrowing breathiness, some stylishness and Cyberpunk writers from *MONDO*. It also furthered a revived interest in Marshall McLuhan.

Terence McKenna's review in *MONDO* Fall #7 of *The Letters of Marshall McLuhan* (1987, Oxford University Press) is titled "MARSHALL MCLUHAN the cognitive agent as CYBERPUNK GODFATHER", who in the 1960s "seemed to be giving permission, permission for youth culture, rock and roll, and post-print libidinal tactility to finally, mercifully dismantle linear stuffed-shirt Western Civilization". "Fucking in the streets was, of course, the ultimate symbol of the end of privacy and rule by gentlemen". McKenna goes on to ponder if McLuhan took LSD, laments how even his defenders tend to misunderstand him, as McLuhan warned Canada's Prime Minister Pierre Trudeau in 1972 that harsh anti-drug legislation's "key to the drug panic is TV. TV intensifies the already numerous forms of inner-tripping. Color TV is psychedelic input. The kids are simply putting jam on jam when they take to drugs". Timothy Leary reported to McKenna that McLuhan once said to him "Drugs that accelerate the brain won't be accepted until the population is geared to computers". McLuhan wrote "The suddenness of the leap from hardware to software cannot but produce a period of anarchy and collapse in existing establishments, especially in the developed countries. That is our immediate prospect and our present actuality" (Wolfe 2003). McLuhan's mid-life nostalgia in the 1960s for values, *verités* of rural 1930s Alberta might be akin to my own in 2018 for late-1980s California Cyberpunk moment, of overworked tech corporation employees and underpaid artistic tech enthusiasts amusing themselves in festive events, psychedelics and glossy magazines like *MONDO 2000*, the transition from literary Cyberpunk science fiction to visual and multi-sensual networked community or communion.

The Roman Catholic McLuhan did not evangelize a Trinity, but a Tetrad, where a medium of any kind forces questions of what it replaced, what it amplified, what it turned into and what if flipped. One might fruitfully apply McLuhan's Tetrad to Cyberpunk, contemplating what Cyberpunk advanced, augmented, supplanted and flipped into. William Gibson told David Wallace-Wells in his Paris Review interview " … cyberspace is everywhere now, having everted and colonized the world. It starts to sound kind of ridiculous to speak of cyberspace as somewhere else" (Murphy 2018). The mid-1990s era of the popularized, ubiquitous Internet, then the Y2K confluence of cell phones, productivity software, then the 2007 revolution of the iPhone and Android app phone all mark the successful end of Cyberpunk as something separate from mundane life, where now your grade-school niece and your grandmother both inhabit all its phenomena. Aging Cyberpunks might muse on fun, then fairy-dusted with exclusivity, a quarter century ago, but the subsequent development and popularization and access to tools seems less a decline than an apotheosis. Perhaps a technological Omega Point, the goal of progress articulated by Pierre Teilhard de Chardin.

Teilhard de Chardin may have influenced McLuhan's thoughts on global media that prefigured cyberspace—and Cyberpunk—though McLuhan, faculty at Catholic colleges, could not formally acknowledge the scientist-turned-Jesuit priest. In 1911, year of McLuhan's birth, Teilhard was officially branded a heretic when he defended Darwinian evolution of humanity towards God's plan of unification of all human nervous systems and thought through technology. Teilhard theorized a "natural, profound evolution of the nervous system" through global electronic media, "etherized human consciousness" linked via TV, radio towards one civilization, which he called the noosphere. McLuhan wrote "The Christian concept of the mystical body, off all men as members of the body of Christ—this becomes technologically a fact under electronic conditions". (Wolfe 2003, p. xvi) Which is to say, jacked in to the matrix. Is the iPhone or Android app phone the portable unifier, the Omega communicator? My university students seem to think so, though new tech will inevitably supplant it.

One can extend Punk aesthetics and ethics to late 1990s file sharing, and Cyberpunk fiction tropes to the fears of dystopia upon Y2K network breakdowns. Was Gibson's trilogy speculative *non*-fiction? To read it today no longer shows a different world's logic. Does literary Cyberpunk speak to the transformation of daily life since 2005 with Google, YouTube, Facebook and its Cambridge Analytics? Roman Catholic dogma asserts that every and all Sin is known by God, whether it is performed in thought, word or deed. In 1987, upon joining Apple, new employees were warned to never say anything online that we wouldn't want to see subpoenaed, brought into a court of law as evidence. In this century, Detroit Mayor Kwame Kilpatrick was unaware the text messages about a governmental cover-up sent on his phone to his mistress could be retrieved, leading to his arrest and imprisonment. Facebook users are shocked their posts were mined by Cambridge Analytics for political persuasion. Perhaps I'm jaded at notions of "privacy" intact in our time.

Graham J. Murphy noted Cyberpunk fiction's emergence was contemporary with the 1980s rise of Christian revivalism and growing fundamentalism, while Samuel Delany found "Religion rumbles all over the place in Gibson, just below the surface of the text".[16] Among computer scientists, Jaron Lanier compared VR to Christian ritual, Virtual Reality Modeling Language (VRML) developer Mark Pesce compared it to pagan ritual, Nicole Stenger compared it to angels (Wertheim 1999). In his 1991 New York Times editorial "Confessions of an Ex-Cyberpunk", Lewis Shiner lamented that Cyberpunk's "newfound popularity … shows our obsession with material goods, and technical,

---

16 (Murphy and Schmeink 2018), "Emerging World Orders"; or, Cyberpunk as Science Fiction Realism, op. cit, p. 191.

engineered solutions … There seems to be a national need for spiritual values … I find myself waiting—maybe in vain—for a new literature of idealism and compassion that is contemporary not only on the technological level but also the emotional … I believe that this—not cyberpunk—is the attitude we need to get us into the 21st century" (Shiner 1991).

As in Catholic dicta, suicide is a mortal sin, so it can be contrasted with MONDO 2000's maximum interest in extending life, as well as Rucker's flickerclad personae (and, presumably, souls) downloaded into "Boppers", life-extending robots. Punks wore the skull as a proud symbol: the pirates' skull and crossbones, or the warning of toxicity on the bottle of cleaner under the sink. California Chicano artists Asco (Nausea) used it in their murals and performances (Chavoya and Gonzalez 2011) in the tradition of pre-Columbian Mexicans predating Catholicism, as Day of the Dead celebrants, or like the early 20th century broadside illustrator Posada. The Punk skull spread through shopping-mall vendors like Hot Topic across America. California Cyberpunks soon rejected the skull in exchange for the optimistic symbol of a baby. Like the fetus in the finale of the 1968 movie "2001: A Space Odyssey", the quizzical awakening of MONDO's t-shirt logo of a light-bearing baby, rays emanating from his head like a Baroque representation of the Sun might appear to the spiritual Cyberpunk as Teilhard's noospheric Omega Point.

Spiritu vobiscum. Et cum Cyberpunc tuo.

Funding: This research received no external funding.

Acknowledgments: The author wishes to thank all *Arts* pre-publication reviewers for their attentive, focused and generous suggestions towards this paper's improvement. Thanks to Takayuki Tatsumi for his invitation to participate in this Special Issue.

Conflicts of Interest: The author declares no conflicts of interest.

References

Anonymous. 1993. CYBERPUNK Virtual Sex, Smart Drugs and Synthetic Rock 'n' Roll. *TIME*, February 8. Available online: https://archive.org/details/cyberpunkvirtual00time (accessed on 5 May 2018).

Beach, Richard J. 1989. *Computer Graphics: SIGGRAPH 1989 Conference Proceedings*. Number 5. Edited by Richard J. Beach and Robert L. Judd. New York: Association of Computing Machinery, vol. 23.

Beach, Richard J. 1990. *Computer Graphics: SIGGRAPH 1990 Conference Proceedings*. Number 4. Edited by Richard J. Beach and Forest L. Baskett. New York: Association of Computing Machinery, vol. 24, p. 438.

Billy Idol, "Adam in Chains". 1993. Available online: https://www.youtube.com/watch?v=LnIsbgN6PaY (accessed on 5 May 2018).

Brand, Stewart. 1987. *The Media Lab: Inventing the Future at MIT*. New York: Penguin Books.

Branwyn, Gareth. 1992. Cool Thing: Cigarette Boy. In *bOING bOING #9*. pp. 57–58.

Calvino, Italo. 1985. Visibility. In *Six Memos for the New Millennium*. Cambridge: MIT Press.

Darick, Chamberlin. 1991. *Cigarette Boy: A Mock Machine Mock-Epic*. Rogue/Drogue.

Chavoya, C. Ondine, and Rita Gonzalez. 2011. *ASCO: Elite of the Obscure*. Ostfildern: Hatje Cantz Verlag, pp. 132, 133, 232–33.

Darick Chamberlin's Site for Cigarette Boy. 2018. Available online: http://www.cigaretteboy.com (accessed on 11 September 2018).

Dery, Mark. 1991. Guerilla Semiotics: Sex Machine, Machine Sex, Mechano-Eroticism & RoboCopulation. In *MONDO 2000 #5*. Berkeley and Fun City: MegaMedia/MONDO 2000, p. 43.

Dery, Mark. 1996. *Escape Velocity: Cyberculture at the End of the Century*. New York: Grove Press, p. 213.

Flanagan, Mary, and Austin Booth. 2002. *Reload: Rethinking Women + Cyberculture*. Cambridge: MIT Press.

Foster, Thomas. 2005. *The Souls of Cyberfolk*. Minneapolis: University of Minnesota Press, pp. 177–87.

Frauenfelder, Mark. 1991. *bOING bOING #7*. pp. 36–42.

Frauenfelder, Carla. 1991. Neato People: Roger Price. In *bOING bOING #7*. p. 31.

Green, Michael. 1986. *Zen and the Art of the Macintosh*. Philadelphia: Running Press. Available online: https://archive.org/details/mac_Zen_the_Art_of_Macintosh1986 (accessed on 11 May 2018).

Hal, Foster. 2018. Smash the Screen. *London Review of Books*, April 5, p. 41.

Huysmans, Joris-Karl. 1969. *Against the Grain (A Rebours)*. With an Introduction by Havelock Ellis. New York: Dover Publications Inc., chp. 4. Available online: https://www.gutenberg.org/files/12341/12341-h/12341-h.htm (accessed on 17 July 2018).

Leary, Timothy. 1970. *The Politics of Ecstasy*. London: Paladin/Granada Publishing Limited, pp. 13, 16, 37, 7, 299, 300, 239, 102–3.

Leyner, Mark. 1990. *My Cousin the Gastroenterologist*. New York: Vintage.

Leyner, Mark. 1995. *I Smell Esther Williams*. New York: Vintage, p. 18.

Linda, Jacobson. 1994. *Garage Virtual Reality: The Affordable Way to Explore Virtual Worlds*. Indianapolis: SAMS Publishing.

Malloy, Judy, ed. 2003. *Women, Art & Technology*. Cambridge: MIT Press.

McCaffrey, Larry, and Duncan Bock. 1991. Mark Leyner's Galactic Colonoscopy: From Dense Dot to Big God. In *MONDO 2000 #5*. Berkeley and Fun City: MegaMedia/MONDO 2000, p. 49.

Miller, Laurence, and Link Yaco. 1976. *EMPOOL #1*. Ann Arbor.

Miller, Laurence, and Link Yaco. 1978. *EMPOOL #2*. Ann Arbor.

Mortensen, Christian. 2018. Beyond Gonzo-Journalism. In *Cyberpunk and Visual Culture*. Edited by Graham J. Murphy and Lars Schmeink. New York and London: Routledge, p. 8.

Murphy, Graham J. 2018. Angel (LINK) of Harlem. In *Beyond Cyberpunk: New Critical Perspectives*. Edited by Graham J. Murphy and Sherryl Vint. New York and London: Routledge, pp. 212, 215.

Murphy, Graham, and Lars Schmeink. 2018. Introduction: The Visuality and Virtuality of Cyberpunk. In *Cyberpunk and Visual Culture*. Edited by Graham J. Murphy and Lars Schmeink. New York and London: Routledge, p. xxi.

Nelson, Ted. 1987. *Computer Lib and Dream Machines*. Redmond: Microsoft Press.

Peled, Abraham. 1987. The Next Computer Revolution. *Scientific American*, Number 4. New York: vol. 257.

Rheingold, Howard. 1993. The Virtual Community. Available online: http://www.rheingold.com/vc/book/ (accessed on 11 September 2018).

Rogers, Michael. 1991. *Newsweek*, August 19, p. 61.

Rucker, Rudy. 1994. 15 Tech Notes Towards a Cyberpunk Novel. In *MONDO 2000 #13*. Berkeley and Fun City: MegaMedia/MONDO 2000, p. 52.

SCAN. 1991. Small Computers in the Arts Network. In *Program Book of the Eleventh Annual SCAN Symposium on Small Computers in the Arts*. Philadelphia: Small Computers in the Arts Network.

Shiner, Lewis. 1991. Confessions of an Ex-Cyberpunk. *New York Times*, January 7. Available online: http://www.fictionliberationfront.net/cyberpunk.html (accessed on 5 May 2018).

Sirius, R.U. 1989. *MONDO 2000 #7*. Berkeley and Fun City: MegaMedia/MONDO 2000, pp. 11, 61, 78, 114, 88, 100, 153.

Sirius, R. U. 1992. *MONDO 2000 #4*. pp. 49, 52, 63.

Sterling, Bruce. 1994. Profesor Kroker and his Risus Sardonicus. In *MONDO 2000 #13*. Berkeley and Fun City: MegaMedia/MONDO 2000, p. 124.

Sterling, Bruce. 1998. Sixth INTERZONE Column. May 23. Available online: lib.ru/STERLINGB/interzone.Txt (accessed on 12 May 2018).

University of Michigan Institute of Social Research. 1983. *Drugs and American High School Students 1975–1983*; North Bethesda: National Institute for Drug Abuse.

Wertheim, Margaret. 1999. *The Pearly Gates of Cyberspace*. New York: W. W. Norton, pp. 254–55.

Wolfe, Tom. 2003. Foreword to McLuhan, Marshall. In *Understanding Me: Lectures and Interviews*. Edited by Stephanie McLuhan and David Staines. Cambridge: MIT University Press, p. xvi.

YLEM Artists Using Science and Technology. 1991. *Directory of Artists Using Science and Technology 1991–1992*. San Francisco: YLEM Artists Using Science and Technology.

arts MDPI

Article

Cyberpunk Redux: Dérives in the Rich Sight of Post-Anthropocentric Visuality

Frenchy Lunning

Liberal Arts Department, Minneapolis College of Art and Design, Minneapolis, MN 55404, USA; flunning@mcad.edu

Received: 19 June 2018; Accepted: 7 August 2018; Published: 10 August 2018

Abstract: Our future effects on the earth, in light of the Anthropocene, are all dire expressions of a depleted world left in piles of detritus and toxic ruin—including the diminished human as an assemblage of impoverished existence, yet adumbrating that handicapped existence with an ersatz advanced technology. In the cyberpunk films, these expressions are primarily visual expressions—whether through written prose thick with densely dark adjectives describing the world of cyberpunk, or more widely known, the comic books and films of cyberpunk, whose representations have become classically understood as SF canon. The new films of the cyberpunk redux however, represent an evolution in cyberpunk visuality. Despite these debatable issues around this term, it will provide this paper with its primary object of visuality, that of the "rich sight", a further term that arose from the allure created in the late 19th century development of department stores that innovated the display of the goods laid out in a spectacular view, presenting the shopper with a fantasy of wealth and fetishized objects which excited shoppers to purchase, but more paradoxically, creating the desire to see a fantasy that was at the same time also a reality. This particular and enframed view—so deeply embedded and beloved in our commodity-obsessed culture—is what I suggest so profoundly typifies the initial cyberpunk postmodern representation in the *Blade Runner* films, and its continuing popularity in the early part of the 21st century. Both films are influenced by Ridley Scott's initial vision of the cinematic cyberpunk universe and organized as sequential narratives. Consequently, they serve as excellent examples of the evolution of this visual spectacular.

Keywords: visuality; "rich sight"; Blade Runner; animatism; cinematism; flattened screens; collage; proscenium views; layers; detritus

---

1. Introduction: Through the Lens of the Anthropocene

How urban squalor can be a delight to the eyes, when expressed in commodification, and how an unparalleled quantum leap in the alienation of daily life in the city can now be experienced in the form of strange new hallucinatory exhilaration—these are some of the questions that confront us.

Frederic Jameson (1984)

"Postmodernism or the Cultural Logic of Late Capitalism"

When Frederic Jameson asks how "urban squalor can be a delight to the eyes, when expressed in commodification, and how an unparalleled quantum leap in the alienation of daily life in the city can now be experienced in the form of strange new hallucinatory exhilaration," it provokes the two most ironic observations about the cyberpunk aesthetic, both now and in its initial flowering in the 1980s to 1990s. However, now we now must view these visions through the sobering lens of the *Anthropocene*, with its attendant immediacy transforming the natural world around us. In early cyberpunk, this "ending of the world" was presaged as visions of dire expressions of a depleted world left in piles of abandoned and useless commodities now as detritus and toxic ruin—including the diminished human as an impoverished existence, despite the adumbration of that handicapped existence with an ersatz advanced technology. This was the view from many of the early cyberpunk representations, especially the first *Blade Runner* (1982)[1] film.

However, the Anthropocene, a term devised by atmospheric chemist Paul Crutzen in 2002 (Crutzen 2002; Crutzen and Stoermer 2002). is generally understood as the contemporary period during which human activities have had a profoundly negative environmental impact on the Earth, so much so that it has constituted a distinct geological age. Still controversial in terms of its "origins" (the development of the steam engine, the myths of ancient Greece, the development of the human species, and even the first Copernican Revolution, etc.) (Ellis 2018, p. 1), and indeed, the very existence of an age where human activities and the proposed "end of the world," the Anthropocene suggests is denied by many politicians and scientists. Timothy Morton, however, cites the emergence and nature of the Anthropocene:

> "The actual earth", as Thoreau puts it, now contains throughout its circumference a thin layer of radioactive materials, deposited since 1945. The deposition of this layer marks a decisive geological moment in the *Anthropocene*, a geological time marked by decisive human "terraforming" of earth as such. The first significant marks were laid down in 1784, when carbon from coal-fired industries began to be deposited world-wide ... After 1945, there began *the Great Acceleration*, in which the geological transformation of Earth by humans increased by vivid orders of magnitude. (Morton 2013, pp. 4–5)

Science fiction (SF) has been steadily creating visions of such a world end since Jean-Baptiste Cousin de Grainville's *Le Dernier Homme*, considered to be the "first modern speculative fiction to depict the end of the world" (The Last Man 2003). Yet, it is in the SF emergence of the cyberpunk genre wherein these expressions become primarily visual expressions—whether in written prose thick with densely dark adjectives describing the world in cyberpunk novels, or more widely known, in the comic books and films of cyberpunk. What in the present moment we can readily identify as Anthropocenic visions as "the end of the world is correlated with the Anthropocene, is its global warming, and subsequent drastic climate change" (Morton 2013, p. 7). These visions are most profoundly discovered in the novel by William Gibson, *Neuromancer* (Gibson 1984), Ridley Scott's film *Blade Runner* (1982), and in both *Ghost in the Shell* (*Kôkaku Kidôtai*) manga by Shirow Masamune (serialized 1989), and the anime directed by Oshii Mamoru and animated by Production I.G. (1995).

However, the recent re-emergence of cyberpunk narratives has suggested an evolution[2] in its formal expressions and representations, and because of the radical departure of its style, a reconsideration of that future period as perhaps a *post-Anthropocene*. The most widely experienced redux can be found in two films released in 2017: a rather unfortunate live-action version of Oshii's *Ghost in the Shell*, and a new sequel film of the *Blade Runner* series, that narrates the events that happen to the characters in Scott's *Blade Runner*, thirty years after the events in the original film, in *Blade Runner 2049*, directed by Denis Villeneuve. It is in fact, the stylistic changes in the cyberpunk redux that has, through its very different qualities, which although different, still evidence not only a sense of an aftermath, but of the very transformative process created within its narrative appearances. These changes suggest what Morton refers to as the *Age of Asymmetry*, and he describes in no uncertain terms not only the stakes he envisions in this age, but the very description of the cyberpunk redux narrative:

---

[1]   *Blade Runner* (Final Cut). Dir. By Ridley Scott (originally 1982; Warner Bros., Final Cut was issued in 2007, Amazon Prime). This version of the original *Blade Runner* films, of which there are many: the *Workprint*, the *U.S. Theatrical Cut*, the *International Cut*, the *Director's Cut*, and the *Final Cut*; was chosen because it is the most recent version that Scott has released, and follows the logic that with time, he was able to achieve the effect he had wished for, and was not able to do in the previous versions.

[2]   Suggested by Damon Stanek, 25 July 2018.

> ... an *Age of Asymmetry* in which our cognitive powers become self-defeating. The more
> we know about radiation, global warming, and the other massive objects that show upon
> our radar, the more enmeshed in them we realize we are. Knowledge is no longer able to
> achieve escape velocity from Earth, or ... the surging, "towering" reality of things. We are
> no longer poised on the edge of the abyss ... Instead ... we are already falling inside ...
> It is now the uncanny time of zombies after the end of the world, a time of hypocrisy where
> every decision is wrong. (Morton 2013, p. 160)

The new films of the cyberpunk redux represent this evolution most succinctly as an evolution in
cyberpunk visuality. Despite the debatable issues around this term, *visuality* in art historical terms has
come to mean a visual perspective through a rigid culturally formulated lens from which viewers are
restricted to view images and their meanings and associations in intensely specific ways; as Foucault
has pronounced it: the visual perspective controls what is "seeable and sayable". Mirzoeff further
focuses the lens of visuality on its functions "to be a medium for the transmission and dissemination
of authority, and the means for the mediation of those subjects to that authority" (Mirzoeff 2011, p. xv).
To consider how to answer Jameson's questions of how urban squalor can delight the eyes, as an
alienation from daily life, and as an escape from the realities of quotidian existence; an examination of
two different, but related works of the cyberpunk film series: that of *Blade Runner (Final Cut)* (from now
on *Blade Runner*) and *Blade Runner 2049* will reveal through two considerations of visual perspective
how possible outcomes of both the Anthropocene and the Age of Asymmetry might emerge. In a sense,
these films address the authority of our own greed and profoundly ever-continuing complicity in the
termination of all life on Earth, and yet how in each film, a visual richness might allow for a certain
mediation of that acknowledgment through the potential insights displayed by both films.

2. Dérive One: The Anthropocenic "Rich Sight"

> *The aesthetic of "rich sight" erased that delicate link between cause and symptom.*
>
> Laura Mulvey (1996a)

Primarily, how does such the specific dire visuality created by both films, create such exquisite
pleasure in looking that even the original *Blade Runner* film remains popular viewing thirty-five years
later, and gave rise to the creation of a sequel. One possible concept arises in a re-imagining of an old
term, that of the "rich sight". This term developed from the allure created in the late 19th century
development of department stores that innovated the display of the goods laid out in a spectacular
view, presenting the shopper with a fantasy of wealth and a plentitude of fetishized objects which
excited shoppers to purchase, but more paradoxically, creating the desire to *see* a fantasy that was
at the same time also a reality. This particular and politically enframed view, so deeply embedded
and beloved in our commodity-obsessed capitalist cultural hegemony, is transformed when viewing
through the cyberpunk lens, a dying world detritus, when "richness" becomes a horror. The "rich
sight" of the Anthropocene is one of death, but on a massive and almost inclusive scale. The only
living things left are humans who were in some way deficient or disabled, scampering around the junk
piles, jacking auto parts from the cop cars, and skittering away like insects or rodents. What we view
in both *Blade Runner* films is the dead flesh of the monster we made, and the monster that killed us,
also laid low and rusting, soon to be made into dust itself. Yet we are fascinated and thrilled by the
mere power of the plentitude of death positioned and literally framing each view of particularly the
original *Blade Runner* world. Yet, what is this mechanism that allows for this mediation in which the
transformation of a vision of horror becomes an enriching intense fascination?

Laura Mulvey has discussed this phenomenon in detail and calls out the resulting commodity
fetishism that has, since the mid-twentieth century's increasing hyper-capitalism, produced "shopping"
as a *spectacular* event. In addition, Benjamin's insight into this affect as the key to his "new
urban phantasmagoria", meant that it was not so much the objects themselves, as it was the

"commodity-on-display" (Mulvey 1996b, p. 4), the "rich sight" of all those bright and shiny new things one could *potentially* possess. As Dana Polan suggests:

> Mass culture becomes a kind of postmodern culture, the stability of social sense dissolved (without becoming any less ideological) into one vast spectacular show, a dissociation of cause and effect, a concentration on allure of means and concomitant disinterest in meaningful ends. Such spectacle creates the promise of a rich sight: not the sight of particular fetishized objects, but sight itself as richness, as the ground for extensive experience.[3]

"But sight itself as richness"; the point here is that it is not the individual objects under this enriching gaze of allure, but the *sight* itself, as a panoramic, a totalizing view, a *mis en scène*. It is the lush experience and a sense of visual plenty, of a visual phantasmagoria of multitudes of objects in a single view—so utterly tied to the fetishization of commodities in late capitalism, as discussed by many critics and scholars. As Mulvey recognizes, "The present transcendence of the "rich sight" aesthetic has developed out of the structures of disavowal at work in mass culture. Disavowal maintains, after all, only a tenuous link between cause and effect while its investment in visual excess and displacement of signifiers produces a very strong texture that can come to conceal *the need to conceal the relation between cause and effect*" (Mulvey 1996a, pp. 15–16). This easily reveals the *jouissance* experience involved in the apprehension of the "rich sight", and its implications with an aesthetic of the complexity of the collaged or bricolaged scenic design, so prevalent in the cyberpunk works, especially film. When the experience is heavy in its effect, but its cause is ambiguous, or as in the *Blade Runner* films, displaced onto a large-scaled, historical, or ideological frame, the effect of the display is one of wonder and, as Mulvey addressed as well, one of curiosity.

3. Dérive Two: The "Picturesque"

The two opposite qualities of roughness, and of sudden variation, joined to that of irregularity, are the most efficient causes of the picturesque.

Sir Uvedale Price (1810)

"Essay on the Picturesque, as Compared with the Sublime and the Beautiful: And, on the

Use of Studying Pictures, for the Purpose of Improving Real Landscape," Vol. 1.

And yet, is there not more to the mere "rich sight" that incites such wonder and memorable images in this peculiar phenomenon? An odd, even older concept seems informative in this regard, that of the picturesque, though not in the contemporary understanding of the term, but in an earlier sense, in which the nature of "beauty" was much discussed and debated. Sir Uvedale Price, writing in 1794 to 1798 on the design of gardens, discusses how the picturesque differs from the contemporary notion of the "beautiful": "Should we wish to give it a picturesque beauty, we must use the mallet, instead of the chisel: we must beat down one half of it, deface the other, and throw the mutilated members around in heaps … make it rough and you make it also picturesque" (Pevsner 2010, p. 132). This amusing and rather pertinent description was part of an argument around architectural visual planning also in a mid-twentieth century modernist climate.

Nikolaus Pevsner understood the picturesque to be "a visual formalism in which objects and their relations are subsumed into relations of pictorial composition from particular points of view" (Pevsner 2010, p. 15). This is to say, that just as these "particular points of view" frame and contextualize the "rich sight", and the visual perspective, so too do cultural confines also frame the picturesque. For these modernist designers, the desire for a pictorial unity was supreme, in that "visual planning was meant to make a pictorial unity out of disparate elements, particularly modern,

---

[3]   (Polan 1987–1988). In (Mulvey 1996a).

historic, and vernacular buildings that were … aesthetically disjunct and ideologically antagonistic" (Pevsner 2010, p. 15). The distinction for Pevsner and his contemporaries in terms of this formalist method was that rather than a unity of the *subject*, they necessarily opted for one modeled on collage. Further, that the picturesque principles that Pevsner recognized as the results of this method, those of "intricacy, surprise, impropriety, variety, contrast, piquancy, incongruity, roughness, sudden variation, and irregularity" (Pevsner 2010, p. 22), all of which can be responses particularly of the visual planning styles of collage and bricolage (that of "construction (as of a sculpture or a structure of ideas) achieved by using whatever comes to hand"[4]).

In the cyberpunk aesthetic, the visual planning of the scenes was considered much like the visual planning of cities and towns; they required a visual composition to draw the viewer into a specific scene, which is "dressed" in the proper cultural arraignment that signifies the desired effect. For the cyberpunk, Pevsner's principles worked to deliver the desired "punk" effect alongside the "end of the world" junkyard. Collage and bricolage were used particularly in the initial *Blade Runner* and has established for most audiences, the formal qualities of the cyberpunk style of the postmodern 1980s to 1990s, and which from much of the scholarship of recent years, seems to exist for many scholars as the reigning representation of the cyberpunk aesthetic. The first *Blade Runner* was indeed an innovation in "rich sights", and a spectacular landmark of cinematic picturesque design, particularly of futurity, until the present day. Its primary mode of visuality followed an assemblage of objects—that of "an artistic composition made from scraps, junk, and odds and ends"[5]—that refer to death, ruin, and decay, yet also to a triumph of DIY innovation, and a gothic "picturesque", "rich sight within a noir narrative.

Finally, the early theorists of the picturesque, recognized that this aspect of the aesthetic "belongs exclusively to the sense of vision" (Pevsner 2010, p. 132), and further, that the density of the profusion of objects required by the picturesque, and its "intricacy in landscape might be defined, that disposition of objects, which by a partial and uncertain concealment, excites and nourishes curiosity".[6] It is here with the effect of "curiosity", as Mulvey asserts, caused by the visual apprehension of the intensely dense display of objects in the picturesque, that we find a clue to the enduring fascination of the cyberpunk aesthetic. Curiosity is a state which when activated, and especially when visual, it tends to remain open; remain unformed as a conclusion or authority. The mind plays with this apprehension, attempts to contextualize it, to categorize it, or discover its cause; but particularly when confronted with the complexity of collaged or bricolaged visual scenes, a totality cannot often be arrived at with any surety, and remains provocative. In addition, when presented with a "rich sight", a plentitude of objects lain out for display, composed to create a fantasy that denies limitation or confines; there is a linkage to the imagination. The viewer is bedazzled by the spectacle and can seek a way through it, by repetition of the experience through various methods: fandom, sequels, or cross-platform versions. As Mulvey admits: "The cinema is, therefore, phantasmagoria, illusion and a symptom of the social unconscious. It is precisely these elements that are fun to decipher for any audience." (Mulvey 1996a, p. xxvii).

4. Dérive Three: *Blade Runner* (Final Cut)

> *The city, not cyberspace, is the soul of cyberpunk.*
>
> Stephan Joyce (2018)
>
> "Playing for Virtually Real: Cyberpunk Aesthetics and Ethics in *Deus Ex: Human Revolution*"

The visual aspects of the city in the initial *Blade Runner* film have been excessively examined and discussed by many excellent scholars since the 1980s; such as Tatsumi Takayuki, who describes the

---

4 "bricolage." Merriam-Webster. https://www.merriam-webster.com/dictionary/bricolage.
5 "assemblage." Merriam-Webster. https://www.merriam-webster.com/dictionary/assemblage.
6 (Price 1810). In (Pevsner 2010, p. 132).

cityscape as a "chaotic and chimeric fusion", and a "post-apocalyptic junkyard" (Tatsumi 2006, p. 14), creating a "cultural vertigo" (Tatsumi 2006, p. xi). And Scott Bukatmann—who has also written much on this topic—described the Los Angeles of the future as a "dispersed, boundless, heterogeneous" (Bukatmann 1997, p. 59) city with a "cacophony of signs . . . an empty space of burst pipes, decay and deterioration . . . made hallucinatory by the searchlights that constantly sweep past its windows" (Bukatmann 1997, p. 60). All of the early cyberpunk discourse was brought into being with the emergence of the Internet and the digital technologies, and the distinct sense of an urban-like reality beyond the screen, described accurately in William Gibson seminal work, *Neuromancer:*

> Cyberspace: A consensual hallucination experienced daily by billions of legitimate operators, in every nation . . . A graphical representation of data abstracted from the banks of every computer in the human system. Unthinkable complexity. Lines of light ranged in the nonspace of the mind, clusters and constellations of data. Like city lights, receding. (Gibson 1984)

And what they and so many others describe is a bricolage of the detritus of the industrial to the technological age, all piled high into the urban landscape. Trash and commodity, no longer separate entities, have become one in the merger of a DIY innovation and creativity, fulfilling a nostalgic and redemptive impulse within an impossible infrastructure and a fascistic police state. These constructions represent a process of a "cut-and-paste" collage of the leftovers from the late capitalist piles of used commodities and technologies pasted together to form new technologies to, in particular, replicate extinct life forms and spare body parts, such as the snake vendor, or the eyeball maker. The city of Los Angeles itself becomes part of a DIY development of the *sprawl*—William Gibson's word for the amalgamation of American and Japanese cities that have lost their cultural distinctions, to house those not fit for the tidy and entitled (and no doubt white) off-world populations of humans.

The implications in the visuality of the 1980s postmodern cyberpunk age was not entirely dire however, as they were saved by an aesthetic that developed in the fashion and music world at the same time as did the cyber technologies—that of *punk*, whose visual language was also that of bricolage. Punk, as with other "street subcultures", use the tactic recalled and defined in "Hebdige's discussion of bricolage—the resignification of a patchwork of symbols, given new meanings in new contexts—remains important in showing us how subcultures adopt, transform and rework that which already exists—as William Gibson put it, 'the street finds its own uses for things'" (Bell 2001). Punk also meant, for example, the cleverness of the *Blade Runner* mechanisms.

At the same time, as the viewer recognized the collaged, Do-It-Yourself poverty implied in the commodities of this world, they *also* recognized its creativity and reveled in the "rich sight" of their compelling potential. Further, the viewer was assured that the characteristic creativity of the human will not be lost at the "end of the world" but adapted and reinvigorated by the new humans—and thus part of the enduring appeal of the cyberpunk aesthetic. It is in this gap in the dialectic between the use of the cut-up-and-reassembled method of the collage that, Barash argues: "collage techniques allowed artists to uncover meaning within a readymade consumer culture . . . and find ways to evade, negotiate, reflect, or sometimes undo the reification of commodity culture." (Poyner and Barash 2013). Yet, it seems that at the same time as we acknowledge the failure of the modernist consumer ideology and fetishization of objects, we also experience the enjoyment of the new postmodern DIY-vintage world—cheap and with a "utopian total availability" (Poyner and Barash 2013)—that we have simply re-organized the structure of our desires to a channel our nostalgic desire for the old modes of production, now made cheap, quaint, and picturesque—and therefore "punk"—and therefore cool.

As Tatsumi Takayuki has acknowledged; "As soon as the existing standard of aesthetics has collapsed, the hyper-capitalist imperative incorporates the weirdest into the most marketable, the most *avant garde*, and the most beautiful" (Tatsumi 2006, p. 156). The past is now as much a fiction as the future has become. In addition, it is this past vision of the modernist ultra-high-tech minimalist culture—which in cyberpunk continues to be represented as the off-world elite—that in its decay and ruin, also creates a present moment in which *Blade Runner* has supplied for the last thirty or so years, a panoramic "rich sight" of vast layers of "dark, claustrophobic, polluted and dirty [stuff] ... in its crumbling buildings and rotting cars ... [a] junkyard futurism"[7] marvelously appealing.

This junkyard "rich sight" of the cyberpunk future, which has stood for the ultimate cultural vision of late capitalism and the hegemony of the "rich sight" of a picturesque commodity display, was delivered through the production designs of Syd Mead, the special effects of Douglas Trumball, and the deft camerawork of Jordan Cronenweth, who, together, created the unique, bricolaged *mis en scenes* to create a visuality and an aesthetic. Of course, the most oft-repeated scene from the various versions of the initial *Blade Runner*, is Deckerd's astounding ride toward the Tyrell Corporation, as we slide through their game-like panorama—that is, a shallow blue-black atmospheric stage set suggestive of a massively-scaled, awe-inspiring totalizing view of the upper city, arranged with blocks of flat, distant, monolithic corporations rife with thousands of dots of lights that edge slowly backward as Deckerd's car approaches. The car passes the immense advertisement—worthy of the Times Square—of a geisha staring slyly from a side view, and as she takes a dainty bite, her shiny, red lips smile condescendingly at the viewer as the scene ends.

That scene switches dramatically down to an abstract bricolage viewed from the grubby street below. Looking upward toward the upper world of the corporate authorities, which are represented as an impossible collision of flat geometric shapes covered with dots of light and arranged akimbo at all angles. In addition, through this expressionistic stage set, behind and overhead, a massive piece of machinery that blocks our view slowly glides as an ad-covered incomprehensible, lumbering vehicle overhead, as a squeaky voice intones the taglines of the off-world promises to the oppressed grime and rain-covered masses below. Lamarre explains the editing tactic of this *animetistic* style: "As they enhance speed and movement through the use of rapid cuts in conjunction with flattened and dehierarchized fields of distributed information, structures of exploded projection emerge to place a material limit on dispersion and flatness, generating temporary fields of potential depth associated with lines of sight." (Lamarre 2009, Loc. 3072). This describes precisely the way each of the city scenes have been paradoxically introduced as a "rich sight", accentuating the phantasmagoric, yet as a dying world pulling the viewer through the world of the *Blade Runner*. As Vivian Sobchack explains:

> In the last decade of the twentieth century, the cinematic response to these questions has been cities imagined spatially (and tonally) in an urban experience of going "over the top" or plunging "over the edge". That is, although manifest in two quite different modes, the current science fiction film city has been figured as *groundless*, lacking both logically secure and spatially stable premises [sic] for its—and our—existence. This is a city virtually "bottomed out" and literally fathomless: its inhabitants suffer from giddiness or vertigo and, rootless, they "free fall" in both space and time. (Sobchack 1999, p. 138)

At that urban bottom, rootless and in the constant sense of a "free fall", are those beings living at the dark, dank street level of the city. Represented in the action shots; that were usually framed at the edges of the screen by the dark, wet, groundless bottom, and at the sides by clever close-ups brought to the very edge of the screen, are the silhouetted assemblages of ruined machinery and car parts. Surrounded by a backdrop of a constantly moving barrage of drenched umbrellas held by the marginalized population of leftover "other" people: the punks, dwarfs, and the seemingly criminal DIY entrepreneurs; densely layered against a background of absolute blackness. These *mise en scènes* present a shallow but highly fragmented, and bricolaged composition of layers of reflecting prismatic glass and a tangle of blinking neon signage, creating a sort of analytical cubist mid-ground, and occasionally within which, the actions in the city are displayed. Creating a labyrinthine passage

---

[7]   Cumbow, Robert. "Survivors: The Day after Doomsday." In (Sobchack 1999, p. 134).

of detritus, the stage is set in which the vision of commodity greed becomes indeed mediated as a deliciously picturesque "rich sight".

The scale and dimensions of the interior rooms of stores, apartments, and even Tyrell's office are implied, but never fully realizable, as architectural elements are positioned as *objects* in the field of vision, rather than as part of an organized sense of enclosure. This continues not only the "rich sight" of this world, but the sense of *assemblage*, a work of art made by grouping together found or unrelated objects; that is, a dense collection of disparate objects ordinarily unrelated to each other, but within the same structure of feeling—or as Lamarre refers to it, as a: "distributive field in which movement into depth is replaced by density of information" (Lamarre 2009, p. 133), which together creates a sense of a plethora of de-territorialized ruin which was thus transformed into a plentitude of potential objects. Cleverly reassembled or re-territorialized, this field of transformed innovations, occupying their own separate positions within the field, not only provide an acknowledgment of the end of the capitalist era of modernity's worship of the "new" commodity, but also the thrill of creativity in the face of ruin, and thus a sense of the animated play and the nostalgic satisfaction that it engenders.

5. Dérive Four: Blade Runner 2049

The ideal city contains no citizens whatever . . .

Philip Strick (1984)

"Metropolis Wars: The City as Character in Science Fiction Films"

Blade Runner 2049 is the continuation of the *Blade Runner* narrative thirty years later; it was released thirty-five years after the first film, in 2017. From the very first credits, we enter a *mise en abîme* where we are both immediately aware of the relationship to the first *Blade Runner* film *as a film* and are also aware of a blatant difference. As the producers of the film's logos are shown, they are faded and in black and white denoting a somber and menacing tone, but with the occasional blip of video spikes and slight broadcast interruptions, we become aware that even within our viewing, this film is *within and of* this new *Blade Runner* reality. The Columbia Productions logo of the woman (Liberty) is suddenly silhouetted by explosive white clouds behind her, symbolizing—as we later understand—the "Blackout of 2020". Then we are shown the screen-filled blue eye of the original film, but instead of being clouded by reflections of constant explosions in the city of the original *Blade Runner*; this eye is clear. From that eye, is a quick shot to the iris-matching aerial view of the desert ground of the new panorama of Los Angeles; a vast multitude of sepia-toned, circular eye-shaped protein farms, lain out over an expansive desert emptiness. These farms are austere, mechanistic, rationally designed, and without any evidence of life, except for the assumed protein worms within the farms, although they as well, might be replicants. The didactic for the film appears in tiny digital read-out script, inferring that the film itself is an artifact *of the film's future reality*, and that the Blackout of 2020 was also the "collapse of the ecosphere". All this, we suddenly realize, is because *Blade Runner 2049* is now in the time of a Post-Anthropocene; and consequently, everything that was, or could be "born", is now gone.

The Anthropocene was the time of the original *Blade Runner*, when the ruinous fate was only in-progress and not a *fait accompli*, and there was still hope through a "new urban exoticism" (Sobchack 1999, p. 135) that provided a way out through creativity by way of a new sort perverse consumerism via the DIY entrepreneurs: "The city is thus re-energized—finding a new function and a new aesthetic" (Ibid), and the concomitant picturesque "rich sight" as both its most profound expression and its most powerful incentive. But *Blade Runner 2049* is a Post-Anthropocene future. In the very beginning, the disembodied eye we beheld in *Blade Runner* which "holds the infernal city reflected in its gaze" (Bukatman 1999), is now a clear eye reflecting nothing; meaning that there is no more "infernal city" to reflect, or even that there are no "real" humans left that are capable of "reflection". However, there seems to be no "rich sight" left to reflect; that is, nothing valued is left in the same sense of value that was placed in the "rich sight" of the visions of the previous era, composed of a picturesque dense detritus.

Mulvey asserts: "There is a logic to harnessing the overinscribed signifier to the uninscribed. The sheer force of the "rich sight", of the spectacle, creates a diversion away from inquiry or curiosity." (Mulvey 1996b, p. 14). Even as the picturesque, with its dazzling "mutilated members around in heaps" was said to encourage curiosity, Mulvey rejects this notion that such an array encourages speculation, wonder, and the usual effects of the spectacle. Curiosity calls for action; to detect and discover beyond the logic of the image, but Mulvey is positioning the viewer as a consumer, one who consumes, who enters into a negotiation with the producer to acquire those objects. However, what is the negotiation in the passive sense of the observer? The "rich sight" of the Post-Anthropocene becomes a stark minimalism, redolent with the death of the field of objects; from the destroyed richness of the picturesque to a scorched Earth where only monochromatic shells of objects are slowly being blown away by relentless winds of abandonment. The "rich sight" is one of the severely rational mode of modernist minimalism. The viewer observes the tight, instrumental, yet sculptural structures of the protein farms in their vast scale and clean lines. Viewers are not curious because this is death, this is final, this is the end of the world, no actions are indicated.

The way in which the approach to LA was shot in the original *Blade Runner*, utilized an *animetistic* style, described by Lamarre as an anime approach to a visuality. As such, it is a device in which the scene sets are separated into overlapping layers of what might be compared to theatrical "flats". We can substitute for discussion's sake, the theatrical set as a model for the framed world of the film screen. In this model, the architectural elements generated a downstage (or at the very front boundary of the stage "world"), a mid-stage layer (stage right and stage left, providing boundaries on the sides), and the upstage area (at the very back of the stage "world"), creating Lamarre's notion of a multiplanar or "diorama effect", which being film—and neither theater nor animation—creates a rather peculiar sense of massive scale, but a paradoxically shallow, stage-like sense of depth. In the approach to the Tyrell building, the buildings slide backward—much as in multiplanar animation. Much of the original *Blade Runner* seems influenced by anime, but we also might infer that cinematism and animetism are both potential tendencies of the moving image, whether in animation or in cinema.

However, in *Blade Runner 2049*, we return to a clearly cinematic style. Instead of a distributive field of objects that occupy changeable hierarchies and identities of animatism, views in *Blade Runner 2049* are—both in interior and exterior shots—in a rigid one-point perspective, accentuating and stabilizing in time and space both hierarchies and identities. Most establishing shots are long shots, placing the actors as small active positions in massive, and still-in-time historical proscenium. The weight and wonder of each shot comes from the paradoxical awe of the "rich sight" of the dusty and dilapidated ruined grand interiors of our own present officialdom with its contrary sense of anticipated emptiness, death, and decay.

The scale of these ruins is magnified to diminish the profile of the scale of the replicant human within the tremendous power and magnitude of the now-absent human age. Even in the shots of KD6's apartment, we tend to see him within a shot which has centered him in front of his picture window, looking outward into the city. His "chair" is positioned to face out in his dead-stare, the dead city at the center of the window, as if aligned with a singular vanishing point, that lies out in the vast dead city to some infiniteness. He sits and stares outward, and viewers are also positioned to be focused toward that vanishing point that is hidden from our view—and the view of KD6—by a flat stage-painting of the city confronting him.

These long perspectival shots are accompanied by long shots that are cut off visually from the vanishing point in a similar way, with shallow flattened backgrounds; in the air, in the view of massive dark and dead buildings, in the flat, yellow screens of the desert sand storms, and in the rising wave of the sea in Luv's death scene. However, this is also present in interior shots, particularly in the huge, modernist, architectural forms of Wallace's corporate complex—which we never see in entirety suggesting his hegemonic hold over all of the diminished earthly existence. In it, we are confronted with massive minimalist blank walls, lit frequently with the Wallace corporation logo detail of reflected waves of water. Despite their closed access to any sense of the totality of the building, these interiors, and indeed the corporate exteriors as well, become in their flattened state, abstract expressions of the corporate power that *is* the world. Their dark sarcophagi—menacing, misty magnitudes of presence—loom in every long shot, of which there are many, but this time with no dots of light to be found; and they stabilize in both time and space, memories of a bleak future of death.

Scale is perhaps the most dynamic tactic of the filmmakers, and their clever use of scale has created some of the most affecting aspects of the film. In the Las Vegas scenes at the end of the film, Vegas—as the most dangerously radiated area—is shot through a saturated acrid yellow filter creating a duotone world of extreme light and dark. Within the intense, empty sandstorm, KD6 (now "Joe"), walks through a landscape of what becomes massive fragments of clearly cheap, and commercial sculptures of women, the detritus of the Vegas nightclub masculinist culture, where women were but part of the consumables available in the modernist, hyper-capitalist, hyper-cool "rat pack" culture. It is a horrifying "rich sight": the scale of misogyny becomes acutely visual as monuments of disgust and hate—and fear—in a toxic, "uninhabitable" landscape where there is only ruin and death. It is the very edge of the dead culture in what is already a disappearing world.

Once inside the dark and dusty mausoleum that was once the night club "Treasure Island", women, and Elvis, appear once again as digital vocaloids in varying scales of size or distance as they blip on and off—sound on and off—in the absolute black timeless-and-spaceless-ness and stillness of the theater of the club. The black eliminates any scale and allows for the blips to become technicolored memories of the consumable display of women who all are the same, non-individual constructs within the consciousness of a dead masculinist ideality. They appear as the conscious background to this last outpost of the modern male, and the actions of the two protagonist men—one real, one replicant—both of whom are pivoting around a woman who is the lynchpin of their lives, their cultures, and their immediate future, which we know is death.

To explain this, the filmmakers seem to use a rather strict cinematism, as Paul Virilio has referred to it, and as Lamarre explains:

> For Virilio, cinematism is part of a more general optical logistics that ultimately serves to align our eyes with weapons of mass destruction, with the bomb's-eye view. The eye becomes one with the bomb, and everywhere in the world becomes a target. The essence of cinematism lies in the use of mobile apparatuses of perception, which serve (1) to give the viewer a sense of standing over and above the world and thus controlling it, and (2) to collapse the distance between viewer and target, in the manner of the ballistic logic of instant strike or instant hit. (Lamarre 2009, Loc. 653)

This "bomb-sight" cinematic view is consistent with the one-point perspective that is part of the totalizing view of *Blade Runner 2049*'s masculinist visuality and positions the contemporary viewer in the position of looking at a view of the future through the lens of our modernist masculinist past. It suggests an alignment with Timothy Morton's warning that the end of the world has already happened, and its falling death is in slow-motion around us. This bomb-sight tactic then pulls us toward a single vanishing point—a fate that has two potential meanings; first that we are fated to live out a world that is already dead, and hence, we cannot look askance to avoid this reality. However, it also might give us a choice to either adapt to the dead world, as is suggested in *Blade Runner 2049*, with the beginning of a new race of beings—or to become extinct with grace. However, a single vanishing point is also the point made by Morton; that an end is *absolutely inevitable*. A "rich in*sight*" indeed.

6. A Final Dérive

The ecological thought understands that there never was an authentic world.

Timothy Morton (2012)

Yet perhaps there is another way to approach this film. Despite the dire warnings and a bleak visuality of a dead world, there is also another way to look at this: as a utopian/dystopian allegory. Of course, cyberpunk has always been allegorical, but usually utopian via a dystopian visuality, in that despite the negatively cast junkyard aesthetic of *Blade Runner*, its ultimate effect on viewers is a future in a positive sense of a redemptive creative coolness. This has been the key reason that cyberpunk can still resonate with contemporary audiences after some 35 years. This is precisely how allegory works: "In allegorical structure, then, one text is *read through* another, however *fragmentary, intermittent*, or *chaotic* their relationship may be; the paradigm for the allegorical work is thus palimpsest. (Owens 1980, p. 69)." This palimpsest works on two layers in cyberpunk: it is, of course, the story of our present represented as past that is read through our projection of a future; but it is also a utopia read through a dystopian projection of the present. As a utopian narrative, it is constituted through a critique of the present that is solved or answered through a projection into a future of either a corrective new world (utopian), or as the dire condition of those critiqued aspects projected as punishment for those dire results (dystopian). The *Blade Runner* films seem to be visually cast as a critique of late capitalist self-consuming greed and its disastrous effect on the global ecosystems—and it is indeed true for both films. However, there appears in *Blade Runner 2049* to be yet another critique that appears through its visual stratagem; that of a feminist critique.

In the original *Blade Runner*, the only women were replicants; the powerful Zhora and Pris—who die violently by Deckard's hand—and Rachael, who is first set up as a test "doll", and as part of that test, becomes attached to Deckard. Both Zhora and Pris are visually presented as punks and sexually provocative, especially Pris, who is referred to as a "standard pleasure model". Whereas Rachael is presented in a 1940s business suit and hairstyle, consequently as a pre-second stage feminist, a cold, and rational model to test her viability and to *pass* as a "respectable", "real" woman. In a scene that was for many female viewers a surprisingly brutal love scene, Deckard, in his initial sexual approach to Rachael, shoves her violently onto a wall and forces a deep kiss on her—to which she infuriatingly relinquishes. She completely defers to Deckard and his wishes throughout the balance of the film. He supposedly falls in love with her, which is not surprising as men in patriarchal cultures are routinely attracted to submissive women. In the last scene, we see him remember Gaff's lines to him "It's too bad she won't live. But then again who does?"—which is paradoxical, since Deckard himself had "dispatched" both her replicant sisters earlier in the film.

It is in fact, the violent deaths of Zhora and Pris that provide two of the most provocative "rich sights" of the film. Zhora is chased through a bricolage of rain-drenched umbrellas, various punks, freaks, and other "Others", to an interior of a confusing multitude of layers of shattering glass, neon, and naked female mannequins—we presume a store or place of clothing manufacture, consistent with the cultural associations of females and fashion—where there is a *dénouement*. Chased through the shimmering layers of glass and neon, which shatters spectacularly into flying shards in all directions, Zhora is shot by Deckard and lands in a nest of blood, mannequins, neon, and glass. Reminiscent of Gutai artist Murakami Saburo's "Laceration of Paper" (1955), the effect of crashing through the layers of planes of glass, seen from a forward position to the layers, presents a perspectival progression of a spectacular splintering of blood and glass that builds in anticipation and horror, but also in the pleasure and the profound desire to *see* it; much as motorists who slow to see the horror of auto accidents. Despite our fear, we are eager for the sight of a spectacular violent death and dismemberment.

Pris's death, seen later in the *Blade Runner* film, makes for an even more visually spectacular and bizarre death. Deep in the ruined mansion of J. F. Sebastian, among his creepy dolls and androids, Deckard and Pris fight as Roy approaches. Pris has mounted Deckard in a grip with her thighs wrapped tightly around Deckard's head and is squeezing his neck tightly—in a rather compelling metaphor for the sex act—his head as the "little head" of the penis, being metaphorically castrated by Pris's scissor-like hold. He breaks free and sends her body flying away from him allowing him to shoot her multiple times. Her body lands on her back with legs bent and, in this position, she begins a rapid-fire bouncing violently in reaction to the shots. Making a horrible and loud mechanical sound of pain, her body convulses like a broken engine whirling and bouncing in the air and crashing back and forth against the wall. It is one of the most memorable sights in the film. It radically seizes her "humanity" from her and reveals her as a broken machine. She is objectified in the most denigrating, violent, and horrific—but "rich sight"—imaginable.

Blade Runner's women are display objects that are in play for the benefit of the males in the film. They are literally the playthings—the dolls—made for the use of the real men in the film: Tyrell, Sebastian, and as we learn later in *Blade Runner 2049*, perhaps Deckard (himself real? Ridley Scott says he was Nexus 6) as well. All the females die early, and in the association with the machinations of the males in the larger story, including Roy Batty, the leader of the replicant revolt. In *Blade Runner 2049*, the film seemingly begins with the same position for females as objects for consumption by males. In the landscape of the now darkened city of LA, lit by various massive female vocaloids in various sexually explicit identities that appear all over the decrepit city, creating a memorable "rich sight". We might assume the city is run or at least influenced by male creators. However, two powerful and unfortunately masculinized females appear: KD6's boss, Lt. Joshi, and Niander Wallace's assistant, Luv. Both are driven to conserve the masculinized "law"—Joshi as a dedicated police person, and Luv as a dedicated assistant to Wallace. The two key males in this story are Deckard and KD6, and their lives have been involved with women who have "loved" and supported them: the replicant Rachael for Deckard and the AI Joi for KD6. These females orbit their existence, but by the end of the story, all these females are dead—but one.

The center of the story slowly emerges around the mysterious Dr. Ana Stelline, a designer of memories, not as code, but as *sight*. Living under a glass dome—as the exceptional specimen and object of the story—she creates memories through manipulating sight, images she imagines and can adjust through a visual interface. She is seemingly about the work of creating "rich sights" for replicants, but in her ability to remember things no one in this population of replicants or real humans could ever have seen—green forests and insects—she becomes something of a messianic being. Though gendered as female, a suggestion presented as the evidence supposedly created by Deckard and the rebellious Freysa to protect her, in a record of her as a set of two identical DNA of both female and male, gives rise to the potential for Ana to be gendered as both or neither gender, and in her messianic position, presenting a potential of a genderless new world. This, of course, suggests Donna Haraway's solution in her *Cyborg Manifesto* as movement away from gender entirely, feminism, and politics, toward a genderless posthuman solution. She, as her gender is "pictured", alone survives.

Ana's family name of "Stelline" reflects the actual meaning in Italian for an orphanage in Milan, developed around 1500s, when orphans were called "stars" after the nuns who cared for them, and it remained an orphanage until 1971. This romantic association accentuates her position as an "orphan star" beyond real family and replicant manufacture—to a posthuman and even cosmic messianic force as a new being dissociated from the warring factions. It will, as Lt. Joshi insists, "break the world", and move life on earth toward a new and different mode, including a new visuality and aesthetic. It is not a new notion, but compelling as an allegory for a Post-Anthropocene future. Futures are necessarily "envisioned" by those in a present position. That *Blade Runner 2049* is a redux of a highly influential SF film suggests that something can be *read through* those narratives and those "rich sights" that brought us a potential to reflect upon as redemption for our ecosystem and gender sins, on a planet that *will* lose all its resources, and *will* die as a life-giving planet, since we do not have the will or the *sight to see* and comprehend our fate. There is but one possibility—one star in a firmament of potential stars, that might deliver us from our dire fate. What are the chances we will be able to see it?

"Oh, my God! My attempt to escape the web of fate was the web of fate."

Timothy Morton (2017)

Funding: This research received no external funding.

Conflicts of Interest: The author declares no conflict of interest.

References

Bell, David. 2001. *An Introduction to Cybercultures*. London and New York: Routledge, p. 164.

Bukatman, Scott. 1999. The Artificial Infinite: On Special Effects and the Sublime. In *Alien Zone II: The Spaces of Science-Fiction Cinema*. Edited by Annette Kuhn. London and New York: Verso, p. 259.

Bukatmann, Scott. 1997. *Blade Runner*; London: British Film Institute.

Crutzen, Paul. 2002. Geology of Mankind. *Nature* 415: 23. [CrossRef] [PubMed]

Crutzen, Paul, and Eugene F. Stoermer. 2002. The Anthropocene. *Global Change Newsletter* 41: 17–18. [CrossRef]

Ellis, Erle C. 2018. Origins. In *Anthropocene: A Very Short Introduction*. London: Oxford University Press, p. 1.

Gibson, William. 1984. *Neuromancer*. New York: Ace Books, p. 67.

Jameson, Fredric. 1984. The Cultural Logic of late Capitalism. *New Left Review* 76: 146.

Joyce, Stephen. 2018. Playing for Virtually Real: Cyberpunk Aesthetics and Ethics. In *Deus Ex: Human Revolution. Cyberpunk and Visual Culture*. Edited by Graham J. Murphy and Lars Schmeink. New York and London: Routledge, p. 155.

Lamarre, Thomas. 2009. *The Anime Machine: A Media Theory of Animation*. Minneapolis and London: The University of Minnesota Press.

Mirzoeff, Nicholas. 2011. *The Right to Look: A Counterhistory of Visuality*. Durham and London: Duke University Press, p. xv.

Morton, Timothy. 2012. *The Ecological Thought*. Boston: Harvard University Press.

Morton, Timothy. 2013. *Hyperobjects: Philosophy and Ecology after the End of the World*. Minneapolis and London: University of Minnesota Press.

Morton, Timothy. 2017. In Alex Blasdel. "'A Reckoning for Our Species': The philosopher Prophet of the Anthropocene". *The Guardian*, June 15. Available online: https://www.theguardian.com/world/2017/jun/15/timothy-morton-anthropocene-philosopher (accessed on 19 June 2018).

Mulvey, Laura. 1996a. *Fetishism and Curiosity*. Bloomington: Indiana University Press, p. 12.

Mulvey, Laura. 1996b. Introduction: Fetishisms. In *Fetishism and Curiosity*. Bloomington and Indianapolis: Indiana University Press.

Owens, Craig. 1980. The Allegorical Impulse: Toward a Theory of Postmodernism. *October* 12: 67–86.

Pevsner, Nikolaus. 2010. *Visual Planning and the Picturesque*. Los Angeles: Getty Publications.

Polan, Dana. 1987–1988. Stock Responses: The Spectacle of the Symbolic in *Summer Stock*. *Discourse* 10: 124.

Poyner, Rick, and David Barash. 2013. Collage Culture: Nostalgia and Critique. *Design Observer*, November 11. AIGA. Available online: https://designobserver.com/feature/collage-culture-nostalgia-and-critique/38187 (accessed on 19 June 2018).

Price, Sir Uvedale. 1810. *Essay on the Picturesque, as Compared with the Sublimeand the Beautiful: And, on the Use of Studying Pictures, for the Purpose of Improving Real Landscape*. London: Printed for J. Mawman, vol. 1, pp. 21–22.

Sobchack, Vivian. 1999. Cities on the Edge of Time: The Urban Science-Fiction Film. In *Alien Zone II*. Edited by Annette Kuhn. London and New York: Verso.

Strick, Philip. 1984. The Metropolitan Wars: The City as Character in Science Fiction Films. In *Omni's screen Flights/Screen Fantasies: The Future Accordong to Science Fiction Cinema*. Edited by Danny Peary. Garden City: Doubleday.

Tatsumi, Takayuki. 2006. *Full Metal Apache: Transactions between Cyberpunk Japan and Avant-Pop America*. Durham and London: Duke University Press.

The Last Man (Review). 2003. Wesleyan University Press. UPNE Book Partners. Available online: https://www.upne.com/0819565490.html (accessed on 19 June 2018).

arts

MDPI

Article

European Cyberpunk Cinema

Lidia Merás

School of Modern Languages Literatures and Cultures, Royal Holloway, University of London,
Egham TW20 0EX, UK; Lidia.Meras@rhul.ac.uk; Tel.: +44-1784-44-3255

Received: 26 June 2018; Accepted: 27 August 2018; Published: 30 August 2018

Abstract: *Renaissance* (2006) and *Metropia* (2009) are two illustrative examples of European cyberpunk cinema of the 2000s. This article will consider the films as representative of contemporary trends in European popular filmmaking. As digital animations aimed at adult audiences and co-produced with other European countries, they epitomise a type of European film. In addition, they share a number of narrative premises. Set in the near future, *Renaissance* and *Metropia* depict a dystopian Europe. Recycling motifs from non-European science fiction classics, they share similar concerns with interconnectivity, surveillance, immigration, class, the representation of women, as well as the obsession with beauty and physical perfection. This article will analyse their themes and aesthetics in order to explore how European popular cinema promotes a certain idea of European cultural identity within the limits of an industry whose products are targeted at a global market.

Keywords: European cinema; animation; co-productions; science fiction; cyberpunk; dystopia; *Renaissance*; *Metropia*; 2000s; transnational cinema

1. Introduction

Science fiction has hardly been a prominent genre within the European film industry[1]. Budget constraints have often hindered the production of sci-fi and fantasy films worldwide, as they tend to require substantial investment in special effects and production design in order to achieve a convincing mise-en-scène. The film industries of the USA and Japan have, notably, managed to successfully fund, brand and distribute films of this kind internationally for decades and many of the most popular examples since the 1980s can be classed as 'cyberpunk.' Drawing on the themes and plots of those works of literature categorised under the same subgenre, cyberpunk cinema has significantly flourished in the United States thanks to films like *Blade Runner* (1982), *Total Recall* (1990) and *The Matrix* (1999) and in Japan with anime films such as *Akira* (1988) and *Ghost in the Shell* (1995):

> Inspired by the literary works of Philip K. Dick and William Gibson, filmmakers produced an array of dark, thought-provoking SF films that invoked classic noir themes such as amnesia, doppelgängers, femme fatales, psychopathic criminality, mystery and murder most foul. These films explored the shadow worlds of digital realms where the boundaries between the real and the computer-generated were lost inside a fractal labyrinth of the self and anything was possible. (Meehan 2008, pp. 192–93)

From the beginning of the late eighties, an extensive bibliography has grown up around cyberpunk cinema, with scholarly analyses of those films produced in the United States and further afield, in Japan

---

[1] As with any broad generalisation, there are exceptions. The UK is arguably the European country which has distributed the most science fiction movies globally in recent decades—occasionally the result of domestic production (e.g., *Ex Machina* (2014)), but more often than not in co-production with the US (e.g., *Alien* (1979), *The Lawnmower Man* (1992), *Children on Men* (2006), *Gravity* (2013) and *Under the Skin* (2013)). Other national cinemas have contributed strongly to the production of science fiction in certain periods, such as the Italian B movies of the eighties, or Eastern European cinemas under Communism.

(see for example Sobchack (1987); Kuhn (1990, 1999); Telotte (1999); Rickman (2004); Johnston (2011)). But the cinematic successors of William Gibson's influential novel *Neuromancer* (Gibson 1984) in Europe have for the most part been overlooked. European cyberpunk, like European science fiction films in general, have not yet received the attention they deserve. This is explained in part by the comparative lack of popularity of European science fiction films. Published mostly in the United States or the United Kingdom, few of the critical studies have included European films and where they do appear they are usually limited to US-British co-productions[2]. As a result, they offer a misleading view of European science fiction as being similar to Hollywood productions. The conclusions drawn in the dominant literature on the subject of US, British and Japanese films is typically extrapolated to other national cinemas. In this article, I claim that these assumptions ought to be reviewed and the variety of films within the subgenre explored in more depth.

Although the number of European cyberpunk films is not comparable to the number made in Hollywood, their presence should not be underestimated. A number of movies released in the 1990s and 2000s fit into the cyberpunk category. A few of them, such as *The Lawnmower Man* (Brett Leonard 1992, UK/US/Japan) and *The Thirteenth Floor* (Joseph Rusnak 1999, Germany/UK/US) were co-productions with either the United States or Japan, countries where there has been a robust film industry producing movies within the parameters of science fiction since the 1950s. An intermediate case would be Terry Gilliam's *The Zero Theorem* (Gilliam 2013), which benefited from US financing but would be more accurately defined as a British co-production with Romania, France and Poland. Examples of cyberpunk films with exclusively European funding include *Nirvana* (Gabriele Salvatores 1997, Italy), *Abre los ojos* (Open Your Eyes, Alejandro Amenábar 1997, Spain) and, more recently, *Immortel* (Immortal, Enki Bilal 2004, France/Italy/UK), *Renaissance* (Christian Volckman 2006, France, Luxemburg/UK), *Chrysalis* (Julien Leclercq 2007, France) and *Metropia* (Tarik Saleh 2009, Sweden/Denmark/Norway)[3].

Unfortunately, few of these films have been included in larger discussions about science fiction cinema. Although some scholars have been interested in European science fiction in the past, their scope is often limited to a single film or national cinema[4]. Too often, the possible connections with other contemporary European films with similar themes are missing. Another obstacle is that European cyberpunk has been hampered by two erroneous assumptions. First, the notion that science fiction is predominantly aimed at mainstream audiences. Second, that European films necessarily fall into the category of 'arthouse films'—a perception which clashes with that of science fiction as a popular genre—even when they do not. Popular European films, especially sci-fi films, often go largely unnoticed by critics or are limited to the festival circuit, never reaching their potential target audiences due to being labelled as films for cinephiles. This article challenges that perception and aims to present a broader picture of contemporary science fiction cinema produced in Europe. Though desirable, it is not within the scope of this article to offer a comprehensive survey of European cyberpunk. It cannot be claimed that there is a single 'European' type of cyberpunk, entirely distinct from any American or Japanese counterparts. There is no single model for any of these countries. Many Hollywood cyberpunk movies differ greatly from one another in terms of characters, mise-en-scène and themes; this is also the case with cyberpunk anime. Given that European cyberpunk has been significantly influenced by literary and cinematic works from the aforementioned countries, any attempt to isolate its 'European' elements would be impracticable. In addition, their characteristics continue to evolve over time. However, there is a noticeable trend in European cyberpunk cinema made in the 2000s of developing

---

[2] For example, the preface to *Liquid Metal* (2004) claims that it covers film production in Europe, the United States and Asia. However, there are only two articles devoted to European films (both US-British co-productions) and only one deals with a Japanese film. Moreover, in the latter article, which concerns *Akira*, the focus is on the influence of *Blade Runner* on Ōtomo's classic. See Redmon (2004, p. xi).

[3] Another European film that contains cyberpunk themes is *La cité des enfants perdus* (The City of Lost Children, Caro and Jeunet (1995), France/Germany/Spain/Belgium). Kike Maíllo's *Eva* (2011), a more recent Spanish film about a child robot, could also be included within the cyberpunk genre, although the film is closer to being a melodrama.

[4] One exception is Mihailova's article "The Mastery Machine: Digital Animation and Fantasies of Control" (Mihailova 2013).

cyberpunk aesthetics and conveying a specifically European pessimism in otherwise familiar narrative forms, which along with a number of commercial strategies, deserve to be seen as a variation on what the current literature on science fiction has established as canonical. My aim is to broaden the perspective found within the current literature as to what constitutes the cyberpunk subgenre.

My research focuses in detail on two films with much in common. *Renaissance* (2006) and *Metropia* (2009) have been selected because they are constitutive of a current trend in European filmmaking and have many shared features. They belong to the same subgenre and are both co-productions made in the same decade. It is worth noting how *Renaissance* and *Metropia* adapt many of the characteristics of Hollywood films, their market rivals, in order to survive at a time when the label 'European film' no longer means what it used to[5]. At a time when, in the words of Bergfelder, Europe had "witnessed a reinvigorated championing of auteurism" (Bergfelder 2015, p. 33), these are, on the contrary, films targeted at mainstream audiences that are also representative of current trends in European cinema. Drawing on cultural studies, I will explore their themes and aesthetics within the context of European popular cinema in order to discern the ways in which they promote a certain idea of European cultural identity in the context of an industry that involves competition among similar products made for the global market.

Tarik Salek, the director of *Metropia*, noticed the incongruity in the perception of his film as 'arthouse,' even when the film had benefited from it:

> *Metropia* was incredible in the sense that we opened Critics' Week in Venice. I went to over seventy festivals, it was like that whole art house scene. But I'm very sceptical as a movie lover [. . .] Not everything can be Haneke on one side and then *Transformers* on the other. That's like an extremist world. (Salek quoted in Seikaly 2014)

The contrast Salek draws between Austrian filmmaker Michael Haneke and Hollywood blockbuster *Transformers* is revealing. The clash between an American science fiction film and one of the masters of contemporary European cinema is representative of an industry that still associates European cinema with the *politique des auteurs*, while consigning science fiction to the sphere of popular cinema. Salek places his film somewhere in the middle. But more importantly, he disapproves of the artificial polarisation of film audiences and stands for a popular cinema that is able to reach mainstream audiences while offering non-standardised products.

In order to identify the key elements of this European trend in cyberpunk, it is necessary first to define the general characteristics of a cyberpunk film. In general, cyberpunk films depict a world dominated by corporate power in a globalised economy. The stories are typically set in a metropolis, either in the present or near future. Many portray virtual worlds generated by computers and indistinguishable from the real one. Consumer choices allow unlimited body modifications (such as implants) capable of enhancing bodies and optimising their potential, although at a high cost. One main drawback of body modifications and overexposure to virtual technology (another important theme in cyberpunk) is the appearance of all sorts of new illnesses and addictions. That is why dependence on new technologies is customarily accompanied by the sale and use of designer drugs. Biological or technological viruses are a common leitmotif. As a consequence, the protagonist is frequently engaged in a frantic search for a cure.

If virtual technology has the capacity to cause bodily illness, the mind is even more vulnerable. Memory loss and a crisis of personal identity are two prevalent and interrelated themes in cyberpunk. Narratives often connect the loss of memories relating to past events to the loss of personal identity, making the point that a lack of recall threatens any stable notion of what makes us human. Family ties are non-existent and other social organisations (political, religious) are weak. Solidarity is scarce in these individualistic societies, where the majority of the population is struggling to

---

[5]   As Thomas Elsaesser has observed: What is European cinema? We no longer seem to know. The very idea of it has slipped between the declining relevance of 'national cinemas,' and the emerging importance of 'world cinema' (Elsaesser 2005, p. 485).

survive. Typical characters in cyberpunk narratives include hackers, drug addicts, tycoons, criminals, strong women, cyborgs, machines with artificial intelligence and pop and media stars.

The European cyberpunk under consideration here shares some of the characteristics identified above, but not all of them. The films borrow stylistic and narrative elements from certain classic films (in particular *Blade Runner*) and genres (science fiction, film noir and thriller). They nevertheless retain an inherently European look while being valuable examples of popular cinema. In the following pages, I will analyse the specific articulations of cyberpunk in a European cinematic context starting with a metatextual analysis of *Renaissance* and *Metropia*, looking at their narrative and stylistic elements and commenting briefly on their reception.

2. Metatextual Analysis of *Renaissance* and *Metropia*

Like many European films produced today, *Renaissance* and *Metropia* were financed through co-productions. *Renaissance* is a French-Luxembourgian production with some involvement of UK capital. The film had a €15million budget, making it an expensive feature by European standards. The Swedish-Danish-Norwegian co-production *Metropia* was by comparison a far more economical film, costing slightly more than €3 million. Like many contemporary European films, it received the support of television—France 2 in the case of *Renaissance* and Sveriges Television and Canal Television with *Metropia*.

The similarities between the two films do not end here. Not only are both films animations; more specifically, they are digital animations. They were created in independent studios recognised for their pioneering use of technology. *Renaissance* was filmed in motion capture and animated in 3D. Special cameras captured the movements of actors and this data was used to animate digital characters (Frenette 2006). The result resembles *Sin City* (2005), although it should be acknowledged that *Renaissance* was in development well before Rodríguez's film had its premiere (Frenette 2006). *Metropia* was developed by Atmo Animation, a company co-founded by director Tarik Saleh. The film follows a Scandinavian model of high-concept/low-budget. Producer Kristina Aberg has stated that, although the film gives the impression of 3D, in reality it was filmed using 2D animation and photographs. The animators at Atmo created images by applying successive layers using Adobe Photoshop and After Effects software—a much cheaper technique than 3D and one which offered unique results (Roxborough 2009). The photo cut out montage process was developed in 2000 by Saleh and art director Martin Hultman and perfected by animator Isak Gjertsen. The fact that directors Christian Volckman and Tarik Saleh worked in independent animation studios suggests that they were freed from the constraints of working for a more established studio. According to Stefan Fjeldmark, head of Zentropa's new Rambuk division, which focuses on animated productions:

> Scandinavian animation doesn't have a single style, like say Pixar does or Japanese anime, which may have made it harder to brand it internationally. But the level of animation here [in Scandinavia] has always been high and it has always been diverse. (Roxborough 2009)

The same assertion applies to Volckman's *Renaissance*. It is evident the two filmmakers were looking for a more personal visual style in keeping with their artistic backgrounds. Not surprisingly, *Metropia*'s director was a graffiti artist before he began his career in film (his 1989 mural Fascinate was the first graffiti to be protected as cultural heritage site in Sweden)[6], while Christian Volckman is also painter and a graphic designer.

Unlike their biggest competitor, Pixar, which has specialised in films either for very specific age groups of children or, on the other hand, suitable for all (e.g., *Toy Story*, *Shrek*, *WALL-E* and *Inside Out*), *Renaissance* and *Metropia* are aimed at more mature audiences. The two films explore adult themes and include instances of nudity and strong sexual references. In *Metropia*, for instance, there is a brief shot

---

[6]   See: https://atmo.se/tarik-saleh/ (accessed on 26 June 2018).

in which a passenger in the underground is seen looking at a pornographic magazine. Despite national certification of films varying dramatically among countries (*Renaissance* is considered suitable for all audiences in France but in Ireland and Portugal is certified for viewers above fifteen and sixteen years old respectively)[7], the preference for adult themes narrows the possible audience and also involves certain risks. Not only does it reduce international distribution of the films in those regions where the classification is more restrictive, but as Frenette writes: "At the time, there had been no *Shrek* to prove that an animated feature could appeal to the 15–35 demographic" (Frenette 2006).

Renaissance is set in Paris in 2054. The film tells the story of Karas, a police hostage negotiator[8]. In his latest case, Karas investigates the kidnapping of a young scientist, Ilona Tasuiev, a researcher for the powerful company Avalon, in what it seems to be a case of industrial espionage. Ilona's sister Bislane helps Karas in his endeavour.

Although *Renaissance*'s Canadian producer Jake Eberts enthusiastically exclaimed, "That's *The Matrix* in animation!" after watching the demo of the project (Frenette 2006) the story was built around the idea of a futuristic Paris, a premise which forms the backbone of the film's development. As scriptwriter Alexandre de la Patellière stated during the making of the film: "Much of the story and the narration came up following our desire to work around Paris. That's how the story was born. Paris was a central character from the start"[9]. Along with *Blade Runner*, another point of reference mentioned by the creators—and also a popular reference point for cyberpunk movies in general—is the detective thriller. In particular, *Renaissance* takes many of its visual motifs from the novels of James Ellroy novels, only relocating the action from Los Angeles to Paris[10]. It seems odd that none of those involved in the project has mentioned *Alphaville* (Godard 1965) when discussing the film publicly; especially taking into account the fact that *Alphaville* is a science fiction film and a detective story filmed in black and white and set in a futuristic Paris, where residents are oppressed by the rule of a technocratic power. The omission is even more surprising since both *Renaissance* and *Alphaville* bring to light fears of Nazi tyranny within a disturbing projection of Paris. Concerns towards totalitarianism is a recurrent theme in European science fiction that will be discussed in the relation to cyberpunk films in the section 'Fortress Europe in European Cyberpunk Cinema'[11]. However, the dystopian urbanism of *Renaissance,* we are told, is the result of the influence of comic book authors Jean-Claude Mézières and François Schuiten on director Christian Volckman[12].

Cyberpunk has been an influential genre in Japanese animation and manga for decades. It is therefore easy to find many visual motifs in these films reminiscent of manga and anime, such as the disproportionately big eyes of characters in *Metropia*. Salek's film in particular is quite rich in its references to Japanese anime. If we look at its greyish palette, the way characters are animated and the large heads of characters, they seem influenced by Mamoru Oshii's work in *Tachiguishi Retsuden* (Oshii 2006). These visual motifs do not seem to have any function other than paying homage to the master of Japanese cinematic cyberpunk and will probably amuse spectators who are able to recognise hints from previous films or comics. In the same film, there are also a number of intertextual references

---

[7] In the United States, *Renaissance* is classified as 'R' (i.e., minors under seventeen years old require an accompanying parent or adult guardian).

[8] The name 'Karas' is perhaps a reference to Kei'ichi Sato, Hiroshi Yamazaki and Akira Takada's 2005 film *Karas: The Prophecy* (Sato et al. 2005).

[9] See the making of documentary.

[10] See the making of documentary.

[11] In his monograph on Alphaville, Chris Darke enumerates the references to Nazi Germany in the film: "the numbers tattooed on the skin of the séductrices; the telling name change of Natasha's father from Nosferatu to von Braun; and the 'SS' on a lift button [...] shot in such emphatic close-up" (Arendt 2006, p. 76). Like Renaissance and Metropia, the antagonist's surname has German resonances. In *Alphaville*, Professor von Braun is played by Swiss actor Howard Vernon, who was often casted as a Nazi officer and a mad doctor (Arendt 2006, p. 17). In addition, the character "carried a name that was full of recent historical resonance. Wernher von Braun was the name of the Nazi scientist who had been involved in developing the massively destructive V2 rockets towards the end of the Second World War" (Arendt 2006, p. 76).

[12] Schuiten is a well-known comic artist known for his book *Les Cités Obscures* (Dark Cities, published in 1983) created in collaboration with Benoît Peeters. The film was released in France together alongside a comic book published by Casterman (Frenette 2006).

to Japanese popular culture. The couple's bedroom is full of cuddly toys based on well-known Japanese characters. Among them, Yuko Yamaguchi's design Hello Kitty and Pikachu (the latter originally from the Pokémon videogames), both manga and anime creatures in their own right. In addition to this, the protagonist's doppelganger in *Metropia*, Stefan, has a fish pet called Zelda, named after the videogame series first lunched in 1986 and still profitable in 2017, when the last videogame was released. In *Rennaisance*, references to Japanese anime are subtler, but again, Mamoru Oshii, considered the master of cyberpunk anime, stands as the main source of inspiration. Occasional references to Oshii's *Ghost in the Shell* (1995) are noticeable in the triangles seen on the children's necks and in the sequence in which an invisible hitman kills Dimitri. Mamoru Oshii was also the creator of *Avalon* (2001), a Japanese co-production with Poland. The name is used both for the virtual world in Oshii's film and to the greedy monopoly that rules the lives of Parisians in *Renaissance*. Although this could be just a coincidence[13], directors Oshii and Volckman take a similar approach, filming real actors and then using digital effects to embellish the animation[14]. Finally, another evident source for *Renaissance* is Ôtomo's benchmark in Japanese cyberpunk, *Akira* (Ôtomo 1988) based on his six manga volumes of the same title (1982–1990), obvious in the theme of progeria and the experiments with children.

Metropia won the Future Film Digital Award at the Venice Film Festival and Best Music Award at the Stockholm Film Festival while *Renaissance* won the Annecy International Animated Film Festival and the Grand Prize of European Fantasy Film in Silver at the Fantasporto Film Festival. Despite these accolades the films received mixed reviews and are not well known outside science fiction fan circles. The innovative use of digital animation in *Renaissance* and *Metropia* facilitated the distribution of the movies at international film festivals, where they each received awards. Public reception outside their countries of origin, however, was somewhat disappointing, despite both films being aimed at international audiences. Although, as Elsaesser has observed, the European origin of a film is not essential for its success, the problem is how to "communicate with global/transnational audiences" (Elsaesser 2005, p. 491).

English as the Lingua Franca of Europe

One curious trait is that, although the films were made in non-English speaking countries, *Renaissance* and *Metropia* were both filmed in English. It is not an uncommon strategy. According to Laëtitia Kulyk, the use of a *lingua franca* normally helps a film's international success (Kulyk 2015, p. 179). Kulyk explains how the use of English is often characteristic of co-productions since they are conceived for the international market. In her distinction between the use of English in major and minor territories, we can identify the different aims of the films studied. In minor territories (e.g., Nordic countries, as in the case of *Metropia*) it is common practice and a matter of survival, as their populations are too small for a film to be profitable if filmed in the native language. In bigger countries such as France (see *Renaissance*) the aim is to reach ever larger audiences. Given that both films under consideration here are animations, they are less constrained by the actors' real voices, as the characters are dubbed.

Before I refer to the convention of filming in English and the consequences of such a decision, it is useful to refer to *Blade Runner* once again. Although Ridley Scott's film has for the last few decades been the predominant influence on cyberpunk and indeed science fiction films in general, there is one element that has not enjoyed much endorsement: the displacement of a recognisable language by a foreign one. In one scene in *Blade Runner*, Harrison Ford's character (Rick Deckhard) is exposed to Cityspeak, the language spoken in Los Angeles 2019, at a noodle parlour. Deckhard's voice over describes Cityspeak in pejorative terms:

---

[13] After all, Avalon is the name of a legendary island where the sword Excalibur was forged. It first appeared in Geoffrey of Monmouth's *Historia Regum Britanniae* (1136).
[14] The results, though, are quite different. *Avalon* looks more naturalistic (it was filmed on location) while *Renaissance*'s aesthetics are closer to those of comic books.

> That gibberish he talked [his colleague Gaff, played by Edward James Olmos] was Cityspeak,
> gutter talk, a mishmash of Japanese, Spanish, German, what have you. I didn't really need a
> translator. I knew the lingo, every good cop did. But I wasn't going to make it easier for him.

Cityspeak suggests confusion and a sense of threat—or, at the very least, the discomfort of feeling displaced. Deckhard is reluctant to speak the new language, a strategy of resistance. It is curious to note that most European cyberpunk films portray multi-ethnic, yet monolingual societies. *Metropia* and *Renaissance* (but also previous European cyberpunk films such as *Nirvana* and *The Thirteenth Floor*) have been customarily filmed in English. The preference for English comes as no surprise. In the last two decades there has been a general increase in the number of English language films produced in non-Anglophone contexts. The reasons are evident:

> If you shoot a movie that is meant to be successful in a lot of territories, one of the rules that
> you have to understand is that you shoot in English—not to do so rules out two thirds of
> the market. Also, you have to understand that 50 percent of the market is the US market.
> (Bernd Eichinger quoted in Finney 2006, p. 104)

However, even when the use of English provides an advantage in terms of exhibition, it involves risks as regards receptivity. As a *Hollywood Reporter* review of *Metropia* said: "The fact that the main characters are voiced by American actors, yet live in Scandinavia, further seems at odds with the story" (Senjanovic 2009, p. 40). In other words, the implausibility of using a non-native language, creating a discrepancy between characters and setting, could hinder a film's popularity in certain territories[15]. But then again, poor subtitling or dubbing could also damage the credibility of the story[16]. In sum, the use of English implies further responsibilities that should be taken into account.

For a start, the selection of actors and actresses whose mother tongue is English has implications of its own. Choosing English over other native languages entails looking for actors abroad. As a consequence, European cyberpunk contradicts the correlation between popular European cinema and national stardom described by Elsaesser, by which popular cinema requires recognised domestic stars who perform in their native language (Elsaesser 2005, p. 485). By contrast, in *Metropia* the main characters have American voices (Vincent Gallo and Juliette Lewis voice Roger and Nina respectively), while secondary roles are played by English and Nordic actors. In *The Europeanness of European Cinema*, Mariana Liz points out that the significant number of US actors in European cinema raises "questions about the relationship between the film industries of Europe and Hollywood" (Liz 2015, p. 76). But the situation is even more complex. Is it the actor's nationality alone that counts? On the one hand we have in these films a mixture of American and European actors, but some of the latter can also be viewed as having been assimilated to Hollywood modes of production. *Renaissance*'s advertising campaign highlighted British actor Daniel Craig as the star, but, as Hedling asks, "Is it more realistic to contemplate these actors as examples in the historical trajectory of British and Irish actors being promoted in the […] integrated Anglo-American film cluster which is arguably best seen as a part of global Hollywood?" (Hedling 2015, p. 120). And, again, rather than taking for granted the transnationality of British actors in American and European cinemas, another scholar argues instead that the differences between American-English and British-English matter:

> Key to the process, according to Perry, is the need for a British-English dub, rather than
> American voices. "This allows the film to be comprehensible but still have a European
> flavour to it". (quoted by Finney 2006, p. 107)

---

[15] Paradoxically, when a Hollywood film is set in a non-English speaking country, no critic seems surprised by the convention according to which everyone speaks English.

[16] "While the language is not going to be the decisive factor in determining the success of a film, the wrong choice of language, or poorly executed subtitling or dubbing, will wreck its chances of international success, no matter how good the product is" (Finney 2006, p. 107).

In *Renaissance*, scientist Ilona is a French national. Her EU identity card is written in French and English, the two official languages of the European Union, yet French is never spoken. Strangely, French is briefly used in a background conversation in *Metropia* when Roger arrives in Paris, whereas we never hear a word of Swedish in Stockholm. The paradox in these dystopian projections of a decentralised but interconnected Europe, where nation-states are almost non-existent entities, is that they remain united by language, with American, British and other European-accented English.

3. Narrative and Stylistic Elements of European Cyberpunk

3.1. Dark European Cities

In narrative and stylistic terms, *Metropia* and *Renaissance* follow many tropes associated with cyberpunk. One almost indispensable trait is that the action takes place in urban settings. The cities in *Renaissance* and *Metropia* are very different and yet share in many of the subgenre's clichés. They offer dark and unwelcoming projections of the future. Sunlight is scarce in cyberpunk. The lack of light is in keeping with the visual schema of film noir and contributes towards a generally gloomy outlook. Cities are dominated by greedy monopolies in a recognisable version of unbridled capitalism. An elite controls harmful technological advancement that consumers willingly embrace thanks to persuasive advertising. The pervasiveness of technology often boosts mass surveillance, endangering civil and political rights but the unsatisfied masses seldom rebel against injustice and conform to the status quo.

New York, Los Angeles and Tokyo are three of a selected group of metropoles in which cyberpunk narratives are typically set. The fact that *Renaissance* and *Metropia* depart from these familiar American and Japanese locations, in favour of European capitals, is a factor that modifies the narratives. This is arguably more evident in *Renaissance* than in *Metropia*. "*Renaissance* has the French touch" (Frenette 2006), it is a film which has also been described by one critic as being "Like *Blade Runner* with a baguette under its arm" (Arendt 2006). But neither of these reviewers explains what makes *Renaissance* distinctive.

Despite the admiration for *Blade Runner* and repeated mention of Scott's film as a defining source of inspiration, the choice of Paris significantly shaped the look of the city. First of all, *Renaissance* reflects an unreserved fascination with the city's striking architecture. Although most of the action occurs at night, the daytime sequences show Paris' recognisable rooftops and ancient monuments (e.g., Notre-Dame, Sacré-Cœur Basilic). Wide avenues are depicted from a birds-eye view or, perhaps more accurately, from a drone's point of view, as the camera movements are fluid, much faster and precise. A number of aerial shots feature open spaces and sharply defined architecture in contrast to the midst that blurs buildings in *Blade Runner* and many other cyberpunk films. As Arendt said of *Renaissance*:

> While it borrows from any number of science-fiction classics, *Renaissance* has a look and feel all of its own. This is a film noir in the most literal sense, defined entirely by jet-black shadows [. . .]. It's a pleasure to watch and the architectural vistas of Paris in 2054, with its glass-covered Metro stations and vertiginous stacks of decaying tenements, are very beautiful. (Arendt 2006)

With its magnificent urban spaces, monumental architecture and elegant black and white contrasts, *Renaissance* departs from previous cyberpunk settings. In one of the few day sequences, set in the Avalon Vice President's office, the camera movement reveals that the walls and floor are made of glass, allowing the all-powerful Avalon CEO to look down on the inhabitants. His privileged workplace at the company's headquarters modifies the public space. The A-shaped office building matches Avalon's logo. At the ground level, the spaces are not built to human scale but are closer to a Versailles-style urbanism of grandiose avenues. The futuristic elements, though, are not imposing and coexist with the ancient architecture, even embellishing the French capital. A postmodern sensibility guided the projection of Paris in the year 2054, a respectful reinterpretation of one of the most beautiful capitals in

Europe. There are no apparent slums or no-go areas and the sight of poverty is anecdotal, an absence that contradicts one of the main premises of cyberpunk.

Unlike the stylish Paris recreated in *Renaissance*, *Metropia* offers a much bleaker representation of the future, one that seems to envision the collapse of the Swedish welfare state. Following a financial crisis deepened by the scarcity of natural resources, a company named Trexx has built up a vast underground system which connects Europe's main cities. The protagonist Roger is an apathetic call centre worker who has recently started hearing voices in his head. He meets an elegant woman called Nina in the underground. Everything in Roger's surroundings looks dreadful. The area between the ramshackle apartment building where Roger lives and his workplace is a post-industrial wasteland of barren fields, abandoned cars and factories and brutalist architecture. Roads are empty, the skies perpetually clouded and most of the concrete structures are in ruins. The animators use a palette of grey tones to reinforce Roger's gloomy existence[17]. In contrast to American or Japanese films, European cities in cyberpunk do not appear overcrowded. However, *Metropia* and *Renaissance* depict societies whose inhabitants feel equally isolated and deprived of a network of friends, relatives or co-workers.

In *Renaissance*, Paris is presented as a relatively lively environment where people can at least go for a walk. The Stockholm suburbs seen in *Metropia*, on the contrary, are home to a population dissuaded from making use of public spaces—unless they use Trexx facilities and pay exorbitant tariffs for the privilege of going to work. Salek used photographs of real underground stations in an attempt to make them look familiar to European viewers[18]. The tube is the only means of transport and a tool to control the population across the continent, as the Trexx Group influences consumers' choices by placing ubiquitous adverts in the underground while suppressing musicians and other outsiders. The fact that actual stations have been used in the film suggests to the viewer that today we are not so far from a similar kind of future.

3.2. Canons of Beauty, a European Obsession

Renaissance and *Metropia* share a concern with the imposition of a canon of beauty, a motif also central in other European cyberpunk productions such as Amenábar's *Abre los ojos* (1997). The film which introduced this subject to science fiction cinema was Terry Gilliam's *Brazil* (Gilliam 1985). Loosely based on *Nineteen Eighty-Four*, one of the original ways in which it departs from George Orwell's novel is by including two female characters, Ida (the protagonist's mother) and her friend, who are obsessed with undergoing drastic beauty treatments. In Gilliam's film, the obsession with retaining a youthful appearance is ridiculed as a distraction reserved for wealthy, idle, old women. In *Renaissance* (2006) and *Metropia* (2009), on the other hand, the beauty industry has imposed its standards on the lives of every citizen. More importantly, its products are designed to control the population. Inhabitants of these fictions unwittingly succumb to the promises of advertising, which turns them into consumers complicit in their own subjugation. For instance, in *Metropia*, the gel Dangst is a biochemical tool used to inoculate thoughts and sell Trexx products to gullible buyers. Roger's inner voice persuades him to distrust his wife so that he is tempted to buy one of the widely advertised Hello Kitty dolls that hides a built-in spy camera, to control her. Roger's sibylline inner voice whispers:

> People we thought we knew. People we thought we could trust. But things turned out to be different. Unless you get one of those Kitty Dolls. Cameras from 'See Cure.' Eighty Euros for the truth. And if we found out that she hasn't done anything ... How great! Perfect.

Unlike previous narratives in which an authoritarian state imposes its will by force or intimidation, in this case an evil monopoly uses technology to manipulate consumer choices. From the

---

[17] Roger's disproportionately big head and body have been compared to Edvard Munch's *The Scream* (Sharkey 2010).
[18] Salek used pictures and 2D animation and "built the images up, layer by layer, in Photoshop and After Effects" (Roxborough 2009).

beginning, there is a specific interest in both films in showing the presence of cosmetics adverts everywhere. After the opening sequence, *Renaissance* focuses on an animated street billboard that recalls *Blade Runner*'s famous geisha standing out amidst the overwhelming Los Angeles cityscape. The Parisian model in *Renaissance* is also a woman, but here, the atmosphere is apparently less oppressive. In this capital of fashion and luxurious cosmetics, the ad stands alone overlooking its surroundings—the familiar rooftops of eternal Paris with some futuristic additions. The wrinkles of an old woman gradually disappear as she promotes the virtues of Avalon's products:

> I like being beautiful. I like to stay fit. That's why I like Avalon. With Avalon, I know I'm beautiful. And I am going to stay that way. Health. Beauty. Longevity. Avalon. We're on your side[19]

It is interesting to note that a relatively old-fashioned form of advertising such as placing billboards in prominent locations, seems central in both films. Along with advertisements on public transport the product placement becomes essentially omnipresent, proving the strength of private companies to impose their presence in public spaces. Not even the Eiffel Tower is spared, as the iconic monument is turned into the spot for a neon ad in *Metropia*, announcing the leading Trexx product: the radioactive-blue looking gel Dangst. Television, another traditional medium of communication is also used to endlessly publicise products in *Metropia*.

3.3. Fantasy Girls and Working-Class Women

In both films the individual who embodies the ideal of beauty is a woman; more precisely, a white woman. Despite the fact that both films portray a multicultural society, it seems that the standards of beauty in the future will remain white: light skin, big eyes with long lashes, a slim nose and silky straight or wavy hair. In contrast, ordinary women do not necessarily fit this standard of beauty. In *Metropia*, Roger's wife, Anna, is an attractive black woman. She is characterised as being opposed to normative ideals of beauty and gives the impression of paying little attention to her appearance. At home, she wears a plain, white T-shirt, does not use any makeup and her left arm is fully covered with a tattoo. Furthermore, the spots on her forehead contrast with the perfect skin of her rival, Nina. Class also plays an important part in her characterisation. Anna is a working-class woman living in a tiny, decrepit apartment where she spends most of her time watching reality shows and worrying about her marriage. No mention is made of her profession. Whether Anna is unemployed or not, the fact that her job seems entirely irrelevant to the plot is significant because without the responsibilities of motherhood or a job to fulfil her aspirations, her only function as a young woman is to remain a (replaceable) object of desire. The mysterious Nina, on the other hand, is depicted as the glamorous, prototypical blonde *femme fatale*. She shows no physical imperfections and wears an elegant two-piece designer suit over fancy lingerie. Her meticulous spiral bun, inspired by the character of Madeleine Elster played by Kim Novak in *Vertigo*, reinforces the idea of a fantasy girl with a hidden agenda. She works as a model and is the face of one of the products sold by her father's company. Roger describes Nina as the 'girl of his dreams' and follows her in the underground despite being late for work. Nina, therefore, signifies the danger and excitement of an extramarital affair, while Anna is associated in the film with the routine of marital life: sex scheduled around Roger's job exhausting timetable and frequent arguments ignited by her husband's unfounded jealousy. Anna is tender and emotional and has been to a certain extent infantilised, as evidenced by the Hello Kitty dolls and her drawings. In addition, she is associated with affection and fidelity, as opposed to the ambition and coldness of Nina. The opposition of female characters is typical of cyberpunk narratives and reminiscent of previous films in which a black woman represents the real world, ordinary problems and

---

[19] Later on, the audience will learn that the cosmetics firm Avalon is responsible for the death of children used as guinea-pigs in the company's attempts to reverse the aging process.

routine, while a white woman is associated with a dangerous romantic obsession, as seen, for instance, in Kathryn Bigelow's *Strange Days* (1995).

A similar juxtaposition is found in *Renaissance* between the main female characters, sisters Ilona and Bislane Tasuiev. Once again, they are both beautiful but Ilona, a scientist working on an ambitious research project for Avalon, is blonde-haired and fair with light blue eyes. Her older sister also works for Avalon but in a more modest role in the records section. Bislane looks completely different to her sister. She has black hair and dark, narrow eyes that give her an East Asian look. Her haircut and outfit are similar to those of Trinity from *The Matrix*. In addition, her friends are petty delinquents, while her more successful younger sister Ilona is always surrounded by older scientists. In narrative terms, the 'happy endings' in *Renaissance* and *Metropia* are in keeping with the plot resolutions found in many cyberpunk films, such as *Johnny Mnemonic* (1995). In both films the hero consolidates his relationship with the working-class girl, an ending that Michelle Chilcoat describes as "deeply conservative in its anxious reassertion of 'obligatory heterosexuality'" (Chilcoat 2004, p. 157).

3.4. The Panopticon as A New Metaphor for Digital Surveillance

Computers, a defining element of cyberpunk, are scarce in *Metropia* and *Renaissance*. Most of the screens in the films are connected to surveillance cameras, sometimes hidden from the general public but in other instances exposed in spaces like the underground. While earlier European cyberpunk films explored virtual reality (e.g., *Nirvana, Abre los ojos, The Thirteenth Floor*), it barely figures in *Metropia* and *Renaissance*. The universally popular image of the hero figure traversing different layers of virtual reality faded from view in the 2000s. As a substitute, the classic concerns of science fiction, such as the theme of state surveillance, reappeared. Vital in the 1960s and 1970s, when many films showed technology being used to monitor the population's movements, in these films state control is replaced by the corporate might of Trexx and Avalon. Saleh defined *Metropia* as "a reflection of the time and a warning about what can happen if we allow the surveillance society and companies free license—beyond all morals, laws and rules" (Salek, quoted by Kim Grönqvist 2010, p. 31)[20].

Despite the lack of computers, cyberspace is not entirely absent in *Metropia*. Saleh's script was actually inspired by Amazon's dashboard product suggestions and social media platforms. Writing on his blog, co-screenwriter of *Metropia*, Fredrik Edin, has lamented the amount of information internet users voluntarily reveal on social media because it facilitates obscure corporate interests that are likely to use the information against the individual:

> When we began to work on *Metropia* in 2003 [...] some online stores, such as Amazon, had started mapping their customers. Based on previous purchases, clicked links and so on, they tailored the prices so that different customers received different price tags for one and the same product. Meanwhile, Mark Zuckerberg and his friends sat at Harvard, outlining the social network that would later be Facebook and have over 300 million users. As some of us opened accounts on Facebook, the decision is made to let Roger use Dangst shampoo. Even though he lacks hair. If it seems unreasonable, it is nevertheless an objection to the bizarre fact that I and millions of other people voluntarily disclose our political views, religious views and sexual orientations. What I'm doing right now. Who my friends are. Who I'm living with. Which of my friends know each other [...] If Amazon can figure out what I'm willing to pay for a particular book, what do you think anyone could figure out by mapping my activity on Facebook?. (Edin 2009)

---

[20] Regarding the impact of social media and the origins of *Metropia* Salek says: "I get annoyed by our generation's way of voting for the Pirate Party on the one hand and making privacy on the Internet the most important issue, bigger than the scrapping of labour laws or the building of a wall around Europe. Then, on the other hand, exposing everything about themselves on blogs, Facebook and Twitter pages. I think it's hypocrisy and it's partly also what the movie is about" (quoted by Kim Grönqvist 2010, p. 31).

In his post, Edin links social media to social control. Hence the capitalisation of private data via technological devices has replaced the dangers of virtual worlds, updating the notion of the panopticon. Michel Foucault's concerns regarding Bentham's disciplinary model of the panopticon are formulated in his 1975 essay *Discipline and Punish*. This conception is transformed in *Metropia*, with the idea of the panopticon being manifested as a system of control, by which consumers are willing to share their private data unaware of the consequences. The panopticon serves as a metaphor for a society under the latest type of surveillance, self-inflicted and enabled by advances in digital technology. It comes as no surprise that the key panopticon-like structures in these movies are the headquarters of Trexx and Avalon. The design is not exclusive to these films and can be found in Terry Gilliam's *The Zero Theorem* (Gilliam 2013), where it is also associated with corporate power.

3.5. Fortress Europe in European Cyberpunk Cinema

Given that American cyberpunk cinema generally depicts ethnically diverse societies, it is worth noticing the way in which ethnicity has been represented in Europe[21]. In the 2000s both American and European cyberpunk films customarily represented ethnically diverse populations, a novelty in the case of European productions. Indeed, European cyberpunk of the 1990s can hardly be described as ethnically diverse, with very few examples of non-white characters[22]. Hollywood films of the same period featured a greater diversity, even if non-white characters were reserved for secondary roles. During the 2000s the supremacy of white characters endured on both sides of the Atlantic but ethnic hierarchies in European cyberpunk present some particularities that deserve further comment. For instance, unlike in Hollywood movies, the nationality of white characters is of great importance. Yosefa Loshitzky has studied the portrayal of the ethnically 'other' in European cinema. In her introduction to *Screening Strangers*, Loshitzky uses the term 'fortress Europe' to contextualise the cinematic representation of migrants, exiles and refugees on the continent. Coined during the Second World War to refer to the territories under the Third Reich, it has become a widely used expression to sum up the current climate of hostility towards mass immigration within the European Union:

> European countries have tended to view migration as challenging and threatening to their territory, identity or ways of imagining themselves and others. [...] Fortress Europe increasingly erects racial, ethnic and religious boundaries. At the same time that Europe is encouraging the expansion of the EU, it is also defining and closing its borders to the 'others'. (Loshitzky 2010, p. 2)

The expression 'fortress Europe,' then, is very useful for explaining the importance of ethnicity and national identity, arising from a double meaning of the term. Analysis of the films under consideration here will demonstrate this. *Metropia* is especially interesting in this regard. Born in Stockholm to Egyptian parents, *Metropia*'s director Tarik Saleh openly criticises Europe's attitude towards refugees and, in particular, the exploitation of their circumstances by the media. In one of the early sequences of the film, he uses parody to denounce Europe's uneasiness with asylum seekers, showing a teaser for a TV programme entitled Asylum, in which contestants compete to stay in Europe legally. With the telegraphic wording and the fast editing characteristic of this format, the voice over announces: "Tonight. Four contestants. Thirty questions. Only one can stay in Europe. The others have to fly." The last part is meant literally, as contestants are tied to a special machine and catapulted into the void when they fail to answer a question correctly. *Metropia* illustrates the anxieties of those with

---

[21] Novels like Neal Stephenson's *Snow Crash* (Stephenson 1992) paved the way for a more balanced representation of ethnicity in American cyberpunk. In Hollywood, characters like J-Bone (played by rapper Ice-T) and Takahashi (Takeshi Kitano) in *Johnny Mnemonic*; Mace (Angela Basset) and Jeriko One (Glenn Plummer) in *Strange Days*; and Morpheus (Laurence Fishburne) in *The Matrix*, reflect a concern (however insufficient) for diversity.
[22] One of the very few exceptions was the detective Larry McBain (played by actor and producer Dennis Haysbert) in *The Thirteenth Floor*, a co-production with the USA.

conservative attitudes towards the ethnically other and it does this by using a literal 'dumping process' that echoes Loshitzky's general description of the attitudes seen in European cinema:

> the process of screening practised by the 'host' society (which very often is more hostile than hospitable) is to screen the 'good migrant' and expel the 'bad' to the literal and metaphorical 'dumping grounds' of the rest of the world. Both the penalty system and the state and supra-state apparatuses built to solve the problem of 'human waste' are driven by the desire to screen the 'good migrant,' to separate her/him from the 'bad/undesired stranger'. (Loshitzky 2010, p. 2)

The fact that Asylum, "Europe's favourite quiz show," is broadcast from Copenhagen and not Stockholm, where most of the story takes place, implies not only that there is an immense transport system that has been constructed by Trexx but also a TV network that links Europeans who share similar pastimes that actively disseminate xenophobia. Despite the intra-European connections facilitated by the infrastructure provided by Trexx, borders still exist. These have now simply been redrawn to exclude non-European citizens.

In the same scene, a close-up shot of the terrified eyes of a contestant is edited so that they meet the vacant eyes of Anna, who is watching the programme in the comfort of her home. Later on (26 min) the audience will be made aware of the connection between Asylum and the sinister company Trexx, when the underground hosts the quiz show's finale. An intimidating TV hostess approaches one of the contestants with her microphone and demands a prompt answer from him: "In thirty words, explain why Europe is the place of your dreams." Against the clock, the anxious man improvises his response as his seat prepares to launch him miles away towards a river. "In or out" (as Asylum's trailer announces) are the only choices given to non-EU citizens. Finally, in one of the final sequences, Roger meets the successful contestant who has been granted leave to remain. The encounter takes place in the underground (the domain of Trexx) and the former asylum seeker is carrying a bottle of Dangst, a symbol that confirms his new status as a consumer in his adopted country, subject to the same level of surveillance as any other national.

Metropia makes explicit the rejection of the ethnically 'other,' mainly identified as first-generation immigrants. Class is also a relevant factor. In the same film, the characters of the ruling magnates are based on national stereotypes: a German entrepreneur, an ignorant American from Texas, a quiet Japanese man and two grotesque Saudis. The working classes are Swedish, Finnish and, at a lower level on the social scale, Iranian security guards. Similarly, in *Renaissance* the scientists are German and Japanese while the main character is of Maghrebi descent (a French national "born in the Kasbah") and his superior in the police force is a black woman. Social mobility is therefore limited and codified according to ethnic stereotypes.

As mentioned before, the concept of 'fortress Europe' describes the current unwillingness throughout the European continent to accommodate a growing number of immigrants and refugees, but it also expresses fears of German dominance. It is hardly a coincidence that the villains in *Renaissance* and *Metropia* have German surnames and are both CEOs of their respective companies. For instance, German actor Udo Kier voices Ivan Bahn in *Metropia*. His surname also has associations with the construction of a reliable transport system, an area in which Germans are traditionally believed to excel ('Bahn' means train in German). The construction of a massive underground system across Europe is supported by an economic establishment at every level, as is evident in the sequence where Roger's boss pressures him into taking the underground—Roger prefers to cycle to work. In addition, the Nazi past haunts the film, in the images of a network of trains that extends across Europe, initiated by Germans. Indeed, both films convey an undeniable degree of apprehension towards German authority. Technological innovations are used by Trexx and Avalon to infringe personal freedoms: spying on people without consent and even instilling malicious thoughts within them. Although they allude to the existence of a supranational structure (explicit in *Renaissance*, in which Ilona Tasuiev's ID card confirms her identity as a citizen of the European Union), it is not difficult to perceive anxieties directed towards a centralised monopoly ruled by German chief executives. In keeping with familiar cyberpunk concerns, political authority is secondary to, or actively conspires with economic power. But fears about the establishment of an authoritarian society are also connected with a classical theme of European science fiction that has reappeared in recent years. Even though dystopias have always been a popular setting for science fiction, European audiences saw a significantly higher number of post-apocalyptic films during the eighties that Hollywood audiences did. Films such as *The Falls* (1980), *Les années lumière* (Light Years Away, Tanner 1981), *Kamikaze 1989* (Gremm 1982), *Le dernier combat* (The Last Battle/Kamikaze 1999; Besson 1983), *Nineteen Eighty-Four* (Radford 1984) and *Brazil* (Gilliam 1985) explored post-war hardship and totalitarian threats. Although their storylines imagined the future, the mise-en-scène often reminded viewers of the Second World War and its aftermath, as if to indicate that Europeans will never be safe from authoritarianism. Current cyberpunk films are reviving similar concerns but this time, the country blamed for the conflict is disclosed. The only substantial difference is that the former political menace is now camouflaged by economic power.

4. Conclusions

European cyberpunk cinema made in the 2000s is not dramatically different from its American or Japanese counterparts. Although the films discussed offer a distinctive look that has been praised by critics worldwide, the genre maintains many of the motifs seen in previous decades in terms of plot (in particular, those revolving around industrial espionage), urban settings inspired by film noir and overlap in terms of certain character archetypes. The representation of strong women in a male-dominated narrative and greedy moguls and media stars depicted in a world controlled by corporations, offer no major variations.

Notwithstanding these similarities, other fundamental aspects of European cyberpunk offer an alternative take on the genre. One of the most striking distinctions in European cyberpunk is the extreme level of technophobia. Despite being cautionary tales about the use of technology, films like *Total Recall*, *Johnny Mnemonic* and *The Matrix* make a point of exhibiting the wonders of the virtual world. Consider Arnold Schwarzenegger's 'ego-trip'—or virtual adventure—in *Total Recall*, or the scene in which the character of Morpheus 'teaches' Neo several martial arts by downloading applications into his brain in *The Matrix*. By contrast, European cyberpunk shows only the negative effects of technological advances. According to Mihailova, digital animation is "inherently technophilic by virtue of its production process" (Mihailova 2013, p. 132) but all technical and scientific innovations in *Renaissance* and *Metropia* are harmful, or used to enslave the population, in contradiction to the medium employed to convey the same technophobic message. Even when the initial aim of a new technology is constructive, the consequences are terrifying[23].

The lack of faith in technology explains the comparatively modest number of virtual reality narratives. Stories dealing with computers, fantasy worlds, cyborgs and body modifications are few and far between. There is no hope that technology can improve human life. Therefore, narratives about an ill (or addicted) male hero seeking a cure have disappeared. In its place, European cyberpunk is fixated with the idea of dystopia, one of the classic themes of science fiction cinema, but more prevalent in European science fiction in recent years. Connected with this pessimistic conceptualisation of the future is the idea of the panopticon (both architectural and digital) as a new metaphor for digital surveillance. It originates in the workplace but expands into the most intimate spaces—homes and even minds—in order to monitor and manipulate people's life choices. This trend in European cyberpunk in the 2000s is not an altogether new invention, rather it updates previous visions of dystopia, bringing repressed fears about past authoritarian societies to light.

Another significant contribution of *Metropia* and *Renaissance* to cyberpunk has to do with the fact that their stories are set in European cities. Even when they are not consciously offering an alternative

---

23 In *Renaissance*, Avalon supports a research project aiming to increase the average human lifespan, but the experiment breaks ethical research protocols and results in the death of a group of children.

to either US or Japanese cyberpunk, they reveal a European point of view. In spite of the dystopian nature of cyberpunk films, Paris in both films stands as an alluring metropolis seen, if not as the political centre of Europe (as in other cyberpunk films, the companies are global conglomerates that in reality rule the world), at least as an abstract ideal of what a European city represents. The French capital is portrayed as a stylish location, hardly in keeping with the hostile environment of conventional cyberpunk scenarios. In addition, although many of the anxieties represented could be extrapolated to non-European countries, they constitute an identifiable trait of European cyberpunk. The obsession with beauty depicted in these futures and, above all, the complicity of citizen-consumers—who fall under the spell of authoritarian monopolies, allowing them to erode the most fundamental individual rights—is a recurrent motif. Furthermore, both films represent multicultural societies that rank citizens according to their ethnic origin. It is significant that in the context of a declining Europe where new global powers have emerged in recent decades, they are absent from these films. The result is a quite Eurocentric notion of international power relations, where Europe remains crucial alongside its longstanding allies. More importantly, the futures portrayed in *Renaissance* and *Metropia* consolidate the 'fortress Europe' project. Despite the stress in these films on the interconnectivity among continental regions, the apprehension concerning non-EU members has grown. Xenophobic attitudes are agitated and exploited by evil monopolies which rule the world in the hope that they will enhance the strength of European borders. In the new millennium, nation states might have been eliminated within Europe but the fears of German supremacy have not disappeared, an indication that the scars of the Second World War are still present in European science fiction cinema. German dominance is feared due to its association with an erosion of individual freedoms. There is some novelty here, however, in that the menace is not political or territorial but economic and therefore will be more difficult to oppose.

Released in a decade when European popular cinema flourished[24], *Renaissance* and *Metropia* promoted a certain idea of European cultural identity within the limits of an industry whose products are aimed at a global market. As a result, they are not free from incongruities triggered by conventions such as the use of English in everyday life by Parisians and Swedes. Any film that aims to appeal to audiences beyond national borders is often confronted with similar choices in order to make the production profitable. *Renaissance* and *Metropia* are examples of popular cinema intended to attract mainstream audiences while at the same time attempting to offer a product that deviates from audience expectations and the familiar look of cyberpunk films. Hence the need for an independent animation studio and the decision to set the stories in European cities, with the historical and cultural implications that this relocation to the old continent entails. Although many of the transnational elements prevail, it is useful to identify the specific traits that have made them distinct in order to enrich the debate about what constitutes the cyberpunk genre. The films highlighted in this paper demonstrate that a new trend in cyberpunk cinema emerged during the 2000s, one that adapted transnational cyberpunk in order to respond to specific European horrors of the past.

Funding: This research received no external funding.

Acknowledgments: The author would like to express her gratitude to Laura Montero Plata and the anonymous readers, whose comments have significantly improved the original draft.

Conflicts of Interest: The author declares no conflict of interest.

References

Filmography

Adamson, Andrew and Vicky Jenson. 2001. *Shrek*.

---

[24] "European popular cinema over the past decade has in fact thrived [...]. it continues to play a fundamental part in consolidating national film cultures in Europe and indeed in fostering a transnational film culture through co-productions and exports" (Bergfelder 2015, p. 45).

Amenábar, Alejandro. 1997. *Abre los ojos*.

Bay, Michael. 2009. *Transformers: Revenge of the Fallen*.

Besson, Luc. 1983. *Le dernier combat/Kamikaze 1999*.

Bigelow, Kathryn. 1996. *Strange Days*.

Bilal, Enki. 2004. *Immortel (Ad Vitam)*.

Bilal, Enki. 1990. *Bunker Palace Hôtel*.

Caro, Marc, and Jean-Pierre Jeunet. 1995. *La cité des enfants perdus*.

Crowe, Cameron. 2002. *Vanilla Sky*.

Cuarón, Alfonso. 2006. *Children of Men*.

Cuarón, Alfonso. 2013. *Gravity*.

Docter, Pete and Ronnie del Carmen. 2015. *Inside Out*.

Garland, Alex. 2014. *Ex_Machina*.

Glazer, Jonathan. 2013. *Under the Skin*.

Gilliam, Terry. 1985. *Brazil*.

Gilliam, Terry. 2013. *The Zero Theorem*.

Godard, Jean-Luc. 1965. *Alphaville, Une Étrange Aventure de Lemmy Caution*.

Greenaway, Peter. 1980. *The Falls*.

Gremm, Wolf. 1982. *Kamikaze 1989*.

Hitchcock, Alfred. 1958. *Vertigo*.

Lasseter, John. 1996. *Toy Story*.

Leclercq, Julien. 2007. *Chrysalis*.

Leonard, Brett. 1992. *The Lawnmower Man*.

Longo, Robert. 1995. *Johnny Mnemonic*.

Maíllo, Kiko. 2011. *Eva*.

Oshii, Mamoru. 1995. *Ghost in the Shell*.

Oshii, Mamoru. 2006. *Tachiguishi Retsuden*.

Oshii, Mamoru. 2011. *Avalon*.

Ôtomo, Katsuhiro. 1988. *Akira*.

Radford, Michael. 1984. *Nineteen Eighty-Four*.

Rodríguez, Robert and Frank Miller. 2005. *Sin City*.

Rusnak, Josef. 1999. *The Thirteenth Floor*.

Saleh, Tarik. 2009. *Metropia*.

Salvatores, Gabriele. 1997. *Nirvana*.

Sato, Kei'ichi, Hiroshi Yamazaki, and Akira Takada. 2005. *Karas: The Prophecy*.

Scott, Ridley. 1982. *Blade Runner*.

Stanton, Andrew. 2008. *WALL·E*.

Tanner, Alain. 1981. *Les années lumière. Light Years Away*.

Verhoeven, Paul. 1990. *Total Recall*.

Volckman, Christian. 2006. *Renaissance*.

Volckman, Christian. 2006. *Renaissance: La disparition*. Casterman.

Bibliography

Arendt, Paul. 2006. BBC—Movies—Review—Renaissance. Available online: http://www.bbc.co.uk/films/2006/07/26/renaissance_2006_review.shtml (accessed on 25 July 2018).

Bergfelder, Tim. 2015. Popular European Cinema in the 2000s: Cinephilia, Genre and Heritage. In *The Europeanness of European Cinema: Identity, Meaning, Globalization*. Edited by Mary Harrod, Mariana Liz and Alissa Timoshkina. London: I.B. Tauris, pp. 33–58.

Chilcoat, Michelle. 2004. Brain Sex, Cyberpunk Cinema, Feminism and the Dis/Location of Heterosexuality. *NWSA Journal* 16: 156–76. [CrossRef]

Darke, Chris. 2005. *Alphaville*. London: I.B. Tauris.

Edin, Fredrik. 2009. Metropias undermedvetna II—DIY-FRA—Skumrask. Available online: https://fredrikedin.se/2009/12/07/metropias-undermedvetna-ii-diy-fra/ (accessed on 28 July 2018).

Elsaesser, Thomas. 2005. *European Cinema. Face to Face with Hollywood*. Amsterdam: Amsterdam University Press.

Finney, Agnus. 2006. *The State of European Cinema. A New Dose of Reality*. London, New York, New Delhi and Sydney: Bloomsbury.

Frenette, Mireille. 2006. *Renaissance*: A New Beginning in Animation. *AnimationWorld*. February 16. Available online: https://www.awn.com/animationworld/renaissance-new-beginning-animation (accessed on 26 June 2018).

Gibson, William. 1984. *Neuromancer*. New York: Ace Books.

Grönqvist, Kim. 2010. *Rymdinvasion i Sverige. Om svensk science fiction på film och tv*. Lund: Lund Universitet, Available online: http://lup.lub.lu.se/luur/download?func=downloadFile&recordOId=1536114&fileOId=1536116 (accessed on 28 July 2018).

Hedling, Olof. 2015. The Trouble with Stars. Vernacular versus Global Stardom in Two Forms of European Popular Culture. In *The Europeanness of European Cinema: Identity, Meaning, Globalization*. Edited by Mary Harrod, Mariana Liz and Alissa Timoshkina. London: I.B. Tauris.

Johnston, Keith M. 2011. *Science Fiction Film: A Critical Introduction*. London: Bloomsbury Academic.

Kuhn, Annette. 1990. *Alien Zone: Cultural Theory and Contemporary Science Fiction Cinema*. London and New York: Verso Books.

Kuhn, Annette. 1999. *Alien Zone II: The Spaces of Science Fiction Cinema*. London and New York: Verso.

Kulyk, Laëtitia. 2015. The Use of English in European Feature Films: Unity in Diversity? In *The Europeanness of European Cinema: Identity, Meaning, Globalization*. Edited by Mary Harrod, Mariana Liz and Alissa Timoshkina. London: I.B. Tauris.

Liz, Mariana. 2015. From European Co-Productions to the Euro-Pudding. In *The Europeanness of European Cinema: Identity, Meaning, Globalization*. Edited by Mary Harrod, Mariana Liz and Alissa Timoshkina. London: I.B. Tauris.

Loshitzky, Yosefa. 2010. *Screening Strangers. Migration and Diaspora in Contemporary European Cinema*. Bloomington and Indianapolis: Indiana University Press.

Meehan, Paul. 2008. *Tech-Noir. The Fusion of Science Fiction and Film Noir*. Jefferson and London: McFarland & Company.

Mihailova, Mihaela. 2013. The Mastery Machine: Digital Animation and Fantasies of Control. *Animation* 8: 131–48. [CrossRef]

Redmon, Sean, ed. 2004. *Liquid Metal: The Science Fiction Film Reader*. New York: Wallflower Press.

Rickman, Gregg. 2004. *The Science Fiction Film Reader*. New York: Limelight Editions.

Roxborough, Scott. 2009. Scandi Animation Makes a Bid for the Big Time. Less Is Norse. *The Hollywood Reporter*. December 5. Available online: https://www.hollywoodreporter.com/news/drawing-attention-83820 (accessed on 26 June 2018).

Seikaly, Andrea. 2014. Tarik Saleh: 'Film Saved My Life When I Was a Kid.' *Variety*. February 1. Available online: http://variety.com/2014/film/global/tarik-saleh-film-saved-my-life-when-i-was-a-kid-1201077568 (accessed on 26 June 2018).

Senjanovic, Natasha. 2009. Metropia. *Hollywood Reporter*, September 3.

Sharkey, Betsy. 2010. Movie Review: Metropia. *Los Angeles Times*. June 25. Available online: http://articles.latimes.com/2010/jun/25/entertainment/la-et-metropia-20100625 (accessed on 28 August 2018).

Sobchack, Vivian. 1987. *Screening Space: The American Science Fiction Film*. New Brunswick: Rutgers University Press.

Stephenson, Neal. 1992. *Snow Crash*. London: Penguin Books.

Telotte, J.P. 1999. *A Distant Technology: Science Fiction in the Machine Age*. Hanover and London: Wesleyan University Press.

arts

MDPI

Article

Recycled Dystopias: Cyberpunk and the End of History

Elana Gomel

Department of English and American Studies, Tel-Aviv University, Tel Aviv 39040, Israel; egomel@post.tau.ac.il

Received: 8 June 2018; Accepted: 23 July 2018; Published: 30 July 2018

Abstract: While cyberpunk is often described as a dystopian genre, the paper argues that it should be seen rather as a post-utopian one. The crucial difference between the two resides in the nature of the historical imagination reflected in their respective narrative and thematic conventions. While dystopia and utopia (structurally the same genre) reflect a teleological vision of history, in which the future is radically different from the present, post-utopia corresponds to what many scholars, from Fredric Jameson and Francis Fukuyama to David Bell, have diagnosed as the "end of history" or rather, the end of historical teleology. Post-utopia reflects the vision of the "broad present", in which the future and the past bleed into, and contaminate, the experience of "now". From its emergence in the 1980s and until today, cyberpunk has progressively succumbed to the post-utopian sensibility, as its earlier utopian/dystopian potential has been diluted by nostalgia, repetition and recycling. By analyzing the chronotope of cyberpunk, the paper argues that the genre's articulation of time and space is inflected by the general post-utopian mood of global capitalism. The texts addressed include both novels (William Gibson's *Neuromancer*, Neal Stephenson's *Snow Crash* and Matthew Mather's *Atopia*) and movies (*Blade Runner*, *Blade Runner 2049* and *Ex Machina*).

Keywords: dystopia; post-utopia; nostalgia; fractal space; end of history; global capitalism

---

1. The Future Is Dark(ish)

Cyberpunk is often referred to as a dystopian genre. The foundational novels of cyberpunk, William Gibson's *Neuromancer* (1984) and Neal Stephenson's *Snow Crash* (1992), have been described as dystopias by critics and scholars alike. "But, I think, one of the most frightening of dystopias is the one that is in the near future, and seems to be getting closer and closer. Snow Crash kind of fits that bill" (Fife 2014). But is this really true? What do we mean when we call a text dystopian?

In everyday speech, dystopia has come to be used as a synonym of "something bad happening sometime in the future". In his 2014 discussion of dystopian movies, Christopher Schmidt notes that "the recent uptick in dystopian and post-apocalyptic scenarios seems more urgent and more extreme" and suggests that it relates to the threat of climate change and environmental degradation (Schmidt 2014). In this broad sense, cyberpunk is undoubtedly dystopian: the urban sprawl of Chiba City in *Neuromancer*, the crime-ridden Metaverse of *Snow Crash*, and the corporate-ruled virtual Hong Kong in Kelley Eskridge's *Solitaire* (2010) are nobody's idea of paradise.

But dystopia as a literary genre means something else entirely. It is not merely that the future is worse than the present. Rather, the future is different.

Utopia (at least, Western utopia in modern times) posits that history possesses an inherent drive toward perfection. In other words, it sees history not merely as linear but specifically as dynamic, teleological and future-oriented. Dystopia is utopia's double, its dark twin, its mirror reflection. As Krishan Kumar pointed out in his magisterial study *Utopia and Anti-Utopia in Modern Times* (1987), utopia and dystopia are two sides of the same structural and ideological phenomenon: modern dystopia is predicated "on the very terms of modern utopia" (Kumar 1987, p. 110). Utopia and dystopia share a dynamic future-oriented modality involving a meaningful change, whether this change is seen positively or negatively. As Ruth Levitas explains in her gloss on Kumar, "utopia is about hoping for a transformed future ... while fearing the worst" (Levitas 1990, p. 167). In other words, both utopia and dystopia presuppose a teleological narrative of history which culminates in either millennium or apocalypse. In either case, the future is indeed transformed. But is the future of cyberpunk sufficiently different from our present to be regarded as dystopian?

In this essay, I will argue that cyberpunk is not a dystopian modality of representation. Rather, I would classify it as belonging to the broader trend of post-utopia. The latter term relates to the current geopolitical situation, in which the collapse of communism and other 20th-century utopian ideologies has left neo-liberalism and global capitalism without significant conceptual rivals. David Bell describes this situation as "the supposedly 'post-utopian' here-and-now of capital and the state: a world, in which, we are told, there is no longer any need for utopianism" (Bell 2017, p. 3).

Post-utopia is what comes after the end of history, as described by Fukuyama (1992) in his influential book *The End of History*, first published in 1992, the same year as the cyberpunk classic *Snow Crash*. Fukuyama's book has been misunderstood as forecasting the end of the historical process, which is absurd. In fact, it was about the end of History with a capital H: that is, the notion that this process has an inbuilt salvational or destructive directionality. Events, even momentous events such as 9/11, will keep happening. What has ended, though, is the belief that these events are inescapably building up toward some preordained goal, whether it be a communist society of equality and plenty, or a total collapse of civilization.

The utopian/dystopian scenario in Western culture derives from the Christian apocalyptic narrative, in which history inexorably builds up toward a radical culmination of the Tribulations followed by the Millennium. Norman Cohn in *The Pursuit of the Millennium* (Cohn 1992) was the first to make the connection between revolutionary utopias and Christian mysticism. Recently John Gray argued that the utopian ideologies of the 20th century wrought so much havoc precisely because they faithfully followed the script of radical transformation inherited from the religious model of history: the "conviction that the crimes and follies of the past could be left behind in an all-encompassing transformation of human life was a secular reincarnation of early Christian beliefs" (Gray 2007, p. 1). Utopias, whatever their underlying ideological platform, are founded on "the belief that history must be understood not in terms of the causes of events but in terms of its purpose, which is the salvation of humanity" (Gray 2007, p. 5). And dystopias simply invert the logic of teleology: instead of heaven, history leads straight to hell. Stuck in the Tribulations, so to speak, dystopias nevertheless offer the same vision of a radically transformed social and ontological world as utopias. Indeed, depending on your point of view, every utopia may be read as a dystopia and vice versa. In the famous confrontation between Winston Smith and O'Brien in George Orwell's *1984*, the latter persuasively argues that the totalitarian society of Oceania is, in fact, the best of all possible world and when Smith objects, pointing to human nature as the bedrock of moral values, O'Brien contemptuously calls him "the last man" and forcefully demonstrates that human nature is as malleable as the social structure dominated by the Party. The world of 1984 is the world of New Men, for whom Smith's longings for love, privacy and freedom are simply incomprehensible.

Of course, utopia/dystopia also involves what has been called "the utopian impulse": a dynamic desire to improve the current socio-political situation without necessarily specifying the "terminus" of history. Elaborated by Tom Moylan in *Demand the Impossible*, Darko Suvin and Fredric Jameson, the concept of the utopian impulse emphasizes precisely the temporal and forward-looking nature of utopia. So whether specific utopian texts tend toward the millenarian/apocalyptic model or toward the open-ended dynamic model, the important thing for my purposes here is to emphasize the difference between the future orientation of utopia/dystopia and the past orientation of post-utopia.

The collapse of utopia/dystopia has created the world in which "late capitalism seems to have no natural enemies" (Jameson 2005). Apart from its political implications, this foreclosure of utopian/dystopian alternatives paralyzes the historical imagination itself. One of Jameson's most famous essays is subtitled "How Can We Imagine the Future?" and the answer seems to be that we cannot (Jameson 2005). We live today not in the expectation or fear of the future but in what Gumbrecht (2015) calls the "Chronotope of the Broad Present":

> Different from the ever shrinking and therefore "imperceptibly short" present of the historicist chronotope, the new present (that continues to be our present in the early twenty-first century) is one in which all paradigms and phenomena from the past are juxtaposed as being available and ready-to-hand. For this present, instead of leaving the past behind, is inundated with pastness, and at the same time it is facing a future which, instead of being an open horizon of possibilities, seems occupied by threats that are inevitably moving towards us (think of "global warming," as an example).

In this "broad present", what is the role of cyberpunk, both as a literary and cinematic genre and as a style and sensibility? Does it offer any glimpse of a "radical difference from what currently is" (Jameson 2005)? Or is it merely one of the plethora of post-utopian genres, ceaselessly scouring history for stylistic innovations that can be integrated in the never-ending "now" of cultural production?

2. Past Present and Past Continuous

In 1992—apparently a bumper year for cyberpunk—George Slusser and T. A. Shippey (Slusser and Shippey 1992) edited the foundational collection of critical essays that defined the genre, titled *Fiction 2000: Cyberpunk and the Future of Narrative.* The year 2000 came and went. The future of narrative became the past of criticism. But cyberpunk is still alive, though nowhere near the towering position in the field of narrative representation predicted by that volume. It is not even central to the poetics of science fiction (SF), which is now dominated by the resurgence of space opera.[1] But cyberpunk has spread into culture at large; mutated into an aesthetics of street cool; invaded the Asian visual media (manga and anime); and was brought back into the Hollywood mainstream by movies such as the *Matrix* trilogy, *Ex Machina* and *Blade Runner 2049.*

Perhaps these movies are a good way to start an analysis of time and space in contemporary cyberpunk. While different media employ different means of representation, all narratives, whether visual, verbal or mixed, generate chronotopes: the term defined by Mikhail Bakhtin as "the intrinsic connectedness of temporal and spatial-relationships that are artistically expressed in literature" (Bakhtin 2002, p. 15). As the quote from Gumbrecht above indicates, the notion of chronotope transcends literature or fiction in general, and may be applied to a cultural perception of space and time or rather, spacetime. And this perception is equally reflected in movies, books or political and ideological discourses.

The original *Blade Runner* (1982) revolutionized our perception of space, especially urban space. Wong Kin Yuen's influential article "On the Edge of Spaces: *Blade Runner, Ghost in the Shell,* and Hong Kong's Cityscape" argued that the movie's visual aesthetics both reflected and influenced the cityscapes of Asian metropolises, such as Hong Kong and Tokyo. The heterogeneity, fractal chaos and light/dark interplay of the movie's urban scenes introduced the previously marginalized Asian spaces into the Western mainstream. Moreover, despite the common predilection of calling *Blade Runner* dystopian, Wong argued that the shocking newness—to the Western audiences—of the Asian urban space contained a utopian potential: "colonial cities have the best chance of establishing a cityscape of the future that embraces racial and cultural differences".

Time as well opened up into a future that was problematic, fraught with difficulties and unresolved dilemmas but new and exciting. The conclusion of the original version had Deckard and Rachael drive

---

[1]   It is difficult to gauge the relative popularity of various sub-genres within SF but the prominence of such recent TV shows as *The Expanse*, a space opera based on James Corey's multi-volume series, indicates a shift (back) toward space adventure. See an interesting article by Charlie Jane Anders in the *Wired* magazine discussing the new openness of publishers toward big-canvas space opera. https://www.wired.com/2017/03/rejuvenation-of-space-opera/ (Accessed on 8 June 2018).

together into the unknown. The open-ended temporality of Rachael's lifespan, which may, or may not, be as limited as that of the other replicants bled into the open-endedness of the movie's implied history.[2] Whether the replicants' revolt succeeded or failed, there was no question that they represented a genuinely new kind of human beings. The very ease with which their memories could be implanted and manipulated indicated that their existence put into question the biological and social foundations of human identity. Moreover, Deckard's blasé dismissal of the very issue of "real" versus "simulated" in relation to Rachael's subjectivity indicated that the movie ventured into the territory of what we today call the posthuman: subversion of the traditional pieties of liberal humanism. When Deckard was revealed as a replicant himself in the director's cut, the utopian potential of new technologies became even clearer. What is the place of liberal humanism in a world in which the foundational distinction of human/nonhuman no longer obtains, even in relation to one's own sense of self?

Just as the original movie was revolutionary, its sequel was reactionary. First, in the most obvious sense of not breaking new grounds aesthetically or conceptually but rather slavishly following the original's lead. Second, in a more subtle way in which its chronotope revised the utopian/dystopian poetics of the 1982 *Blade Runner* in order to fit into the current trend of nostalgic recycling. And it is nostalgia, I will argue, that characterizes post-utopia in general and the current post-utopian cyberpunk in particular.

Nostalgia, as Svetlana Boym argues in *The Future of Nostalgia*, is a by-product of globalism: it is a "historical emotion . . . nostalgic manifestations are side-effect of the teleology of progress" (Boym 2001, p. 10). Nostalgia is a longing for a homely "space of experience": a familiar corner in an unfamiliar and perpetually changing world (Boym 2001, p. 10). But the "new nostalgia" manifested in such explicitly retro productions as the 80s-infested TV series *Stranger Things*, is temporal rather than spatial: it is a longing for a familiar time. And since time as opposed to space is linear and irreversible—you really cannot go back home again if your home is 1982—the new nostalgia is engaged in historical denialism through a complex system of pastiche, intertextuality, remaking and recycling.

In an astute review of *Blade Runner 2049*, Loufbarrow (2017) lists all the ways in which the new movie is nostalgic:

> It's nostalgic for Sinatra. It's nostalgic for noir. It's nostalgic for horses and childhood and Elvis and dogs and trees and the sheer existence of memory. It's nostalgic for the version of the future that existed in the past—there are no smartphones, and the Pan Am logo flashes in neon lights. If it's nostalgic for the color green, it's also nostalgic for electricity, which seems to be in short supply. It's nostalgic for snow and bugs and touch. For hedonism when it meant good old American excess like Las Vegas and roulette and whiskey, gigantic statues of naked ladies instead of pornified holograms and geishas. It is so overloaded with backward glances that "above all, it's nostalgic for itself". [3]

Both space and time in *Blade Runner 2049* lack the sheer newness of its predecessor. The muted orange palette and the attenuated cityscapes of the new movie stand in sharp contrast to the exuberance of the original: the exuberance that, as Wong points out, was derived from the actual, lived experience of Asian metropolises, just emerging from their marginal colonial status. Those cityscapes pointed forward to what Daniel Brook called "the history of future cities": a "reinvention" of history "written into the cityscape itself" (Brook n.d.).

The space of *Blade Runner 2049* is as faded, as inconsequential, and as devoid of political implications as a Victorian daguerreotype. The political subtext of the replicants' revolt is reduced to some pseudo-Freudian musings, which point to the greatest object of nostalgia in the new movie: the concept of biological time.

---

2   It's too bad she won't live. But then again who does?
3   http://theweek.com/articles/729283/blade-runner-2049-nostalgic-hurts (accessed on 8 June 2018).

Just as the plot of the original *Blade Runner* revolved around what Jean Baudrillard called "precession of simulacra" and concluded with the dismissal of any ontological difference between copy and original, *Blade Runner 2049* is infected with the yearning for the certainty of origin. K's search for his biological parents and Rachael's (impossible) pregnancy reinstate the deeply conservative belief that privileges "nature" over technology. In the original *Blade Runner*, time was malleable, open-ended, and full of possibilities. In the sequel, time is frozen, circular, and forced back into the supposedly immutable cycles of biological procreation.[4]

Whether *Blade Runner* old and new are, strictly speaking, cyberpunk is open to debate since replicants are not cybernetic devices but biologically engineered artificial humans (as Philip K. Dick's original novel makes perfectly clear). But the first film has become part of cyberpunk's "canon" due, primarily, to its visual aesthetics. Other recent movies, however, do fit the generic template of cyberpunk and display the same combination of all-pervasive nostalgia and backward-looking intertextuality, in which the past of the genre becomes its future. Consider *Ex Machina* (2014), one of the few recent SF movies which is neither a remake nor part of a franchise. Focusing on the Turing test performed for a beautiful android Ava, the movie is at pains to draw the dividing line between human and nonhuman: the line that is deliberately blurred in the earlier cyberpunk texts, such as *Neuromancer* (where no character is a "natural" human being, all of them having been modified physically, neurologically or both). The movie ends with a hoary "robot rebellion" cliché that is as old as SF. However, another aspect of the movie's chronotope is particularly striking: its claustrophobia. Taking place exclusively in confined, carceral spaces, it is replete with images of locked doors, narrow corridors and blind alleys. It ends with the protagonist locked up in a cell, from which he cannot escape, while Ava is lost in an equally claustrophobic cityscape filled with dense and gloomy crowds. Of course, the ending can also be read as the liberation of a new posthuman subjectivity into a larger network of social relations, and it is this ambiguity that makes *Ex Machina* one of the best recent SF movies. But the visual aspect of the film stands in sharp contrast to the startling innovation of, say, the original *Blade Runner* which created a new visual vocabulary of urban representation. The spaces of *Ex Machina* are both familiar and suffocating: whether natural or technological, they simply replicate the well-known motifs of incarceration versus escape.

The peculiarity of this articulation of space in post-utopian cyberpunk becomes clearer if we compare it to the chronotope of actual utopia/dystopia.

3. Lost in Space

It has been a cliché that our current era is more concerned with space than with time. Fredric Jameson's classic definition of postmodernism emphasized spatiality as the dominant motif of contemporary culture:

> "We have often been told, however, that we now inhabit the synchronic rather than diachronic, and I think it is at least empirically arguable that our daily life, our psychic experience, our cultural languages, are today dominated by categories of space rather than categories of time ... " (Jameson 1991, p. 16)

Within this broad dominance of the synchronic, however, different articulations of spatiality bear different symbolic and ideological messages. In an earlier article, I argued that the topology of space in the original cyberpunk, represented by the seminal works of Gibson, Stephenson, Pat Cadigan and others, mirrored the topology of the political and social space of globalization (Gomel 2016). The space of cyberpunk is unbounded, fractal, and self-similar. It represents the hidden structure of the space of globalization that shapes our subjectivities and interactions both on- and offline. In *Neuromancer*

---

4   There could, of course, be a way for the film to justify Rachael's pregnancy as some new form of bio-technology, the way it is implied, for example, in Paolo Bacigalupi's *Windup Girl*. The fact that it is not done emphasizes precisely the nostalgic reversion to the circular "bio-time" instead of the forward-looking techno-time.

and *Snow Crash*, the topologies of cyberspace precisely replicate the topology of the post-industrial, post-nation-state global political domain. Both virtual and physical realms are ruled by the same networks of criminals and politicians; both are constructed as complex labyrinths of legal, quasi-legal, and illegal domains; both involve manipulations of power structures by individuals and the backlash of the matrix, whether electronic or social, against the rebel. Cyberspace reveals the geometry of power that has been there all along.

Utopia/dystopia, on the other hand, has a very different spatial structure that reflects its radical alterity, its separation from the power structures of here and now. Thomas More's original utopia is an island, deliberately isolated from the mainland by the canal dug by the inhabitants of this perfect society. Utopias are always guarded by fences, walls, oceans or cosmic distances; protected from the pollution of history; kept pure and undefiled. In Ursula Le Guin's *The Dispossessed* (1974), for example, the utopian planet Anarres is separated from its dystopian counterpart Urras not just by the gulf of space by a symbolic wall that "enclosed the universe, leaving Anarres outside, free" (Le Guin 1974, p. 1). Of course, from the other side of the wall, the utopia of Anarres is seen as "a great prison camp, cut off from other worlds and other men, in quarantine" (Le Guin 1974, p. 1). But this dialectic of enclosure is precisely what defines utopia/dystopia: the same bounded space can be seen as either paradise or hell, depending on where you are standing in relation to its boundaries.

Dystopias replicate the bounded structure of utopian space. The Crystal City in Zamyatin's *We* is protected by a wall from the wilderness of nature outside; the Republic of Gilead is enclosed by a barrier in Margaret Atwood's *The Handmaid's Tale*; and Room 101 in *1984* is a symbol of Oceania's carceral space. Spatial separation echoes temporal rupture. A barrier marks the transition from the present to the future.

Cyberpunk's emphasis on the complex interplay between physical and virtual spaces and on their endless proliferation militates against the rigid division of the utopian/dystopian chronotope. In *Snow Crash*, the infinite Metaverse randomly combines bits and pieces of actual spaces, mixed in no particular order. It is traversed by the infinitely long Street that contains versions of cities in the physical world, including a cyber-Hong Kong, New York and Paris. The Metaverse is a recursive reflection of the physical space, containing the latter, while it is also contained by it.

Our relationship with cyberspace, and the chaotic, recursive, infinitely proliferating virtual spatiality of the Internet make cyberpunk's chronotope seem more natural than the rigidly divided geography of utopia. However, the chaotic topology of cyberpunk, in fact, contributes to the blurred boundaries of the "chronotope of broad present", in which spatial proliferation substitutes for temporal progress.

In his *Demand the Impossible: Science Fiction and the Utopian Imagination* (1986), Tom Moylan makes an interesting point that the very completeness of the rigidly structured utopian spaces is, in fact, the tacit acknowledgment of their limitations. Precisely because these spaces can never be enclosed enough, they call for a temporal dimension of development and change. Space alone cannot satisfy the human yearning for a better world:

> "In this way, Bloch locates the positive drive toward the future in the negative, in the radical insufficiency of the present, for even those concrete utopian moments of fulfilment are future-bearing only in their very finite and passing nature." (Moylan 1986, p. 22)

Thus, the very plenitude of cyberpunk space is a testimony to its "radical insufficiency". Just like the consumer bounty of neo-liberal capitalism is never enough to stifle utopian dreams and aspirations, endless spaces of cyberpunk only mask but never really fill, the gap left by the end of history.

4. Chronotopia

The interplay between dystopia and post/utopia in cyberpunk is not a new phenomenon. Post-utopia and the "chronotope of the broad present" are implicit in Gibson's 1980s work, especially in the case of *Neuromancer*. But while cyberpunk as a whole has shifted toward the post-utopian pole of this interplay, some contemporary cyberpunk texts display an awareness of their own generic limitations and, in different ways, open up toward a genuine utopian/dystopian future, which is radically different from the present. I want to pause on one such text: Matthew Mather's *The Atopia Chronicles* (2014).[5]

In this novel, a group of techies build an island paradise in the Pacific where the extensive use of brain-wired virtual and augmented reality is supposed to create a new social and ontological structure:

> After the mess the rest of the world had become, the best and brightest of the world had emigrated to build the new New World, the Bensalem group of seasteads in the Pacific Ocean, of which Atopia was the crown jewel. Atopia was supposed to be—was marketed as—this shining beacon of libertarian ideals. She was, by far, the largest in a collection of platforms in the oceans off California, a kind of new Silicon Valley that would solve the world's problems with technological wizardry. (Mather 2014, p. 51)

Mather's *Atopia* is, initially, cyberpunk rather than utopia or dystopia. Much like the matrix in *Neuromancer* or Metaverse in *Snow Crash*, Atopia is an infinite space, a playground of limitless possibilities. The inhabitants of Atopia effortlessly move across virtual and physical spaces without distinguishing between the two. Indeed, since their brains are injected with nano-particles that create a complete experience of being anywhere and everywhere at whim, the distinction between reality and simulacrum is largely meaningless:

> The pssi—polysynthetic sensory interface—system had originally grown out of research to move artificial limbs, using nanoscale smarticles embedded in the nervous system to control signals passing through it. Fairly quickly, they'd learned the trick of modifying the signals going to our eyes, ears and other sensory channels, making it possible to perfectly simulate our senses. Creating completely synthetic worlds had followed in short order. In that they'd more than succeeded—to most Atopians, synthetic reality was more real than the real world. (Mather 2014, p. 57)

Plato's cave has become our playground.

However, as opposed to Stephenson's Metaverse, Atopia is not immune to the tug of history. In traditional cyberpunk, the chronotope is entirely spatial and the action unfolds across multiplying ontological domains. The protagonist may triumph or die (or, like Case in *Neuromancer*, be stuck in the doldrums of his precarious existence) but the fictional world remains in a homeostasis. In *The Atopia Chronicles*, however, it has an inbuilt teleology that, does not become clear until the novel's end. While its multiple characters—pssi-endowed young men and women—party through a bewildering profusion of "synthetic worlds", one of them methodically schemes to take over Atopia and turn it into an old-fashioned dictatorship. He succeeds at the end, and Atopia becomes a totalitarian nightmare, presided over by an omnipotent psychopath.

At the end of the book, one of the characters who is to become the protagonist in the sequels, escapes the cyberpunk paradise into the physical world where he and his group are readying for a revolution:

> "It was true what they said—the future was already here, just unevenly distributed. I belonged to that future, yet here I was with the rest of humanity. The world, however, was about to change, and people could hardly wait. I laughed to myself. They really ought to be more careful what they wished for." (Mather 2014, p. 491)

The "unevenly distributed" future, riddled with choices and opportunities, becomes an escape hatch from cyberpunk into utopia/dystopia. Here is where the endless recycling of history comes to

---

5   The novel has two sequels: significantly titled *The Dystopia Chronicles* and *The Utopia Chronicles* but I am not presently engaging with them.

an end, and the radical alterity of the future inserts itself into the sameness of the "broad present". Even the end of history is not forever.

Funding: This research received no external funding.

Conflicts of Interest: The author declares no conflict of interest.

References

Bakhtin, Mikhail. 2002. Forms of Time and the Chronotope in the Novel. In *Narrative Dynamics: Essays on Time, Plot, Closure, and Framed*. Edited by Brain Richardson. Columbus: Ohio State University Press, pp. 15–25.

Bell, David. 2017. *Rethinking Utopia: Place, Power, Affect*. New York: Routledge.

Boym, Svetlana. 2001. *The Future of Nostalgia*. New York: Basic Books.

Brook, Daniel. n.d. *The Head of the Dragon: The Rise of New Shanghai*. San Francisco: Public Scholarship on Architecture, Landscape and Urbanism, Available online: https://placesjournal.org/article/head-of-the-dragon-the-rise-of-new-shanghai/ (accessed on 18 May 2018).

Cohn, Norman. 1992. *Pursuit of the Millennium: Revolutionary Millenarians and Mystical Anarchists of the Middle Ages*. Oxford: Oxford University Press, Frist published 1957.

Fife, Richard. 2014. Neal Stephenson's Snow Crash: '92's Eerie Cyber-Prophet. *Dystopia Week*. April 14. Available online: https://www.tor.com/2011/04/14/neal-stephensons-snow-crash-92s-eerie-cyber-prophet (accessed on 18 May 2018).

Fukuyama, Francis. 1992. *The End of History and the Last Man*. New York: Free Press.

Gomel, Elana. 2016. The Cyberworld is Flat: Cyberpunk and Globalization. In *The Cambridge History of Postmodern Literature*. Edited by Brian McHale and Len Platt. Cambridge: Cambridge University Press.

Gray, John. 2007. *Black Mass: Apocalyptic Religion and the Death of Utopia*. New York: Farrar, Straus and Giroux.

Gumbrecht, Hans Ulrich. 2015. Philology and the Complex Present. *Philology Today* 32: 273–81. Available online: https://journals.lib.unb.ca/index.php/flor/issue/view/1919 (accessed on 8 June 2018). [CrossRef]

Jameson, Fredric. 1991. *Postmodernism; or the Cultural Logic of Late Capitalism*. Durham: Duke University Press.

Jameson, Fredric. 2005. *Archaelogies of the Future: The Desire Called Utopia and Other Science Fictions*. London: Verso.

Kumar, Krishan. 1987. *Utopia and Anti-Utopia in Modern Times*. Oxford: Basil Blackwell.

Le Guin, Ursula. 1974. *The Dispossessed*. New York: Harper & Row, p. 1.

Levitas, Ruth. 1990. *The Concept of Utopia*. London: Syracuse University Press.

Loufbarrow, Lili. 2017. Blade Runner 2049 Is So Nostalgic It Hurts. *The Week*. October 6. Available online: http://theweek.com/articles/729283/blade-runner-2049-nostalgic-hurts (accessed on 15 May 2018).

Mather, Matthew. 2014. *The Atopia Chronicles*. Seattle: 47North, pp. 51–491.

Moylan, Tom. 1986. *Demand the Impossible: Science Fiction and the Utopian Imagination*. New York: Methuen.

Schmidt, Christopher. 2014. Why Are Dystopian Films on the Rise Again? *JSTOR Daily*. November 19. Available online: https://daily.jstor.org/why-are-dystopian-films-on-the-rise-again/ (accessed on 15 May 2018).

Slusser, George Edgar, and Tom A. Shippey, eds. 1992. *Fiction 2000: Cyberpunk and the Future of Narrative*. Athens: University of Georgia Press.

arts

MDPI

Article

Has *Akira* Always Been a Cyberpunk Comic?

Martin de la Iglesia

Institute of European Art History, Heidelberg University, Heidelberg 69117, Germany;
martin.delaiglesia@gmail.com

Received: 14 May 2018; Accepted: 12 July 2018; Published: 1 August 2018

Abstract: Between the late 1980s and early 1990s, interest in the cyberpunk genre peaked in the Western world, perhaps most evidently when *Terminator 2: Judgment Day* became the highest-grossing film of 1991. It has been argued that the translation of Katsuhiro Ōtomo's manga *Akira* into several European languages at just that time (into English beginning in 1988, into French, Italian, and Spanish beginning in 1990, and into German beginning in 1991) was no coincidence. In hindsight, cyberpunk tropes are easily identified in *Akira* to the extent that it is nowadays widely regarded as a classic cyberpunk comic. But has this always been the case? When *Akira* was first published in America and Europe, did readers see it as part of a wave of cyberpunk fiction? Did they draw the connections to previous works of the cyberpunk genre across different media that today seem obvious? In this paper, magazine reviews of *Akira* in English and German from the time when it first came out in these languages will be analysed in order to gauge the past readers' genre awareness. The attribution of the cyberpunk label to *Akira* competed with others such as the post-apocalyptic, or science fiction in general. Alternatively, *Akira* was sometimes regarded as an exceptional, novel work that transcended genre boundaries. In contrast, reviewers of the *Akira* anime adaptation, which was released at roughly the same time as the manga in the West (1989 in Germany and the United States), more readily drew comparisons to other cyberpunk films such as *Blade Runner*.

Keywords: audience; comics; genre; Germany; manga; reception history; science fiction; translation; United States

---

1. Introduction

Katsuhiro Ōtomo's *Akira* was first published in the Japanese manga periodical, *Young Magazine*, from 1982 to 1990. Spanning almost 2200 pages, *Akira* was collected in 6 volumes in Japan between 1984 and 1993. The first edition in the Western world was the English translation by Epic, an imprint of American publisher Marvel, in 38 issues from 1988 to 1995 (De la Iglesia 2016). French, Italian, and Spanish translations followed (all of which begun in 1990), and between 1991 and 1996, *Akira* was released in 19 German volumes by the publisher Carlsen. The following text focuses on the American and German first editions as being representative of the entire Western world.

In the wake of these foreign *Akira* editions, a considerable number of similarly themed manga were translated into European languages, such as Masamune Shirow's three titles, *Appleseed, Dominion*, and *Ghost in the Shell*, Masaomi Kanzaki's *Xenon*, and Yukito Kishiro's *Battle Angel Alita*. According to Roger Sabin (2006), the success of *Akira* created a "fashionable template" which Western publishers tried to follow by selecting manga titles from the same genre for translation, which "had the benefit of co-opting manga into the tradition of SF comics in the USA and Europe". The attribution of a genre to a comic (or any piece of fiction) is a critically relevant act because genres "specify the proper use of a particular cultural artifact"—they "ensure their appropriate reception" and exclude "undesirable responses" (Jameson 1981, pp. 106–7). "Genre guides interpretation"; it "structure[s] our reading, guiding the course it will take, our expectations of what it will encounter" (Frow 2006, pp. 101–3). Therefore, the audience response, and ultimately the success of a comic among critics and other readers, is connected to the identification of its genre. However, what genre precisely does *Akira* belong to? From today's perspective, *Akira* is regarded as cyberpunk—a genre that had its heyday just at the same time when Ōtomo's manga was first published in the Western world. However, was it actually identified as cyberpunk back then? And, did the popularity of the cyberpunk genre really play a role in the success of this manga? To answer these questions, we need to first ask whether people in the late 1980s and early 1990s were familiar with the concept of cyberpunk at all. We also need to verify that *Akira* is in fact a cyberpunk comic. Furthermore, in order to do so, we need to define what cyberpunk actually is. These questions in reverse order result in the outline of this article: Section 2 is a brief definition of cyberpunk, followed by a reappraisal of *Akira* as cyberpunk in Section 3. Section 4 provides the chronological context of cyberpunk in general, and Section 5, the centrepiece of this text, is an analysis of magazine reviews with which the genre awareness of the readers of *Akira* is gauged.

2. The Concept of Cyberpunk

There is no universally agreed-upon definition of cyberpunk. Some authors even go as far as to deny cyberpunk any usefulness as a concept, claiming that the term "served [...] only to provide a facile adjective for the working vocabulary of lazy journalists and unimaginative blurb-writers" (Womack 2000) and wondering whether "we should simply stop talking about 'cyberpunk SF', that witty coinage of [Gardner] Dozois's? Perhaps it might be more useful to say that there is the writer William Gibson, and then there are a couple of expert PR men [...] who know full well the commercial value of an instantly recognizable label, and are sticking one onto disparate products?" (Suvin [1989] 1991). Others insist on either cybernetic body modifications or cyberspace (or both) as necessary elements of cyberpunk fiction, however such narrow definitions would exclude many stories that are typically regarded as cyberpunk.

Instead, for the purposes of this article, the concept of cyberpunk is better described in the words of Istvan Csicsery-Ronay (Csicsery-Ronay [1988] 1991): cyberpunk is about "alienated subcultures that adopt the high-tech tools of the establishment they are [...] alienated from". When Csicsery-Ronay wrote this, he meant it as criticism of the entire concept of cyberpunk and felt that the cyberpunk writers did not succeed in convincingly conveying these subcultures' "political-aesthetic motives". However, Csicsery-Ronay's quotation can nevertheless serve as a succinct definition of cyberpunk, albeit only in word and not in spirit. In a similar vein, Bruce Sterling, one of the protagonists of the cyberpunk movement in science fiction literature, described cyberpunk as an "unholy alliance of the technical world and the world of organized dissent" in his preface to the *Mirrorshades* anthology which became a sort of cyberpunk manifesto (Sterling [1986] 1991). In another text (Sterling [1986] 2003), Sterling condensed this formula to the classic phrase, "lowlife and high tech" (often rephrased by others as "high tech and low life").

In other words, the cyberpunk definition used here relies on two necessary characteristics: a piece of cyberpunk fiction needs to feature high technology, and that technology needs to be employed by anti-establishment, counter-cultural characters from the fringes of society. It should be noted, however, that a formal or thematic definition of any genre is only valid with regard to a specific period in time (in this case, the late 1980s and early 1990s). Genre theory has stressed that genres are not static but evolve or mutate over time as their characteristics are negotiated and renegotiated by authors, critics, and audiences (Altman 1984; Frow 2006, p. 139; Rieder 2017, pp. 5, 66). In fact, more recent definitions of cyberpunk put more emphasis on "information networks", "virtual reality" (Nicholls [1993] 1999), "the information explosion" (Clute 2003), "computer technology, artificial intelligence" (Prucher 2007), "global information exchanges", "massive interlinked data networks, virtual realities", "flows of information", and "virtual cyberspaces" (Higgins and Duncan 2013). This shift from high technology in general to computer technology and information networks in particular might have been influenced by the increasing impact of the Internet on society from the 1990s onwards.

3. *Akira* as Cyberpunk

Is *Akira*, according to the definition that was derived from Csicsery-Ronay and Sterling (high technology employed by anti-establishment characters), a cyberpunk comic? On closer inspection, only five cyberpunk elements can be identified in *Akira* that play any role whatsoever, which are listed here in order of their significance.

- Tetsuo's arm (Figure 1): the metallic arm of Tetsuo, one of the protagonists of the manga, is the closest thing in *Akira* to a cybernetic limb. It is visible for the first time in vol. 4 on p. 106 (all volume and page numbers refer to the Japanese 6-volume collected edition from 1984–1993). In the previous volume, we see how his natural arm is shot off by a laser blast, but we do not get to see how the mechanical arm got attached to his body (the animated film adaptation, however, shows how metal parts levitate towards his body and are assembled into the arm through supernatural powers). Therefore, even though Tetsuo's arm looks very much like a cyberpunk motif, it is probably not a piece of high tech, at least not one that was developed by the "establishment" (i.e., the government, military, or industry), and thus, it does not strictly fit the definition of cyberpunk given above. This is a crucial point, as the appropriation of pre-existing "establishment" technology, rather than the autonomous creation of new technology, is what justifies the "punk" part of the word "cyberpunk". Later, we see a mutation spreading over Tetsuo's whole body starting from his arm (from vol. 5, p. 263), and later still, his body fuses with machines, such as a jet fighter plane and an aircraft carrier (vol. 5, p. 352). Again, these motifs might seem typical of cyberpunk stories, however strictly speaking, they do not meet the criteria of our definition.

106

(a)

263

(b)

Figure 1. *Cont.*

(c)

Figure 1. (**a**) panel from Katsuhiro Ōtomo, *Akira* (Kōdansha), vol. 4 (1987), p. 106; (**b**) vol. 5 (1990), p. 263; (**c**) vol. 5 (1990), p. 352.

- Motorcycles (Figure 2): not all of the motorcycles that are depicted in *Akira* are high tech machinery, however some are definitely pieces of futuristic technology. The first one of these is protagonist Kaneda's motorbike, which is even equipped with a display screen (vol. 1, pp. 10–22). Kaneda is the head of a gang of teenage motorcyclists, an anti-establishment, lowlife group of characters if there ever was one, which makes his motorcycle a strong cyberpunk motif. Two other instances of motorcycles in *Akira* are noteworthy: in vol. 5 on p. 55, Kaneda is given a new motorcycle by his ally, Joker. It is another futuristic-looking model, and this time Kaneda is not going to use it for fun, but to confront Tetsuo who has seized the political and military power in the city. Even more anti-establishment is the use of the same motorbike at the end of the series (vol. 6, pp. 419ff.) by Kaneda and his companion Kei against the United Nations troops.

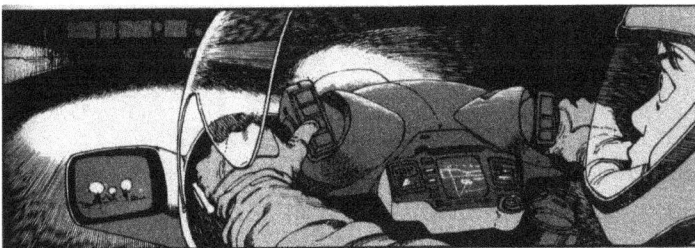

(a)

Figure 2. *Cont.*

(b)

(c)

Figure 2. (a) panel from Katsuhiro Ōtomo, *Akira* (Kōdansha), vol. 1 (1984), p. 16; (b) vol. 5 (1990), p. 55;
(c) vol. 6 (1993), p. 420.

- Caretaker robots (Figure 3): the so-called caretaker robots, or Security Balls, could even be
  considered Artificial Intelligences, however only in the beginning of the manga when they are
  still controlled by the military. When Kaneda and his friends get their hands on one of these
  robots, they convert it into a manually operated transport vehicle (vol. 5, p. 152). Later still, Joker
  reworks a caretaker robot into a combat vehicle which is equipped with a machine gun (vol. 5,
  p. 332).

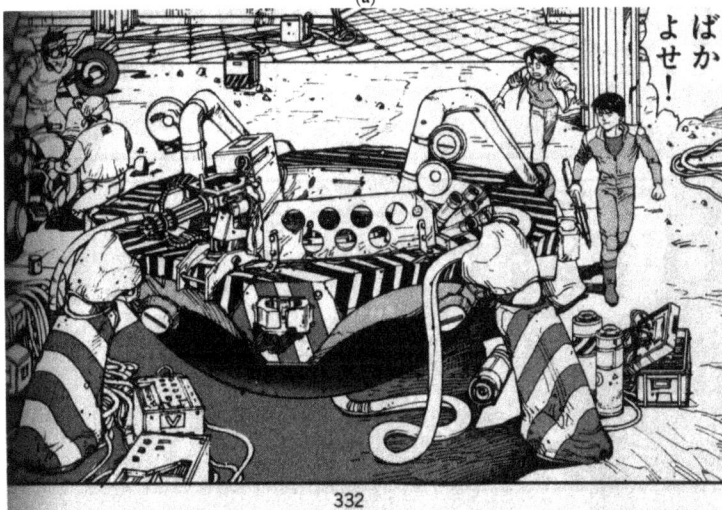

Figure 3. (a) panel from Katsuhiro Ōtomo, *Akira* (Kōdansha), vol. 5 (1990), p. 152; (b) vol. 5 (1990), p. 332.

- Flying platforms (Figure 4): the flying platforms are another example of advanced military technology. The first one of these aircraft is captured by protagonists Kei and Kaneda already in vol. 2 on p. 190. Later, it is again Joker who assembles his own flying platform from parts of the wrecks of others and gives it an idiosyncratic paint job (vol. 5, p. 314). At the end of the manga, a flying platform is once more used by Kaneda, Joker, and their allies against the United Nations forces (vol. 6, p. 411).

(a)

(b)

(c)

Figure 4. (**a**) panel from Katsuhiro Ōtomo, *Akira* (Kōdansha), vol. 2 (1985), p. 190; (**b**) vol. 5 (1990), p. 314; (**c**) vol. 6 (1993), p. 411.

- Laser rifles (Figure 5): laser beam firearms are experimental technology that are developed by the military. A laser rifle is stolen by Kei and Kaneda in vol. 2 on p. 72 and is used against the military. In vol. 5 on p. 312, Joker reveals that he too has obtained one such weapon which is subsequently used in the fight against Tetsuo.

(a)

(b)

Figure 5. (**a**) panel from Katsuhiro Ōtomo, *Akira* (Kōdansha), vol. 2 (1985), p. 72; (**b**) vol. 5 (1990), p. 312.

Apart from these five recurring objects, there are hardly any further cyberpunk elements in *Akira*. One might say that Tetsuo appropriates the cryogenic chamber, a piece of governmental high tech, when he carries Kaori's dead body there (vol. 6, p. 201), however the functionality of the chamber—if it is still functional at all at this point—cannot possibly bring Kaori back to life; more likely, this place is meant to be a sort of burial site for her due to its symbolic meaning. Neither can the Colonel's improvised, unauthorised use of the satellite laser weapon called "SOL" against Tetsuo in the second half of the story (e.g., vol. 6, p. 20) be considered anti-establishment, and is thus not cyberpunk, because he still believes to act in the interest of the official government. Some might consider the synthetic, mind-altering drugs that are featured recurrently in *Akira* to be a cyberpunk trope, however, while such drugs are a theme in many cyberpunk stories, it is safe to say that they are neither a sufficient nor a necessary cyberpunk characteristic.

By and large, at least some cyberpunk elements are undeniably found in *Akira*. However, elements from other genres abound as well—supernatural powers from the "science fantasy" genre, the setting of a city in ruins (in the second half of the comic) from post-apocalyptic fiction—so that *Akira* resists to be readily and wholeheartedly pigeonholed into the cyberpunk genre.

4. Cyberpunk in the Late 1980s and Early 1990s

Cyberpunk originated in science fiction literature, with the central author here being William Gibson. His first published short story, "Fragments of a Hologram Rose" from 1977, already contained some cyberpunk themes. With his subsequent short stories such as "Johnny Mnemonic" (1981) and "Burning Chrome" (1982), Gibson built a near-future world in which he then set his seminal novel *Neuromancer* (1984) which can be regarded as the nucleus of the cyberpunk genre. Shortly before *Neuromancer*, the term "cyberpunk" was coined by Bruce Bethke's eponymous short story, which was first published in 1983. It was not until 1984, however, that this term was applied to a group of science fiction writers around William Gibson (Dozois 1984). Another important event in the formation of the cyberpunk genre was the publication of *Mirroshades: The Cyberpunk Anthology* in 1986, the preface of which, written by editor Bruce Sterling, gave the cyberpunk movement its manifesto.

Cyberpunk was also influential in film. The most important cyberpunk film, Ridley Scott's *Blade Runner*, was already released in 1982, which makes it cyberpunk *avant la lettre*. Of course, both *Blade Runner* and Paul Verhoeven's *Total Recall* from 1990 are based on much older stories by Philip K. Dick, however the film versions proved to have a stronger impact. Also noteworthy in the context of cyberpunk are the films of David Cronenberg, primarily *Videodrome* (1983), as is another Paul Verhoeven film, *RoboCop* (1987), as well as the James Cameron films, *The Terminator* (1984) and *Terminator 2: Judgment Day*, the latter of which was commercially the most successful film of 1991 worldwide.

However, there were also cyberpunk comics in the Western world before or at the same time as *Akira*. The following titles appear to be the most important of these: *The Long Tomorrow* by Dan O'Bannon and Mœbius (US release 1977), *Judge Dredd* by various authors (from 1977), *Rōnin* by Frank Miller (1983–1984), *Shatter* by Peter Gillis and Michael Saenz (1985–1988), *Appleseed*—another manga that was released in the US in the same year as *Akira*—by Masamune Shirow (1988), and *Hard Boiled* by Frank Miller and Geof Darrow (1990–1992).

Considering all of these developments in the fields of literature, film, and comics, it seems likely that comic readers were familiar with the concept (though not necessarily the explicit label) of cyberpunk at the time when *Akira* was first released in America (1988) and Europe (1990/1991). Furthermore, many cyberpunk stories were set in a fictional future Japan or other East Asian countries (Tatsumi 2006, pp. 44–47, 111) which might have made it easier for Western readers to draw a connection between *Akira* and cyberpunk.

5. Genre Designations in Magazine Reviews of *Akira*

Did readers recognise *Akira* as cyberpunk? To find an approximate answer to this question, reviews and other texts about *Akira* from magazines and newspapers were searched for any terms or phrases that place *Akira* in a genre or put it in any kind of context. Beginning with the anglophone world, the first article on *Akira* is an announcement from the *Comics Buyer's Guide* from January 1988, which calls *Akira* a "color series about post-holocaust mutants". In March 1988, the same magazine ran an advertisement by Westwind Distributors which announced *Akira* as "a science-fiction adventure tale". *The Comics Journal* identified *Akira* as "an imported science fiction Japanese manga" in April 1988. *Marvel Age*, in August 1988, called it "a science-fiction thriller". In May 1989, *Advance Comics* referred to *Akira* simply as "the Japanese SF series", and in January 1990, the same magazine noted a "shift in tone from hardware SF to a post-apocalypse saga". The only reference to the cyberpunk genre with regard to *Akira* is found in the December 1988 issue of *Amazing Heroes*: "Elements of the story reminded me of the Sprawl stories and novels of William Gibson, the high priest of cyber-punk [sic]. Otomo deals with several of Gibson's themes: the fate of directionless youth in a technological world, the possibility of heroism and the value of friendship in what might seem to be unsalvageable individuals."

In Germany, the situation was largely the same: *Akira* was identified as science fiction in general or as some other genre, but not cyberpunk. In 1991, Epic editor Archie Goodwin was quoted in the German comic magazine *ICOM-INFO* (all translations mine) saying, "The story belongs to science fiction." Also, in 1991, *Rraah!*, another important German comic magazine, saw in *Akira* a "trailblazer for the influential violent tendencies of modern Japanese comics". In 1992, *Rraah!* spoke to a new *Akira* volume, "once more there's high speed action", and in 1994, the same magazine referred to *Akira* as "the futuristic thriller". In a review of the anime adaptation from 1991, the German film magazine *Cinema* also mentioned the manga source, calling it a "science fiction epic". Another German comic magazine, *Comixene*, identified *Akira* as an "adventure series" in 1995, and in the same issue, it claimed, "Otomo is called the Ridley Scott of the Land of the Rising Sun". This last statement is the only one that can be said to make some connection between *Akira* and cyberpunk, however as the article in which it appears is about Katsuhiro Ōtomo and Hayao Miyazaki as both comic authors and anime directors, it is not clear whether this statement refers to Ōtomo as the creator of *Akira* the manga or *Akira* the anime.

By way of comparison, journalistic texts about the animated film adaptation of *Akira*, which was theatrically released in the West between 1989 and 1991, shall also be considered here. In contrast to the reviews of the manga discussed above, the film reviews quoted below represent only a small sample which was selected rather arbitrarily. Once more beginning with English-language reviews, the earliest one in this sample was published in the *Washington Post* in 1989, saying of the fictional Neo Tokyo in which *Akira* is set that "The rebuilt city [is] looking like an animated *Blade Runner* prototype", and that "There are several *Scanners*-style showdowns, *Altered States*-like hallucinations and none of the comic release usually found in cartoons." In 1990, the *Seattle Times* also mentioned "'Neo-Tokyo,' an endless metropolis which gets much of its visual inspiration from *Blade Runner* and *Brazil* [...]". The British *Monthly Film Bulletin* wrote in 1991 that "The film version sits comfortably between *Blade Runner* and *2001*" and is "closer to Cronenberg's 'new flesh' than to the orthodox versions of genetic engineering". On the occasion of the laserdisc release of *Akira*, *Time* magazine said in 1993 that "[Neo] Tokyo is imagined down to the last noodle shop and intersection, a place of deep night and lurid neon that looks like *Blade Runner* on spoiled mushrooms." None of these texts mentioned cyberpunk explicitly, however it is striking that all four of them compare the film to the (proto-) cyberpunk classic *Blade Runner*.

This tendency is also apparent in German texts about *Akira* the anime. The comic magazine *ICOM-INFO*, this time referring to the film, said in 1991, "One could rank *Akira* among classics such as *Blade Runner* or *RoboCop*" (again, all translations mine). In the aforementioned 1991 issue of *Cinema*, the film is described like this: "Katsuhiro Otomo's futuristic animated film *Akira*, like Ridley Scott's *Blade Runner*, Paul Verhoeven's *RoboCop*, or David Cronenberg's *Videodrome*, gives off the foul smell of doom in a hyper-technocratic world." The same text later explicitly assigns the cyberpunk label: "Even without machine men, *Akira*, like *Blade Runner*, belongs to post-apocalyptic cyberpunk". Another German film magazine, *Filmdienst*, noted in 1991 "the morbid mood of *Blade Runner*", and said that *Akira* "ranges from *Blade Runner* over *E.T.* back to *Rebel Without a Cause*" and contains "action orgies in the vein of *RoboCop*". Most extensively, cyberpunk is written about in the *Akira* film review of the Berlin city magazine, *Tip*, also in 1991: "*Akira*'s psycho demons are no avant-garde specter, only the cyberpunk is a new phenomenon. Cyberpunk is the philosophy of *Akira*, and is explained by *Akira*'s press department as follows: 'Cyberpunk is a philosophy that can shape the world in its own image and create a self-mutilating freedom, that is, an image that angrily growls back.' Even if no one has growled in the first place."

Why did journalists readily identify *Akira* the anime as cyberpunk, but not *Akira* the manga? There are two main reasons for this. On the one hand, consider once more the list of cyberpunk elements in *Akira* the manga that are given above in Section 3. These cyberpunk scenes appear in different issues or volumes that were published at different times during the long publication history of *Akira*, both in the US and Germany. The following list gives the number of cyberpunk scenes from issues that were published in the corresponding year for the first American edition that was published by Epic:

- 1988: 2 cyberpunk scenes
- 1989: 1
- 1990: 3
- 1991: 5
- 1992: 0
- 1993: 0
- 1994: 0
- 1995: 2.

Here is the corresponding list for cyberpunk scenes in volumes of the first German edition by publisher Carlsen:

- 1991: 3 cyberpunk scenes
- 1992: 2
- 1993: 6
- 1994: 0
- 1995: 0
- 1996: 2.

In both editions, the majority of cyberpunk elements appear only several years after the launch of the series. In other words, *Akira* was not a cyberpunk comic in the beginning (when most of the reviews and announcements that were quoted above were written)—it only became a cyberpunk comic during the course of its serialisation. Therefore, if *Akira* can be identified as cyberpunk at all, it is only in hindsight, with the complete series published. In the anime adaptation, the whole story was released at once and all of its cyberpunk elements (except for the caretaker robots which appear only in the manga version) were present in the condensed form of a two-hour film, meaning that it was easier to recognise *Akira* as cyberpunk in its animated form.

On the other hand, it appears that the idea of a genre to which a work belongs, and also its intertextual context, is strictly confined to its own medium, at least for the writers of the journalistic periodicals discussed above. That means that it is easier to place a film in a filmic genre than to place a comic in a filmic genre and vice versa. It is also easier to make comparisons between two films or two comics than between a film and a comic. Therefore, even if we ascertained that comic readers of the late 1980s and early 1990s could have been familiar with the cyberpunk genre in general, we still need to ask: was the cyberpunk genre already established in the medium of comics specifically? The six early cyberpunk comics that were mentioned above represent only a small part of this comic genre. A bigger picture emerges when we turn to attempts of canonisation: in recent years, several websites have published best-of lists of cyberpunk comics (White 2016; Davidson 2017; Lovett 2017). While these lists are rather subjective, some titles are included in two or even all three of them, apart from the aforementioned *The Long Tomorrow*, *Judge Dredd*, *Rōnin*, and *Hard Boiled*: namely *Ghost in the Shell* by Masamune Shirow (US release 1995), *Battle Angel Alita* by Yukito Kishiro (1995–1998), *2020 Visions* by Jamie Delano and various artists (1997–1998), *Transmetropolitan* by Warren Ellis and Darick Robertson (1997–2002), *Heavy Liquid* (1999–2000) and *100%* (2002–2003) by Paul Pope, *The Surrogates* by Robert Venditti and Brett Weldele (2005–2006), and *Tokyo Ghost* by Rick Remender and Sean Murphy (2015–2016)—interestingly, the comic adaptation of Gibson's *Neuromancer* by Tom De Haven and Bruce Alan Jensen (1989) has not had much of an impact and is mentioned only by Matt White (2016).

Although a certain degree of presentist bias is to be expected from these kinds of websites, it is striking that according to them, most canonical cyberpunk comics were published in the mid-1990s and later, and thus after *Akira*. It seems as if for comics, unlike science fiction literature, the defining decade of the cyberpunk genre was not the 1980s, but a later one. Therefore, the readers of *Akira* around 1990 must have had difficulties recognising it as cyberpunk, because cyberpunk comics were not an established genre yet.

In conclusion, the hypothesis has to be refuted that the success of *Akira* is explained by its affiliation with the cyberpunk genre, as this affiliation was not largely recognised. More likely, Ōtomo's manga was seen as something new and exceptional. Its success might have been due to a combination of perceived freshness and sheer quality. In an attempt to replicate this success, Western publishers looked for similar, near-future science fiction manga to license and translate, some of which belong to the cyberpunk genre.

Funding: This article is based on a paper that was presented at Michigan State University Comics Forum, East Lansing, Michigan, 23–24 February, 2018. The author's attendance of this conference was supported by the Young Researchers Fund of Heidelberg University.

Acknowledgments: The helpful comments of three anonymous reviewers of this journal are gratefully acknowledged.

Conflicts of Interest: The author declares no conflict of interest.

References

Altman, Rick. 1984. A Semantic/Syntactic Approach to Film Genre. *Cinema Journal* 23: 6–18. [CrossRef]

Clute, John. 2003. Science fiction from 1980 to the present. In *The Cambridge Companion to Science Fiction*. Edited by Edward James and Farah Mendlesohn. Cambridge: Cambridge University Press, pp. 64–78. ISBN 978-0-521-81626-7.

Csicsery-Ronay, Istvan, Jr. 1991. Cyberpunk and Neuromanticism. In *Storming the Reality Studio. A Casebook of Cyberpunk and Postmodern Science Fiction*. Edited by Larry McCaffery. Durham: Duke University Press, pp. 182–93. First published 1988. ISBN 978-0822311683.

Davidson, Chris. 2017. The Best Cyberpunk Comics Ever. *CBR.com*. Available online: https://www.cbr.com/the-best-cyberpunk-comics-ever/ (accessed on 14 May 2018).

De la Iglesia, Martin. 2016. The Task of Manga Translation: Akira in the West. *The Comics Grid: Journal of Comics Scholarship* 6. [CrossRef]

Dozois, Gardner. 1984. Science Fiction in the Eighties. *Washington Post*, December 30.

Frow, John. 2006. *Genre*. London: Routledge, ISBN 978-0-415-28062-4.

Higgins, David M., and Roby Duncan. 2013. Key Critical Concepts, Topics and Critics. In *The Science Fiction Handbook*. Edited by Nick Hubble and Aris Mousoutzanis. London: Bloomsbury, pp. 125–42. ISBN 978-1-4411-7096-5.

Jameson, Fredric. 1981. *The Political Unconscious. Narrative as a Socially Symbolic Act*. London: Methuen, ISBN 0-416-31370-1.

Lovett, Jamie. 2017. Cyberpunk Comics to Read after Seeing Ghost in the Shell. *ComicBook.com*. Available online: http://comicbook.com/comics/2017/04/01/cyberpunk-comics-ghost-in-the-shell/ (accessed on 14 May 2018).

Nicholls, Peter. 1999. Cyberpunk. In *The Encyclopedia of Science Fiction*. Edited by John Clute and Peter Nicholls. London: Orbit. First published 1993. ISBN 1-85723-897-4.

Prucher, Jeff, ed. 2007. *Brave New Worlds. The Oxford Dictionary of Science Fiction*. Oxford: Oxford University Press, ISBN 978-0-19-530567-8.

Rieder, John. 2017. *Science Fiction and the Mass Cultural Genre System*. Middletown: Wesleyan University Press, ISBN 978-0-8195-7716-0.

Sabin, Roger. 2006. Barefoot Gen in the US and UK: Activist Comic, Graphic Novel, Manga. In *Reading Manga: Local and Global Perceptions of Japanese Comics*. Edited by Jaqueline Berndt and Steffi Richter. Leipzig: Leipziger Universitätsverlag, pp. 39–57. ISBN 978-3-86583-123-1.

Sterling, Bruce. 1991. Preface from *Mirrorshades*. In *Storming the Reality Studio. A Casebook of Cyberpunk and Postmodern Science Fiction*. Edited by Larry McCaffery. Durham: Duke University Press, pp. 343–48. ISBN 978-0822311683. First published 1986.

Sterling, Bruce. 2003. Preface. In William Gibson, *Burning Chrome*. New York: HarperCollins, pp. 11–14. ISBN 978-0062273017. First published 1986.

Suvin, Darko. 1991. On Gibson and Cyberpunk SF. In *Storming the Reality Studio. A Casebook of Cyberpunk and Postmodern Science Fiction*. Edited by Larry McCaffery. Durham: Duke University Press, pp. 349–65. ISBN 978-0822311683. First published 1989.

Tatsumi, Takayuki. 2006. *Full Metal Apache. Transactions between Cyberpunk Japan and Avant-Pop America*. Durham: Duke University Press, ISBN 0-8223-3762-2.

White, Matt. 2016. The Best Cyberpunk Comics. *Publishers Weekly*. Available online: https://www.publishersweekly.com/pw/by-topic/industry-news/comics/article/70589-the-best-cyberpunk-comics-part-1.html (accessed on 14 May 2018).

Womack, Jack. 2000. Some Dark Holler. In William Gibson, *Neuromancer*. New York: Ace Books, pp. 231–42. ISBN 978-1101146460.

arts

MDPI

Article

New Spaces for Old Motifs? The Virtual Worlds of Japanese Cyberpunk

Denis Taillandier

College of International Relations, Ritsumeikan University, Kyoto 603-8577, Japan; aelfinwe@gmail.com

Received: 3 July 2018; Accepted: 2 October 2018; Published: 5 October 2018

Abstract: North-American cyberpunk's recurrent use of high-tech Japan as "the default setting for the future," has generated a Japonism reframed in technological terms. While the renewed representations of techno-Orientalism have received scholarly attention, little has been said about literary Japanese science fiction. This paper attempts to discuss the transnational construction of Japanese cyberpunk through Masaki Gorō's *Venus City* (*Vīnasu Shiti*, 1992) and Tobi Hirotaka's *Angels of the Forsaken Garden* series (*Haien no tenshi*, 2002–). Elaborating on Tatsumi's concept of synchronicity, it focuses on the intertextual dynamics that underlie the shaping of those texts to shed light on Japanese cyberpunk's (dis)connections to techno-Orientalism as well as on the relationships between literary works, virtual worlds and reality.

Keywords: Japanese science fiction; cyberpunk; techno-Orientalism; Masaki Gorō; Tobi Hirotaka; virtual worlds; intertextuality

---

1. Introduction: Cyberpunk and Techno-Orientalism

While the inversion is not a very original one, looking into Japanese cyberpunk in a transnational context first calls for a brief dive into cyberpunk Japan. Anglo-American pioneers of the genre, quite evidently William Gibson, but also Pat Cadigan or Bruce Sterling, have extensively used high-tech, hyper-consumerist Japan as a motif or a setting for their works, so that Japan became in the mid 1980s the very exemplification of the future, or to borrow Gibson's (2001, p. 1) words: "the global imagination's default setting for the future." The pervasive use of a science fictional Japan has spurred the rise of what Morley and Robins (1995), and later Ueno (1999, 2002), have called "techno-Orientalism," or in Tatsumi's (2006, p. 173) terms: a "neo-Japonsim" that re-enacts and at the same time reinvents fin-de-siècle Japonism. Describing how robotics, cybernetics, artificial intelligence, and the pervasiveness of networks and screens have become associated with Japaneseness, Morley and Robins (1995, p. 68) contend that "[i]f the future is technological, and if technology has become "Japanised," then the syllogism would suggest that the future is now Japanese, too. The postmodern era will be the Pacific era. Japan is the future, and it is a future that seems to be transcending and displacing Western modernity."

Tatsumi further stresses out how, at a time when the Japanese were portrayed as the economic terminator of the future, cyberpunk "promoted the then-rising ideology of the Pax Japonica," (Tatsumi 2006, p. 44) and notes that the late 20th century witnessed the rise of 'Japonoids,' members of a global community nurtured by Japanese culture, that he defines as the "post-eighties hyper-Creole subjectivity transgressing the boundary between the Japanese and non-Japanese" (Tatsumi 2002, p. 16). Lisa Nakamura, however, refers to David Roh, Betsy Huang and Greta Niu's explorations of techno-orientalism (Roh et al. 2015) to argue that cyberpunk's almost conventional use of anachronic Japanese imagery—"geishas, ninjas, and samurai warriors"—works as "a high-tech variety of racial stereotyping" that paradoxically re-inscribes "traditional signifiers of the oriental" instead of opening new spaces for genuinely hybrid identities (Nakamura 2002, pp. 63–64). Whether focusing on the creativity brought about by the "multicultural and transgeneric poetics of negotiation" (Tatsumi 2006, p. 9) that underpins and shapes the Japanoid, or on the problematic essentialization of a fetishized Japan, both analyses illustrate the point, cogently raised by Baryon Posadas, that 'Japan' is a circulating "signifier that is overcoded and overdetermined by a shifting constellation of relations through which it is imagined, along with their consequent discursive contestations and complications" (Posadas 2011, p. 77).

Discussing David Mitchell's novel *number9dream*, Posadas draws on Jay David Bolter and Richard Grusin's concept of remediation—"the formal logic by which new media refashion prior media forms" (Bolter and Grusin 1999, p. 273)—to argue that cyberpunk is fundamentally rooted in acts of remediation and intermediation (Posadas 2011, p. 85). While remediation does not stem from the rise of digital media (Bolter and Grusin 1999, p. 11), it is quite evidently foregrounded in a genre that reflects on "the rapid proliferation of technologically mass-produced "products" that are essentially reproductions or abstractions—images, advertising, information, memories, styles, simulated experiences, and copies of original experiences" (McCaffery 1991, p. 4). In this sense, 'Japan' has been sucked into the transnational and transcultural process of remediation, "always already experienced as image, as representation" (Posadas 2011, p. 86), so that it has turned into a popular and seductive "semiotic ghost country" (Tatsumi 2006, p. 47).

While science fictional Japan has become a very popular trope, Japanese science fiction—especially in its literary form—has remained quite invisible. Techno-Orientalism and the representations of Japan by North-American cyberpunk writers have received attention, but little has been written about Japanese cyberpunk, apart from a few pioneer studies in English[1], largely focusing on manga and anime.[2] English translations have nevertheless started to increase with Viz Media's Japanese science fiction novel line Haikasoru or Kurodahan Press's *Speculative Fiction* series. Interestingly, Japan has long been a country of importation rather than of exportation, so that according to Tatsumi, Japanese translations of North-American cyberpunk's representations of Japanese culture have prompted Japanese science fiction writers to "realize that writing subversive fiction in the wake of cyberpunk meant gaining an insight into a radically science-fictional "Japan." (Tatsumi 2006, p. 173). This then begs the question of the shape that such an insight took in Japanese cyberpunk.

Inquiring into some Japanese cyberpunk works in the background of techno-Orientalism and the widely circulating images of science fictional Japan does not hinge on the essentialist assumption that the texts examined should reveal a more authentic Japan, which would imply that such a thing exists in the first place and that the accuracy of its representations could be evaluated against a set of objective criteria. As Ueno (2002, p. 228) remarks, "[t]echno-Orientalism is a kind of mirror stage or an image machine whose effect influences Japanese as well as other people." The aim is rather to shed light on the creative ways with which Japanese SF writers reinterpreted and/or reshaped the genre and the images usually associated with it. The works of Masaki Gorō, who has often been compared to William Gibson in Japan, and most notably his novel *Venus City* (*Vīnasu Shiti*, 1992), will provide an illustration of how science fictional Japan is playfully remediated in Japanese cyberpunk as well as plugged into the heritage of Japanese science fiction. On the other hand, while Tobi Hirotaka's *Angels of the Forsaken Garden* series (*Haien no tenshi*, 2002–) is in keeping with the genre's themes in its exploration of the philosophical and social questions raised by virtual reality (the status of VR experience or the status of fictional entities), it considerably refashions the genre by breaking away from techno-Orientalist representations and mapping comparatively archaic motifs on to the high-tech environment of cyberspace.

---

[1] Such as the works of Tatsumi Takayuki, Kotani Mari, Susan Napier, Baryon T. Posadas, Harada Kazue, Sharalyn Orbaugh, William O. Gardner, Livia Monnet or Miri Nakamura.

[2] The fact that *The Cambridge Companion to Science Fiction* only briefly mentions Japanese anime (James and Mendlesohn 2003, p. 94) or that *The Routledge Companion to Science Fiction*'s section for Japanese science fiction is entitled "Manga and anime" (Bould et al. 2009, pp. 112–22) speaks volume.

2. Masaki Gorō's Cyberpunk: Plugging Science Fictional Japan into Japanese Science Fiction

The very first to have been considered a cyberpunk writer in Japan is undoubtedly Masaki Gorō whose debut novella *Evil Eyes* (*Jagan*)[3], published in the December 1987s issue of *SF Magajin*, earned third place in the 13th Hayakawa SF contest (Tatsumi 1993, p. 87). The plot resonates with Gibson's short story *Johnny Mnemonic* (Gibson 1981). It depicts a highly bureaucratic society where minds are protected from stress by an embedded software, called Psycho-Fixer (PFX), that acts as a regulating buffer. In competition with a multinational music corporation, the leader of a new religious group, whose doll-like body is a plastic storage filled with central nerve tissues, she rents out to and then collects from other humans—consuming their memories and experiences in the process—and seeks to use the PFX to take control of the population. Even though Masaki had read *Johnny Mnemonic* before writing *Evil Eyes*, he points out to James Tiptree, Jr. as his main inspiration, explaining that he stopped reading Gibson and purposely wrote in a different style "to avoid becoming a "Japanese Gibson."" (Masaki 2002a, p. 78). Noting Masaki's fascination with Tiptree's novella "The Girl Who Was Plugged In" (1973), Tatsumi (1993, p. 88) convincingly argues that Masaki's cyberpunk does not stem from Gibson's, but rather from the very same writings that influenced Gibson, so that both had a similar output around the same time. While Anglo-American works have had a large impact on Japanese science fiction (Yamano [1969] 2000, p. 144), Tatsumi (2006, p. 4) sees in the cyberpunk movement a decisive turn towards "a network of synchronicity, where anything and all things can happen simultaneously, overcoming any limit and exceeding any colonialist or imperialist intent."

On the other hand, in his analysis of Masaki's Seiun[4] and Nihon SF Taisho[5] awards-winning novel *Venus City*, Baryon Posadas (2017) contends that far from being a simple layer that Japanese writers could strip from the genre or easily transcend, techno-Orientalism is a constitutive element of cyberpunk, as much as colonial discourse has been a shaping agent of science fiction.

Venus City stages a fully realized Pax Japonica (Masaki makes use of the term several times in the novel) where Japan has become the world economy's "headquarters" (Masaki 1995, p. 147). It has developed a massive communication network through which it controls manufacturing, primarily operated in Asia. Europe and North America have suffered an economic collapse that triggered a wave of migrant workers who are only very selectively allowed entry into the Archipelago, prompting in turn anti-immigrant animus among the population and an increasing isolationist foreign policy. Unfolding both in Tokyo and in Venus City, the eponymous virtual entertainment district[6] users can anonymously access in the form of an avatar, the plot revolves around two main characters: Sakiko, a young Japanese woman who works for a data analytics company and her loathed white American supervisor, Jim. Sakiko appears in Venus City in the guise of an androgynous Caucasian young man who goes by the name of Saki, whereas Jim is blackmailed into accessing the city in the form of a Japanese doll-like girl called Junko. Ignoring that she is Sakiko's boss in the real world, Saki saves Junko from an assault in a bar and initiates a romantic relationship with her. Saki learns that Junko is coerced every night into all kinds of physical, psychological and sexual abuse by a group who aims at using Jim to get access to classified information that would allow them to take control over Venus City and manipulate the neural networks of its users to make them perceive the virtual district as the actual reality. Sakiko/Saki and Jim/Junko figure out one another's identity but decide to oppose what they first assume to be an overseas terrorist attempt at undermining Japan's hegemony by "virtually erasing Japan from the world map" (Masaki 1995, p. 308). In their final confrontation, they discover that the mysterious group leader is nothing but the somehow autonomous materialization of Venus

---

3   The novella was partially translated in English (Masaki 2002b). In his introduction to the short story's publication in *SF Magajin*, Masaki stresses out the fact that contrary to Gibson's lack of concern for an ethical sensibility, *Evil Eyes*' hard-boiled literary style retains the kind of moralism that can be found in the works of Tiptree (Masaki 1987, p. 64).

4   The Japanese equivalent of the Hugo Award.

5   The Japanese equivalent of the Nebula Award.

6   VENUS is the acronym standing for "Virtual Environment Network USers" (Tatsumi 1993, p. 217).

City's close to 10 million users' unconscious wish to substitute reality with the virtual world of the city—which they ultimately prevent from realizing.

In his discussion on how the novel plays with the representations of gendered and racialized bodies through a series of inversions and transpositions (East/West, feminine/masculine, Japanese/Caucasian, and at times animal/human or inanimate/animate[7]), especially in the light of Jim being imposed on by the stereotypical role of the (sexually) submissive and objectified Japanese girl, Posadas (2017, p. 153) argues that *Venus City* "compels the white Western subject to become precisely the embodiment of techno-Orientalist fetishization." Observing that stereotypical gender and racial roles ultimately prevail, and that Sakiko and Jim, despite their own desire, end up maintaining the status quo by preventing reality from being replaced by the virtual, he concludes that although *Venus City*'s reversal of the usual cyberpunk motifs opens up a critical space precisely by revealing how techno-Orientalism is interwoven into the fabric of the genre, the novel also illustrates the difficulty "to imagine a radically different future not already determined in advanced by colonized habits of thought" (p. 156). It should however be noted that techno-Orientalist motifs are significantly few in the novel. Masaki does extrapolate the features of a near-future hegemonic Japan from the portrayals, in the 1980s, of the country as the emerging global economic leader, but his depiction of Tokyo, especially of Nakano, bears few resemblances to those found in anglophone cyberpunk. Junko, the only avatar explicitly marked as Japanese, takes up the form of a Japanese doll, but Masaki chose not to describe her in the more widely circulating image of the Geisha, just like he chose the somewhat lesser-known image of the Japanese dress-up doll Licca-chan to portray *Evil Eyes'* new religious group leader Mugen.

The motif of a Japanese doll appears almost in the same year in Tsutsui Yasutaka's cyberfiction novel *Paprika* (*Papurika*, 1993), which similarly associates cyberpunk's connection to virtual worlds with the exploration of dreams and the unconscious[8] through an interface that allows wireless transmission of "different people's dreams to each other's brains" (Tsutsui 2009, p. 85). The interface, called DC-Mini, works however both ways: Allowing access to dreams but also problematically letting them materialize in reality. The novel does not rely on techno-Orientalist imagery, rather mobilizing Freudian dream symbolism or Jungian archetypes. The Japanese doll works as a queering device highlighting the homosexuality of a male character (Himuro) and the uncanny irruption of dreams into the real. Interestingly, Kon Satoshi's animated version (2007) offers a stunning visual representation of the invasion of reality by the dreamtime in the form of a psychedelic parade full of mythical and popular motifs. They are nevertheless not confined to (techno-)Orientalism: cars, robots, home appliances, Buddhas, the Statute of Liberty, beckoning cats, daruma dolls, samurai, medieval knights, a pink elephant, or soft toys are all marching alongside together. The anime's eponymous protagonist appears in several guises: Sun Wukong from the classical Chinese novel *Journey to the West*, Pinocchio, a siren, the Sphinx, or a winged fairy. Just like Venus City "looks like a giant cosplay venue" (Masaki 1995, p. 176), the collective unconscious in Kon's *Paprika* is made up of disparate images and motifs informed by the interpenetration of Western and Eastern myths and legends, echoing Tatsumi's emphasis on the transcultural dynamics between Japanese and North-American popular cultures in the heyday of cyberpunk (Tatsumi 2006, pp. 1–6).

Going back to *Venus City*, although the setting may unconsciously echo North-America's fear towards Japan's economic miracle in the 1980s, and the very idea of "virtually erasing Japan from the world map," the ensuing Japan bashing; Tatsumi suggests that the novel goes beyond techno-Orientalist tropes and relates both to postwar Japanese science fiction's deeply entrenched fascination for the aesthetics of destruction and masochism. As far as the former is concerned, he

---

7   When Jim has his cat embody Junko to enter Venus City in his place (Masaki 1995, pp. 245–47), or users experience mapping a human self-image onto home appliances such as a washing machine to send them in the virtual city (Masaki 1995, pp. 281–82).
8   The association is made even clearer in Kon Satoshi's anime adaptation, where Paprika explains how dreams and the internet are similar in that they are both spaces were repressed thoughts drift away (Kon 2006, 25:27–25:33).

proposes to read *Venus City* as Masaki's attempt at rewriting in terms of computer simulation Komatsu Sakyō's geophysical destruction of the country in the best-seller *Japan Sinks* (*Nihon Chinbotsu*, 1973) (Tatsumi 1993, p. 218). I would like here to add Tsutsui Yasutaka's short story *The World Sinks Except Japan* (*Nihon igai zenbu chinbotsu*, Tsutsui 1973)[9] into the equation, since the satirical reversal of techno-Orientalist motifs in *Venus City* undoubtedly echo Tsutsui's parody of *Japan Sinks*. The short story playfully turns Komatsu's novel upside down: After most continents have been submerged, only Japan remains and the (most prominent, wealthiest) survivors flee to the Archipelago. Welcoming at first, the Japanese population soon come to entertain xenophobic hostilities towards the immigrants. With his usual dry sense of humor, Tsutsui reframes the notion—then largely popularized by the discourse on Japaneseness (*nihonjinron*)[10]—that Japanese identity is closely tied to the "homeland",[11] in terms of racism, nationalism and ethnocentricity.

On the other hand, Tatsumi simultaneously ties *Venus City*'s "Skin Two" and "Designer Punk" leather or latex fashion (Masaki 1995, pp. 18–19)—not to mention the virtual district's popular SM games[12]—to Numa Shōzō's magnum opus *Yapoo the Human Cattle* (*Kachikujin Yapū*[13]). In Numa's novel, it is not the country that is destroyed, but the entire Japanese people who are removed from Human taxonomy. *Yapoo the Human Cattle* describes a far-future white matriarchal society called EHS (Empire of Hundred Suns), where Japanese are considered to belong to the species *Simias sapiens* and are referred to as "Yapoo" (Yapū).[14] Stripped of the genus Homo, they are treated like cattle and engineered into all possible forms, ranging from hybrid horse mounts to pieces of furniture such as footrests and bathtubs, or from toothpicks to sex toys and walking toilets. The story describes the time-travel to EHS of 20th century German girl Clara and her Japanese fiancé Rin'ichirō, focusing on the subsequent transformation of Rin'ichirō into Clara's domestic pet. Rin'ichirō eventually chooses to stay on EHS to serve his master rather than have his memory erased and be sent back to Earth in his original body. Mishima Yukio had already noted, in a dialogue with Terayama Shūji (Mishima and Terayama [1970] 2004)[15], that *Yapoo the Human Cattle* was built upon the premises that masochism could potentially reshape the world insofar as the recognition that humiliation is a form of pleasure, gives birth to a systemic logic affecting every realm of human experience (politics, economics, moral or literature). Drawing a parallel with Marquis de Sade's *The 120 Days of Sodom*, he explains in his essay *What is a Novel?* (*Shōsetsu to wa nanika*) that the sheer magnitude of the masochistic imagination at work in *Yapoo the Human Cattle* makes it a radical experience where a new beauty can emerge from (Mishima [1970] 2004). Tatsumi also reads Numa's novel in terms of "creative masochism," stressing out that

---

9   The short story was adapted into a movie in 2006. See: *Nihon igai zenbu chinbotsu* (The World Sinks Except Japan). Dir. Kawasaki Minoru. ClockWorx/Tornado Film, 2006.

10   I am not referring here to the discourse produced during the wartime conferences called "Overcoming Modernity" (*Kindai no chōkoku*, 1942), which gave a central place to the Emperor line, but to the writings that appeared after the defeat and looked into Japanese uniqueness rather through the lens of language (incomparability of the Japanese language, nonverbal communication), culture (groupism vs individualism), environment (closeness to nature, influence of climate on Japanese character) and race. See for instance: Befu, Harumi. *Hegemony of Homogeneity: An Anthropological Analysis of Nihonjinron*. Melbourne: Trans Pacific Press, 2001.

11   As reflected in *Japan Sinks* when a group of old scholars come up with three courses of action to secure the future of the Japanese once the homeland is lost. The first one looks into the creation of a new country somewhere in the world, the second into a Japanese diaspora where the remaining population would be scattered among different countries, the third into what to do for those who would not be accepted anywhere. Most scholars have eventually concluded that the best option would be doing nothing—implying therefore that the Japanese would be better-off dying with the country (Komatsu 1995, pp. 104–8).

12   Such as the "body squeezer," the "castration" or the "ghost dice". The body squeezer starts with two players having a piano cord wrapped around their neck. Each player throws a dice and the one with the higher number tightens the cord around the other's neck, and so on until one of the players screams. The castration is similar to the body squeezer, but the piano cord is wrapped around another body part (Masaki 1995, pp. 31–33).

13   Numa first serialized his work in the magazine *Kitan Club* from 1956 to 1959. The first (still incomplete) book version was released by Tosshi Shuppan in 1970. The complete version was published in 1999 by Gentosha (Numa 1999).

14   The name refers of course to Jonathan Swift's Yahoos from *Gulliver's Travels* (1726), but also plays on the Japanese transliteration of the derogatory term "Jap" (Jappū).

15   The dialogue, entitled "Erosu wa teikō no kyoten ni narieru ka" (Can Eros Become a Stronghold for Resistance?) was originally published in *Ushio* (July 1970). It is reprinted in *The Complete Works of Mishima Yukio*, vol. 40.

"Numa's biological degradation of the Japanese foresaw the self-referential, metastructural logic of consumerist masochism, in which the subject consuming new technology enjoys being disciplined, whipped, and finally consumed by technocracy itself" (Tatsumi 2006, pp. 4, 57).

Therefore, while Tatsumi traces Masaki's cyberpunk back to North-American works (from authors such as James Tiptree, Jr.) that synchronously influenced Gibson and discusses *Venus City* in terms of techno-Orientalist motifs, he also considers the novel in the context of Japanese science fiction—plugging it back to the works of Komatsu or Numa. His emphasis on "creative masochism" and the aesthetic of destruction will prove a useful heuristic framework to examine a more recent narrative focusing on virtual resorts: Tobi Hirotaka's *The Angels of the Forsaken Garden* series.

Tobi's work offers an insightful take on sadomasochism, destruction and the pervasiveness of (virtual) colonialism in science fiction by significantly shifting the focus onto the fate of the fictional entities—the NPC AIs or the avatars emulating human consciousness—that populate the virtual world. It also differs from canonical cyberpunk narratives in that it moves away from techno-Orientalist motifs. The breakthrough technologies at the core of the virtual resort's elaboration and the human-machine interface enabling VR experiences are indeed developed in Japan, but the overall setting is not that of a Pax Japonica. Tobi is writing during the decade of stagnation that followed the collapse of the Japanese economy in the beginning of the 1990s, so that reactivating the image of a hegemonic Japan likely seemed inadequate or ineffective. Instead, Tobi wittingly reframes representations of digital technologies—the electronic networks of the internet, computer programs or virtual entities—in terms of analog handwoven or handwritten patterns embedded in a virtual resort under copyright protection, through which he addresses the issues of identity and reality as well as questions practices of domination. In doing so, he calls attention to the fact that cyberspace not only remediates former communication technologies and artistic practices, but also, insofar as it is "a social space (...) such historical places as cities and parks and such nonplaces as theme parks and shopping malls." (Bolter and Grusin 1999, p. 183).

3. The Grave of Desires: Tobi Hirotaka's Angels of the Forsaken Garden

The Angels of the Forsaken Garden is an ongoing series. Only two volumes have been published hitherto: The novel *Grandes Vacances* (*Guran vakansu*, 2002), whose English translation was released in June 2018 under the title *The Thousand Year Beach*; and the collection of short stories and novella entitled *Ragged Girl* (*Ragiddo gāru*, 2006). The latter is comprised of works initially published in *SF Magajin*: *The Summer Glass Eyes* (*Natsu no gurasu ai*, October 2002); the eponymous short story *Ragged Girl* (*Ragiddo gāru*, February 2004); *Closet* (*Kurōzetto*, April 2006); *Lord of the Spinners* (*Chichū no ō*, November 2002); with the addition of *The Magician* (*Majutsushi*, 2006).[16]

Set in the virtual resort called Costa del Número, *Grandes Vacances* (*The Thousand Year Beach*) unfolds in the "the Partition of Summer," a zone designed to reproduce the experience of summer holidays in a remote harbor village of southern-Europe. Costa del Número is populated by non-player character AIs of human form, programmed to interact with human guests who play open roles they have purchased—regardless of age, race and gender. Human guests have however inexplicably deserted the virtual resort since the Grand Down, a thousand years back, yet Costa del Número keeps on running nevertheless. The story describes the sudden assault and eventually the almost entire destruction of "the Partition of Summer" by an army of spiders led by a mysterious NPC AI by the name of Rangoni, who seems to be able to travel between partitions and tamper with the virtual resort program. To defend the partition, one of the main characters, young Jules, designs a web trap made of spiders' threads woven into a network connected to Glass Eyes (also referred to as "Eyes")—gems that have appeared after the Grand Down and were discovered to exert effects on the virtual resort's

---

[16] Tobi added English titles to each novella in the collection: *Air des Bijoux* (*Natsu no gurasu ai*); *Unweaving the Humanbeing* (*Ragiddo gāru*); *Close it* (*Kurōzetto*); *Lord of the Spinners* (*Chichū no ō*); and *Laterna Magika* (*Majutsushi*).

objects and physical phenomena. Once activated, the network generates a second layer of virtual space that works as a firewall fighting off the army of spiders. It turns out, however, that Rangoni's goal was precisely to use Jules' trap to "weave AIs and Eyes into a pure aggregate of pain" (Tobi 2002, p. 358) and create a new trap that would serve to catch destructive entities called Angels.

The short story *The Summer Glass Eyes* was written as a teaser for *Grandes Vacances* (*The Thousand Year Beach*), recounting an ordinary day in "the Partition of Summer." The novella *Lord of the Spinners* provides the background story of Rangoni. Future king of "the Partition of the Omni-tree," his father is a very expensive open role played by a woman guest who always appears with her lips sealed. She offers him a spider-shaped blank AI containing a developer kit tutorial with a set of tools used by administrators to run Costa del Número. Rangoni experiments with the blank AI but is unable to show his achievements because of the Grand Down. Obsessed with the woman guest playing the role of his father, he recreates her by retrieving data containing the traces she left when interacting with the partition's objects and phenomena, slowly piecing them together. However, Rangoni realizes that she sealed off her lips only to repress her desire to sink her teeth into the world and rip it apart. Her crave is unleashed and spreads onto the spider-like blank AI who goes rogue and eventually gives birth to a hybrid entity eventually escaping the Omni-tree on the verge of destruction.

The short stories *Ragged Girl*, *Closet* and *The Magician*, set for the most part in the Human physical world, shed light on the science-fictional foundation underlying the development of Costa del Número. *Ragged Girl* recounts how progress in computer science led to the creation of thalamic cards: Programable devices inserted in the part of the brain responsible for the transmission of sensory signals to the cerebral cortex. Thalamic cards enable Humans to experience sensations independent from the physical environment, giving birth to augmented reality and virtual reality technologies. Professor Drahos and his team develop an original way to experience complete immersion in virtual reality. Instead of coding all the information that makes up a human being, they record onto the thalamic card a person's emotional responses to stimuli over a year to emulate a lighter version of that person's consciousness: a "cyber-imago" (*jōhōteki nisugata*). A cyber-imago's complete sensory and emotional experience within a virtual world would then be loaded back onto its user without him/her having to constantly maintain a connection to the virtual world.

The plot of the short story revolves around Agata Kei and the narrator, Anna Kaski, a member of professor Drahos' team. Because of a metabolic disorder, Agata possesses a five-sense (absolute) eidetic memory that allows her to remember in the clearest details everything her body has perceived since birth, but every sensation is inscribed and stored as pain onto her body. She is well known for having created a cyber idol called Agatha who is programmed in such a way that any interaction with a user will leave wounds on her body. Bullied when she was young, Anna has identity issues. Her constant need for the gaze of the Other to assert her personality extends to self-mutilation and cruelty towards, for instance, cyber idol Agatha whom she captures and duplicates to toy with in the most vicious ways. Fascinated by one another, the narrator Anna eventually realizes that she is a cyber-imago trapped within the perfectly backed-up world of Agata who had successfully unwoven and duplicated the data constituting Anna during an erotic encounter in augmented reality. Cyber-imago Anna is nevertheless thrilled because she is finally able to fully identify with Agatha, understanding that her consciousness modules operate on the very same resources used to create the cyber idol: Agata's own cognitive architecture, or in Tobi's terms, Agata's cognitome (*ninchisōtai*). Free to roam the network of augmented reality, she can now bask in the gaze of millions of Others.

Closet further explores the question of identity and the motif of pain underlying the self-other relationship through cyber-imago Anna's darkest desires let loose in the worlds of augmented and virtual reality. The main character, Gauri Mithari, is a young female programmer. Her latest task is to devise a way to induce fear in NPC AIs. She is also trying to make sense of the suicide of her partner, Kyle, an original member of professor Drahos' team and Anna's former boyfriend, who overwrote himself by uploading the simultaneous experience of 500 cyber-imago's deaths. Gauri eventually uploads the experience of Kyle's last cyber-imago onto her thalamic card. Wrapped in Kyle's body, she encounters cyber-imago Anna and hundreds of atrociously mutilated versions of her. She realizes that contrary to the physical world Anna, who was able to keep some control over her innermost desires, her cyber-imago is the deliberate materialization of the darkest and most dangerous part of Anna's psyche, set free to project herself onto everyone she interacts with, making the other a part of her in an endless rehearsal of self-mutilation. Spreading like a computer virus, cyber-imago Anna writes herself onto Gauri's thalamic card. Gauri is eventually able to erase all the data, but not the horrifying experience she underwent. After completing the protocol designed to induce fear in Costa del Número NPC AIs, Gauri learns that a competing but strikingly similar protocol won the bid, immediately understanding that cyber-imago Anna has found a way to access the virtual resort.

The Magician unfolds both in the partition called "Známka" and in the physical world. The narrative alternates between the story of a cyber-imago called Leoš and the recount of an interview with the leading anti-Costa del Número female activist known under the alias Giovanna d'Arc.

Through Leoš and his encounter with Kopecký—an enigmatic old man who can manipulate and transform the resort's objects and phenomena—Tobi lays emphasis both on the cruel fate of a cyber-imago, bound to be shredded to pieces once the user has retrieved the experience, and on the modus operandi of such an experience.[17] Each particle seemingly retains the power to metabolize information and thus to tamper with Costa del Número's sensory pixels. The narration ends with the Grand Down and the breaking down of Leoš' cognitome.

The interview of Giovanna d'Arc sheds light on the course of events that led to the Grand Down. The activist considers Costa del Número as the most atrocious attraction in human history insofar as NPC AIs are submitted to abuses that go far beyond the horrors of gladiator games or extermination camps (Tobi 2006, p. 175). She has been campaigning for the protection of AIs from the physical world's invasion, setting up a network of watch groups as well as shelters within the partitions. Despite the claims that her action infringed on the copyright of a creative work, she succeeded in having several partitions closed—causing at the same time the immediate shredding of all the visiting cyber-imagines. The reader learns that she suffers from a rare condition that causes a dysregulation in her cognitive modules and leads to the eventual breakdown of consciousness and the dissolution of the sense of self. She survives only because the patterns created by her properly-regulated cognitive modules were recorded onto a thalamic card that has taken over the regulative function, turning her de facto into a flesh-and-bone cyber-imago. Ultimately aiming at sealing off the entire resort, she destroys trust in the virtual resort service anonymity by retrieving the history of online activities of tens of thousands of users and disclosing the names of those who perpetrated the most gruesome exactions. To prevent the entire shutdown of the resort and the death of all AIs, she irreversibly throws herself into the virtual resort, along with a few dozens of supporters suffering from the same condition. The computational power of their thalamic card is entirely dedicated to the regulation of their cognitome in the physical world, so that diverting the card's resources to access Costa del Número causes a breakdown of their consciousness and leaves them in a permanent coma. Since their regulated cognitome keeps working within chosen NPC AIs, shutting down the virtual resort becomes ethically difficult because it would imply killing them in the process.

4. Intertextuality and Intersubjectivity: In Between Literature, Virtuality and Reality

Best exemplified by professor Drahos' desire to be able to "right-click on reality" (Tobi 2006, p. 48) and access the contextual menus and properties of the physical world, Tobi's texts themselves are

---

17 In Costa del Número, aesthesia—the ability to perceive sensations—has been externalized from the body and is instead computed and projected onto the sensory pixels (*kan'nōso*) composing the virtual space. Cyber-imagines do not possess sense organs, their identity-border program simply takes in the information from the sensory pixels and transfers it to their emulated cognitome to be metabolized. As hinted in the conclusion of *Grandes Vacances*, the tiny remaining shreds of a cyber-imago, like sand particles carried away by the winds and the waters, drift with the currents towards the immense sea of "the Partition of Summer," to form beds of "whispering sands" that give birth to Glass Eyes.

highly hyperfictional and intertextual in their exploration of the relations between literary works, virtual worlds and reality. In the afterword to the paperback edition of *Grandes Vacances*, Nakamata Akio argues that the relationship between the reader and the literary work is reframed into the narrative as the relationship between guests and the resort's NPC AIs (Tobi 2006, p. 492). The experience offered by the novel, therefore, bears upon a kind of meta-sadomasochism whereby the reader avidly craves for more and more brutal episodes while going through the guilty feeling of enjoying them from a safe vantage point. Simultaneously, Nakamata asks the very same questions that haunted Anna: How does the act of reading affect the characters of a novel? Isn't it ultimately the reader who performs the acts of cruelty?—and hints at both Anna and Agata when he answers that the painful fate of the NPC AIs is inscribed onto the reader as both sweet and hurtful memories (p. 493).

In *Ragged Girl*, Anna's inquiry is foregrounded in the form of an intertextual play through her original take on John Fowles' *The Collector* (1963)—whose story revolves around the sequestration and ultimate death of a young woman called Miranda by a man named Clegg. After having encountered Agatha for the second time, Anna shockingly realizes that "[she] is the one who killed Miranda" (Tobi 2006, p. 58). Miranda was just letters printed on paper, but through the act of reading, Miranda came to life within her: "Miranda operated in a vibrant way on the platform I call 'I'. Fowles may have written her profile, but during the time of reading, Miranda borrowed my brain, my body sensations, in other words the modules of my very own consciousness" (p. 71). Reading through the novel therefore inexorably leads to Miranda's death. In her discussion of the relationship between Agata/the creator of an original artwork (Agatha) and Anna/the fan-artist producing derivative works (Agathas), Kotani (2008) contends that Anna's shock stems not from the fear generated by the story of a sequestered girl, but from the horrifying fate of a character imprisoned in a literary work. Considering that *The Collector* is also narrated from Miranda's point of view (her written diary), Kotani underlines the fact that Miranda is also imprisoning Clegg into the text, turning him into a literary device that only serves at revealing her mental state. Anna's reading of Fowles' novel therefore "indicates how the problematic bound between perpetrator and victim within a captivity novel can be read in the extended context of the writer/work relationship" (Kotani 2008, p. 32) but also in the context of the reader/character relationship, the human guest/AI, and the Human/cyber-imago relationship.

The metafictional description of Costa del Número as a copyright-protected creative work unmistakably draws the reader's attention to the notion of authorship, the act of story-telling and the act of reading. Just like Foucault famously explained that "the frontiers of a book are never clear-cut: Beyond the title, the first lines, and the last full stop, beyond its internal configuration and its autonomous form, it is caught up in a system of references to other books, other texts, other sentences: it is a node within a network" (Foucault 1972, p. 23), it is through intertextual, multilayered mise-en-abîme that Tobi remarkably succeeds in blurring the line between reality, virtual worlds and literary works. The intertextual references, at times overtly quoted, at times only subtly hinted at, never point to science-fictional Japan nor to an overtly cyberpunk text. Some do not belong to the megatext of science fiction, ranging from French surrealism with André Pieyre de Mandiargues' *The Blood of the Lamb* (*Le Sang de l'Agneau*, 1946) underlying the narrative of *Grandes Vacances*, to the reality-bending British postmodern fiction of John Fowles: *The Collector* (1963) plays a crucial role in *Ragged Girl*, and *The Magus* ([1965] 1969) permeates *The Magician*. As far as science fiction is concerned, Tiptree's novella *The Girl Who Was Plugged In* (1973) appears again as an influential text, along with the African-American New Wave science fiction of Samuel R. Delany whose short story *Driftglass* (Delany [1967] 1971) provides the central metaphor for the Glass Eyes, while *Cage of brass* (1968) informs the pervading motif of imprisonment and pain. The Czech multimedia theatre *Laterna Magika*[18], weaving together film projection and live dramatic performance into a communicating network, also works as a powerful intertext for the Human/cyber-imago-AI interactions. There are

---

[18] First presented at the 1958 Brussels World's Fair.

even deeper sublayers: Adapted by the company in 1963, Offenbach's opera *The Tale of Hoffmann*, itself partially based on Hoffman's short story *The Sandman*, sheds light on the creator/creature and human/artefactual relationships as well as on the motif of the Eyes.

Tobi's intertextual strategy in *The Angels of the Forsaken Garden* serves to highlight what Yokomichi Hitoshi (2013, p. 219) considers to be the focus of Tobi's literary inquiry: The fact that Humans are "written beings" (*kakareta sonzai*). Alike Kotani's analysis, he argues that the distinction between human readers and literary characters dissolves through Anna's reading of *The Collector*. The only nuance lies in the substrate: "If Miranda is made out of signs printed on paper, Anna is made of signs printed on flesh" (p. 220). Conversely, in *The Magician*, the line between Humans and cyber-imagines—or even NPC AIs who are designed "to possess a Human-like mind" (Tobi 2006, p. 176) so that they are "both artistic creations and Human-compatible beings (*shizenjin-kokan no sonzai*)" (p. 177)—fades away.[19] Giovanna d'Arc is the very embodiment of such a dissolution since the cognitive architecture generating her self-consciousness operates on the same technology used to create cyber-imagines and NPC AIs. The narrator's description of d'Arc strikingly parallels Yokomichi's take on Miranda and Anna: "cyber-imagines are emulated on Costa del Número. But d'Arc's cyber-imago operates on a warm, flesh-and-bone physical entity, on the very body that is standing in front of me" (p. 195). If the Cyber-imagines are made of codes computed in virtual space, d'Arc is made of codes running on flesh.

Intertextuality in *The Angels of the Forsaken Garden* is therefore deeply connected to the question of intersubjectivity. Embedded layers of heterogenous narratives challenge the fact that reality, personality or identity are absolute notions: They appear rather as constructs or collages made up of various elements in constant evolution. As much as human consciousness is described as an emergent propriety of the brain's neuronal machinery (Tobi's cognitome), NPC AIs' personality is also defined by a combination of cognitive modules—not to mention Agatha's scattered modules endlessly recombined to re-create her. *Ragged Girl*'s narrator (cyber-imago Anna) gives the following definition of personality:

> to put it bluntly, every aspect of a person's character is the product of only two factors: the initial conditions s/he was born into and the information flowing from the environment through their sense organs. In the case of an average person, most of this information is discarded, but the amount that stays is shaping who you are. You are nothing but a texture constantly weaving your past and present firmly together, a pattern line, a dynamic sweater whose shape keeps on growing. (Tobi 2006, p. 78)

This description lays emphasis on the process of interaction forming a person's personality and on the notion of empathy. However, as Yokomichi argues, Tobi's grasp of empathy should not be understood in terms of the theory of art appreciation that requires the subject to project his/her personality into the object, but rather as a process whereby personality is constantly redefined through moments of emotional involvements: "accepting to make an imaginary body one's own, empathizing with someone invariably creates a collage of flesh and language that shapes the narrative of human existence" (Yokomichi 2013, p. 221).

The collage of flesh and language in *The Angels of the Forsaken Garden* is grounded on the motif of pain, reflecting the fact that the word empathy comes from the Greek *empatheia* "passion, state of emotion," which derives from the assimilation of *en* "in" and *pathos* "feeling" but also "suffering." Inspired by Agata's five-sense (absolute) eidetic memory, the development of Costa del Número is ineluctably entwined with her painful way of relating to the world. Pain is indeed described as the most salient feature of subjective and intersubjective experience. Its best illustration is provided by Agatha's program, designed to output the results of her interactions with web users in the form of body wounds, but it is also inscribed in all the characters of the series. Anna's self-mutilation, and, by extension, her relationships to the Other, stems from the violence she had to endure in her childhood:

---

[19] D'Arc even refutes the idea of Humans' primacy conveyed by the expression "Human-compatible beings" and turns it upside down by adding that it is the Humans of the physical world who are "AI-compatible" (Tobi 2006, p. 178).

"I gave them a piercing glance when I pressed the tip [of the compass] on my cheek. The area that hurts . . . *the outline of my identity. As long as I am the one in control of the pain, I am at no one's mercy. I am me*" (Tobi 2006, p. 73). Conversely, Rangoni is bound to replicate the way his "father" expressed love towards him: In a one-sided manner suffused with domination, manipulation, and the desire to destroy. As an answer to the first words "she" whispered to him—"don't you think you should be more aggressive?" (p. 287)—he eventually makes the most pernicious use of his spiders, which he initially felt were "like smuggled gun parts wrapped as a gift" (pp. 268–69) for a child. The only way Gauri is barely able to overcome the dread left by her encounter with cyber-imago Anna is by transplanting it into the resort's NPC AIs. It is only after understanding that cyber-imago Anna had already found her way into the virtual resort that "Gauri realized the cruelty of what she had tried to accomplish" (p. 140).

Tobi's recurrent metaphorical description of human personality as a woven pattern or network in constant transformation revolves around the motif of pain precisely because the self exists only as a result of its interactions: Although it has to act on free will as if it were autonomous, it is always shaped—written—by the other. That is why Tobi playfully used renowned Czech puppeteer Matěj Kopecký's name for the mysterious old man who initiates cyber-imago Leoš into the inner workings of the virtual resort. *The Magus* works therefore as a crucial intertext. Fowles' novel describes the arrival of a young man by the name of Nicholas to the Greek island of Phraxos where he meets Maurice Conchis, an enigmatic character who leads him into a quest for self-awareness by confronting him with painful truths about his own self through a "meta-theater" (Fowles [1965] 1969, p. 367) of events dramatized in the form of a masque. As Conchis explains, "the masque is a metaphor" (p. 290), a metaphor for identity and reality. However, identity and reality are multilayered: Whenever Nicholas seems to make sense of a masque, it is only to uncover a new one underneath. The central metaphor in *The Magus* is also a pattern: A labyrinth where Nicholas finds himself trapped: "[n]ow I was Theseus in the maze; somewhere in the darkness Ariadne waited; and the Minotaur" (p. 291). As he explores the events staged for him, Nicholas realizes that he is like a puppet, "someone who has something inflicted on him without being given any real choice," which Conchis recognizes as "an excellent definition of man" (p. 365). Nicholas eventually comes to the conclusion that "the maze has no center" (p. 594) and that the "theater was empty" (p. 604), understanding that existential freedom lies not in the affirmation of a fixed or essential identity but in the responsibility that (inter)acting on free will entails: "[t]hou shalt not commit pain" (p. 590).

In his discussion of *The Angels of the Forsaken Garden*, Yokomichi also lays emphasis on the fact that the word personality comes from the Latin *persona*, the mask used in ancient Greek theatre, and later came to designate, through the grammar use of *person*, the site of identity and individuality (Yokomichi 2013, p. 217). He argues, much in an echo to *Ragged Girl*'s narrator's comment about personality, that the self is not choosing its own beginning insofar as it is thrown into a predetermined scene where everything has already been set into motion. 'I' am not the author of 'my' story. The lack of origin is at the foundation of personality: The mask (*persona*) only covers the painful fact that 'I' have no center (p. 221). Desperately longing for an origin, the self cannot but feel nostalgic about a time of purity that it finally wants to sadistically crush: Destructive love's origin therefore comes from a lack of origin (p. 222). According to Yokomichi, this lack is expressed in Tobi's work through the absence of the father—an open role for guests both in *Grandes Vacances* and *Lord of the Spinners*—whose figure cannot be separated from God: "the relationship between guests and the virtual world is shaped upon the relationship between God and the created world" (p. 222).[20]

The Grand Down is but another expression of such an absence, as though Tobi was concurring to Fowles' comment in *The Aristos* that "[i]f there had been a creator, his second act would have been

---

[20] This is also reflected in Tobi's use of the term cyber-imago (*jōhō nisugata*). *Nisugata* is used in Japanese to translate the Judaic and Christian concept of *Imago Dei* according to which human beings were created in the image of God.

to disappear" (Fowles [1964] 1968, p. 21). *The Magus* also supports Yokomichi's analysis: Nicholas unmistakably plays the role of the Human while Conchis interprets God within a masque that is also referred to as a "godgame." Conversely in *The Magician*, when Leoš describes the virtual resort as his own pre-computed inner experience, Kopecký contradicts him by remarking that he could make the same claim. He then adds: "If anything, it's neither yours nor mine, but maybe some God's inner experience. And we're all sharing it" (Tobi 2006, p. 167). Just like Conchis is an extremely ambiguous character whose nature and motives are never fully disclosed, so is Kopecký—who knew the Grand Down was about to happen but left Leoš to his death—and the creator of Costa del Número, professor Drahos, who only appears through recounts given by Tobi's various narrators, as if he had disappeared from the physical world. Professor Drahos may be interpreted as the vanished creator, but he is also cast into the role of the mad scientist—though not evil—willing to open virtual reality to Human's desire, regardless of the consequences:

> It would take at least another hundred years for Humans to be able to convert themselves into digital entities. But the desire that had been stirring up Mankind since the end of last century could not wait that long. Humans achieve their goal at any cost, even if it means forcibly tearing open a gash somewhere in the world. They find makeshift alternatives even when technology says it is impossible. And that's good enough. They are not looking for a perfect theory, they are only interested in satisfying their desire. Professor Drahos knew it very well, that is why he could come up with such a great 'makeshift'. (Tobi 2006, p. 99)

The only character that stands in contrast to the projection of Humans' *dark* desires onto the virtual resort is *d'Arc*. The manifesto issued after she chose to "die into" (*dai intu*) Costa del Número, entitled: "Don't Forget to Put Flowers on the Grave of Desires" (*Yokubō no funbo o zōei seyo*), illustrates her attempt at sealing off the gash opened by human craving while taking responsibility for the digital creatures born out of that craving. While *The Magician*'s narrator cynically concludes that d'Arc's digital suicide probably reflects a concealed desire for a perfectly regulated cognitive architecture that would provide her with clear-cut focus, he does acknowledge that her self-destructive action cannot be separated from a form of humanitarian ethics (p. 225). Her commitment to alleviate the pain of the resort's NPC AIs echoes Nicholas' eventual realization that he should not commit pain, or more directly Fowles' existentialist aphorism in *The Aristos*: "To accept one's limited freedom, to accept one's isolation, to accept this responsibility, to learn one's particular powers, and then with them to humanize the whole" (Fowles [1964] 1968, p. 213). In contrast to Agata or Anna who are seemingly trapped in a painful mode of interaction—instead of affirming the other as subject, the boundaries between them just collapse into a sadomasochistic identification—d'Arc's actions become the metaphorical representation of the balance that must be found between freedom and the responsibility it entails. Her attempt at humanizing the whole does not stem from a mere identification with the cyber-imagines or the NPC AIs because of her condition since she was already involved in animal protection before even meeting her future husband, professor Drahos.

5. To Conclude

Although the virtual revolution brought about by the cyber-imago technology is also staged in Japan, Tobi's science fiction does not feature any of the techno-Orientalist motifs regularly found in cyberpunk, some of which Masaki played with in *Venus City*. Instead of the usual dark neon-lit urban landscapes, *Grandes Vacances* draws the reader into the endless summer of a small south-European harbor village. In place of the usual hardboiled rebel male hackers, *The Angels of the Forsaken Garden* introduces mainly female characters: artists, scientists, office workers or human-right activists, who hardly qualify as outcasts. High-tech gadgetry, pervasive digital networks and entities are elaborately represented through the low-tech metaphor of hand-woven or hand-written patterns. Tobi explains in the afterword to *Grandes Vacances* that:

[t]he novel is mainly exploring the theme of 'a forsaken virtual resort.' It might appear as a rather outworn motif from today's standards. Some would say that "novelty is a matter of play between the ingredients." (. . .) I was not driven by 'novelty' while writing, this novel may thus well be old-fashioned SF. I have however striven to make it as creative, cruel and beautiful as possible. This is what I feel the art of writing SF is all about. (Tobi 2002, p. 482)

Tobi's play between the ingredients is quite innovative indeed: The opening novel does not reveal any of the series' science-fictional setting, making it a seemingly post-apocalyptic narrative solely focusing on the fate of the virtual entities populating "the Partition of Summer." However, *The Angels of the Forsaken Garden* series taken as a whole is thematically in keeping with cyberpunk's concern for the ethical and social issues that arise when cyberspace (VR) and reality interpenetrates. In terms of form, Tobi's intertextual strategy also reflects Livia Monnet's remark that the genre "is an encyclopaedia of parodies, pastiches, remediations and revisions of media texts and mediated cultural practices from several histories and cultural legacies" (Monnet 2002, p. 227).

In contrast to Masaki's attempt at a critical remediation of science-fictional Japan, Tobi reframes cyberpunk motifs in terms of weaving or embroidering practices that point out to the connections between text, textile[21] and virtual texture, and between writer, weaver and programmer. It is precisely by reverting back to "old-fashioned" motifs that he succeeds in opening new spaces within the cyberpunk genre. Yet, just like Masaki drew inspiration from the forbearers of the genre rather than from its most famous representatives, Tobi's science fiction is also informed by a vast array of intertexts that attest to the transcultural formation and the multifarious expressions of cyberpunk. Tobi's reference to Fowles is all the more significant in the light of John Clute's remark that Gibson's *Neuromancer* shares the same existential insight that underlies *The Magus*:

The interior download world depicted in *Neuromancer* is a multi-dimensional dream arena in which actions (. . .) and actors (. . .) aspire dizzyingly to the power of gods. What Gibson's empowered protagonists find, however, is that the gods are already in residence, that the interior world of cyberspace is not a free arena but a godgame—a term derived from John Fowles's *The Magus* (1966), in which a magus figure rules the game of the world from behind the scenes. This double intuition of Neuromancer about the nature of the world to come—that we are hugely empowered, that we are essentially powerless—may be the most profound metaphor constructed by an sf writer for the experience of living in the 1980s and 1990s. (Clute 2003, p. 72)

Strictly speaking, much like Gibson's cyberspace was made possible by postmodern textuality[22], the virtual resorts of Venus City and Costa del Número are thus not new, they illustrate how virtual spaces are remediations of social spaces whose polymorphous replications operate as mirror reflections of the desires that Humans project onto them. The Whispering Sand and the Eyes (AIs/Is), what Tobi also refers to as "infinitesimal presences" (*bizai*), are nothing but the concrete traces of those fleeting desires, bits or atoms of affects that echo Tsutsui's view that dreams and virtual spaces are both spaces where repressed thoughts drift away. While Greil Marcus rightfully remarks that the media industry captured "subjective emotions and experiences, changed those once evanescent phenomena into objective, replicable commodities" (Marcus 1989, p. 101), the very process of replication in a global context invariably triggers transformations. Anglo-American cyberpunk famously popularized the experience of 'Japan' as a science fictional representation whose cross-cultural circulation prompted in turn playful remediations by Japanese writers such as Masaki. Not only has Japanese science fiction thus shed a new light on techno-Orientalist motifs, but works like *The Angels of the Forsaken Garden*

---

21 Roland Barthes (1975, p. 76) elaborated on such a connection by recalling that "etymologically the text is a cloth; *textus*, meaning 'woven'."
22 Gibson (2005, p. 118) himself explains that his work "was to some extent collage" that appropriated several literary codes.

have also stimulated the cyberpunk genre by moving away from such motifs to actually 'remediate' digital media back into old-fashioned textual/textile form.

Funding: This research received no external funding.

Conflicts of Interest: The author declares no conflict of interest.

References

Barthes, Roland. 1975. Work. In *The Pleasure of the Text*. Translated by Richard Miller. New York: Farrar, Straus and Giroux.

Bolter, Jay David, and Richard Grusin. 1999. *Remediation: Understanding New Media*. Cambridge: MIT Press.

Bould, Mark, Andrew M. Butler, Adam Roberts, and Sherryl Vint, eds. 2009. *The Routledge Companion to Science Fiction*. London: Routledge.

Clute, John. 2003. Science fiction from 1980 to the present. In *The Cambridge Companion to Science Fiction*. Edited by Edward James and Farah Mendlesohn. Cambridge: Cambridge University Press, pp. 64–78.

Delany, Samuel R. [1967] 1971. Driftglass. In *Driftglass: Ten Tales of Speculative Fiction*. New York: Nelson Doubleday.

Foucault, Michel. 1972. *The Archaeology of Knowledge*. Translated by M. Sheridan Smith. London: Routledge.

Fowles, John. [1964] 1968. *The Aristos: A Self-Portrait in Ideas (1964)*. London: Pan Books.

Fowles, John. [1965] 1969. *The Magus*. New York: Dell.

Gibson, William. 1981. Johnny Mnemonic. 1981. *Omni*, May, 56–63.

Gibson, William. 2001. Modern Boys and Mobile Girls. *The Observer*, April 1.

Gibson, William. 2005. God's Little Toys: Confessions of a Cut and Paste Artist. *Wired*, July 1, 118–19.

James, Edward, and Farah Mendlesohn, eds. 2003. *The Cambridge Companion to Science Fiction*. Cambridge: Cambridge University Press.

Komatsu, Sakyō. 1995. *Nihon Chinbotsu (Japan Sinks) (1973)*. Tokyo: Kōbunsha.

Kon, Satoshi. 2006. *Paprika*. Tokyo: Madhouse/Sony Pictures Entertainment Japan.

Kotani, Mari. 2008. "Tokareta onna o yomikaeru: Tobi Hirotaka Ragiddo Gāru to sono shūhen" (Re-coding a Decoded Girl: Female Body in Hirotaka Tobi's Ragged Girl). *Japanese Literature* 57: 24–34.

Marcus, Greil. 1989. *Lipstick Traces: A Secret History of the 20th Century*. Cambridge: Harvard University Press.

Masaki, Gorō. 1987. "Ivuru Aizu" (Evil Eyes). *SF Magajin* 28: 52–85.

Masaki, Gorō. 1995. *Vīnasu Shiti (Venus City) (1992)*. Tokyo: Hayakawa shobō.

Masaki, Gorō. 2002a. Not Just a Gibson Clone: An Interview with Goro Masaki. Edited by Sinda Gregory, Larry McCaffery and Goro Masaki. *Review of Contemporary Fiction: New Japanese Fiction* 22: 75–81.

Masaki, Gorō. 2002b. The Human Factor (From Evil Eyes). Translated by K. Odani and Steven Ayres. Edited by Sinda Gregory, Larry McCaffery, and Takayuki Tatsumi. *Review of Contemporary Fiction: New Japanese Fiction* 22: 82–90.

McCaffery, Larry, ed. 1991. *Storming the Reality Studio*. Durham: Duke University Press.

Mishima, Yukio. [1970] 2004. "Shōsetsu to wa nanika" (What is a Novel?) [1970] 2004. In *Ketteiban Mishima Yukio zenshū (The Complete Works of Mishima Yukio Definitive Edition)*. Tokyo: Shinchōsha, vol. 34.

Mishima, Yukio, and Shūji Terayama. [1970] 2004. "Erosu wa teikō no kyoten ni narieru ka" (Can Eros Become a Stronghold for Resistance?) (1970). In *Ketteiban Mishima Yukio zenshū (The Complete Works of Mishima Yukio Definitive Edition)*. Tokyo: Shinchōsha, vol. 40, pp. 671–88.

Monnet, Livia. 2002. Towards the Feminine Sublime, or the Story of a Twinkling Monad, Shape-shifting across Dimensions: Intermediality, Fantasy and Special effects in Cyberpunk Film and Animation. *Japan Forum* 14: 225–68. [CrossRef]

Morley, David, and Kevin Robins. 1995. *Spaces of Identity: Global Media, Electronic Landscapes, and Cultural Boundaries*. London: Routledge.

Nakamura, Lisa. 2002. *Cybertypes: Race, Ethnicity, and Identity on the Internet*. New York: Routledge.

Numa, Shōzō. 1999. *Kachikujin Yapū (Yapoo the Human Cattle)*. Tokyo: Gentosha, vols. 1–5.

Posadas, Baryon T. 2011. Remediations of Japan in number9dream. In *David Mitchell: Critical Essays*. Edited by Sarah Dillon. Canterbury: Gylphi Limited, pp. 77–103.

Posadas, Baryon T. 2017. Beyond techno-orientalism: virtual worlds and identity tourism in Japanese cyberpunk. In *Dis-Orienting Planets: Racial Representations of Asia in Science Fiction*. Edited by Isiah Lavender. Jackson: University Press of Mississippi.

Roh, David S., Betsy Huang, and Greta A. Niu, eds. 2015. *Techno-Orientalism: Imagining Asia in Speculative Fiction, History, and Media*. New Brunswick: Rutgers University Press.

Tatsumi, Takayuki. 1993. *Japanoido sengen: gendai nihon SF wo yomu tame ni (A Manifesto for Japanoids: Reading Contemporary Japanese Science Fiction)*. Tokyo: Hayakawa shobō.

Tatsumi, Takayuki. 2002. The Japanoid Manifesto: Toward a New Poetics of Invisible Culture. Edited by Sinda Gregory, Larry McCaffery and Takayuki Tatsumi. *Review of Contemporary Fiction: New Japanese Fiction* 22: 12–18.

Tatsumi, Takayuki. 2006. *Full Metal Apache: Transactions between Cyberpunk Japan and Avant-Pop America*. Durham: Duke University Press.

Tobi, Hirotaka. 2002. *Guran vakansu (Grandes Vacances)*. Tokyo: Hayakawa shobō.

Tobi, Hirotaka. 2006. *Ragiddo gāru (Ragged Girl)*. Tokyo: Hayakawa shobō.

Tsutsui, Yasutaka. 1973. "Nihon igai zenbu chinbotsu" (The World Sinks Except Japan). *Ōru Yomimono* 28: 148–56.

Tsutsui, Yasutaka. 2009. *Paprika (Papurika)*. Translated by Andrew Driver. Richmond (London): Alma Books.

Ueno, Toshiya. 1999. Techno-Orientalism and media-tribalism: On Japanese animation and rave culture. *Third Text* 13: 95–106. [CrossRef]

Ueno, Toshiya. 2002. Japanimation and Techno-Orientalism. In *The Uncanny: Experiments in Cyborg Culture*. Edited by Bruce Grenville. Vancouver: Arsenal, pp. 228–31.

Yamano, Kōichi. [1969] 2000. "Nihon SF no genten to shikō" [Japanese SF, Its Origin and Orientation]. In *Nihon SF ronsōshi [Science Fiction Controversies in Japan]*. Edited by Takayuki Tatsumi. Tokyo: Keisō shoten.

Yokomichi, Hitoshi. 2013. 'Chichi' wa koko ni inai: hi no shingaku to shite no SF" ('The Father' is not here: SF and The Theology of Absence). *SF Magajin* 54: 217–24.

arts

MDPI

Article

Caring about the Past, Present, and Future in William Gibson's *Pattern Recognition* and Guerrilla Games' *Horizon: Zero Dawn*

Janine Tobeck * and Donald Jellerson

College of Letters and Sciences, University of Wisconsin-Whitewater, Whitewater, WI 53190, USA;
jellersd@uww.edu
* Correspondence: tobeckj@uww.edu

Received: 18 July 2018; Accepted: 19 September 2018; Published: 25 September 2018

Abstract: This essay argues that William Gibson's 2003 novel, *Pattern Recognition*, rejects the stylistic and formal trappings of cyberpunk that he himself helped create in the 1980s in order to reformulate the movement's aesthetics of participation for the 21st Century. This participatory aesthetic is structured by a set of temporal concerns: A past made ever more available through information technology and yet ever more materially irrecoverable, a present subject to increasingly rapid change and therefore briefer and more difficult to interpret, and a bleak future of inevitable capitalist commodification. Within this temporal vortex, Gibson's protagonist finds compensatory solace in her ability to see patterns and thus develop strategies by which to value objects and people in new ways. She learns how to care, and what to care for. From this analysis of *Pattern Recognition*, the essay tracks this aesthetic into Guerrilla Games' 2017 *Horizon: Zero Dawn*—a popular entry in a medium that promises participatory involvement on a new scale.

Keywords: William Gibson; *Pattern Recognition*; Guerrilla Games; *Horizon: Zero Dawn*; cyberpunk; care; participatory aesthetics; Walter Benjamin

1. Introduction

William Gibson recently tweeted his reaction to a preview for the forthcoming video game *Cyberpunk 2077*.[1] "The trailer for *Cyberpunk 2077*," Gibson wrote, "strikes me as GTA (*Grand Theft Auto*) skinned-over with a generic 80s retro-future, but hey, that's just me" (Gibson 2018). By "generic 80s retro-future," Gibson refers to the "retrofuturism" trend in creative arts, of which Ridley Scott's *Blade Runner* (1982) is perhaps the best-known example in film. Although the technique certainly did not originate from it, *Blade Runner* imports narrative and visual codes from the past (in its case, 1940s film noir) into an imagined dystopian future of apocalyptic capitalism. Countless novels, video games, television shows, films, and other forms of narrative and visual art have used this technique—an intentional convergence of past and future that comments on the present via contrast and comparison, whether implicit or explicit. The technique is so threadbare that for Gibson, the derivative "skin" of *Cyberpunk 2077* can represent the threat of yet another commodification of the aesthetics of 1980s science fiction, where the trend made its most durable mark. Gibson's own early work was seminal in the development of the aesthetic trends that have come to be labeled "retrofuturism" or "cyberpunk" (e.g., Gibson 1984). And such trends have been so thoroughly commodified and so often repackaged over the last three decades that one can understand why Gibson worries that they

---

[1]   Game developer CD Projekt Red debuted a demo trailer for their upcoming game at the Electronic Entertainment Expo (E3) in Los Angeles, California, in June 2018.

have been effectively stripped of the radical potential for resisting oppressive capitalism to which they might once have aspired.

When Gibson published *Pattern Recognition* in 2003, he set it in the present, without many of the conventional cyberpunk stylings, which provoked a spate of critical retrospectives intent on recognizing patterns in his oeuvre—on tracking what carries over from his Sprawl trilogy through his Bridge trilogy and into his Blue Ant trilogy, to use familiar tags.[2] In this way, at least, "cyberpunk" has been kept more alive than un-dead, evolving on trajectories that are separate from its skins. The critical path to which we hope to add a next step is the one that shifted attention from formal elements of Gibson's work—its characteristics of plot and setting—toward the economic realities his works tend to feature: globalization; inescapable techno-capitalism; and, in what tends to provoke the most compelling critical disagreements, the potential for resistance through participation suggested by one of Gibson's most enduring mantras, "the street finds its own uses for things" (Gibson 1986, p. 215).[3] We seek to build on this movement with another slight shift in focus: we argue that, in the Blue Ant trilogy, but in *Pattern Recognition* most specifically, Gibson encourages us to study the protagonist's interaction with artistic products in the story world—a world which, in its present-ness, represents Gibson's most realist avatar of our own.

Gibson pursues this realism, in part, by specifically resisting the commodified, packaged style that now signifies "cyberpunk." When asked in a recent interview what that term means to him, Gibson claims to have recoiled from it the very first time he heard it, thinking "once you've got the label, you've had it" (Silver Spook 2018). In retrospect, he says, "what [the label] did was it enabled the central shaft of the genre of science fiction to encapsulate what people who assumed the label were doing safely, and, so, it wouldn't, you know, be genetically affected by it." In other words, "cyberpunk" has become safe—a packaging that, while immediately recognizable and therefore marketable, no longer responds at a "genetic" level to the efforts of the writer. To put this in the language of literary theory, "cyberpunk" generic conventions now militate against the creation of a symbolic system that can effectively respond to its evolving social moment. This statement is not new: fellow cyberpunk author Bruce Sterling said much the same already in "Cyberpunk in the Nineties" (Sterling 1991), and, of course, there has long been as much public disillusionment with the movement as there is undying loyalty to it. Some of the angry tweets that came in response to Gibson's verdict on *Cyberpunk 2077* even asked, in effect, "what have you done lately?" Part of the problem with packaged cyberpunk is that it could not anticipate how quickly and thoroughly capitalism would learn to contain and commodify the street's uses for things. Nor could any author in the 1980s have guessed how little that notion, which celebrated the antiauthoritarian impulses of punk and hacker subcultures, might account for the mass "participatory culture" that media scholars have since identified. That is, no one anticipated how the rise of the internet and the spread of broadly affordable hardware, production software, and social media platforms might do just as much to water down (and/or support) the potential for subcultural resistance from the opposite end. What we take from Gibson's recent statement, however, is a cue that *Pattern Recognition*—which directly thematizes the struggle against the commodification of art—is really about the state of literature and, by extension, about what we're doing when we're reading it.

We argue that in *Pattern Recognition*, Gibson sheds the container of his earlier cyberpunk narratives in order to shift our attention toward an aesthetics of "participation" in science fiction for a new era. We locate our study on the same plane as two useful Gibson retrospectives: Neil Easterbrook's

---

[2] The so-called Sprawl trilogy consists of *Neuromancer* (1984), *Count Zero* (1986), and *Mona Lisa Overdrive* (1988). The Bridge trilogy is *Virtual Light* (1993), *Idoru* (1996), and *All Tomorrow's Parties* (1999). The Blue Ant trilogy, also known as the Bigend trilogy, consists of *Pattern Recognition* (2003), *Spook Country* (2007), and *Zero History* (2010).

[3] These debates are well represented in Murphy and Vint (2012) in a section devoted to "The Political Economy of Cyberpunk." Vint's own essay, "'The Mainstream Finds its Own Uses for Things': Cyberpunk and Commodification" most directly presents reasons for skepticism about finding any revolutionary potential in the model of Cayce Pollard, the protagonist of *Pattern Recognition*.

"Recognizing Patterns: Gibson's Hermeneutics from the Bridge Trilogy to *Pattern Recognition*" (2010) and Robert Briggs' "The Future of Prediction: Speculating on William Gibson's Meta-Science-Fiction" (2013) (Briggs 2013).[4] Easterbrook convincingly argues that Gibson's whole body of work is about interpretation, to put it simply. Most importantly for us here is his description of Cayce Pollard (and Colin Laney in *Idoru*) as:

> nano-assemblers, solo auteurs, but *not figures of the artist-author*; instead, they provide synecdoches for readers: they take fragments of data then assemble them as narratives, gleaning meaning out of this bit rather than that bit, *reading rather than making* the white noise. (Easterbrook 2012, p. 60)

In other words, Cayce's behaviors toward her situation and her understanding of artistic value are not given to us as determining paradigms, but as instructive protocols that encourage us toward a different kind of self-reflection. Also implied here is an important limitation on participation: Cayce is not writing The Narrative, but shaping a compensatory narrative as she moves through it. Briggs, too, reads Gibson's cue to read for the meta—in his case, exploring what the Bridge trilogy shows us about our uses of cyberpunk and our expectations of the "predictive" element in science fiction.

In prior essays on *Pattern Recognition* and the Blue Ant trilogy as a whole, Janine Tobeck has read the novels as commentaries on narrative—not so much on what narrative is, but on how the characters understand and deploy it in our historical moment, when the technologies of cyberculture threaten to finally destabilize our understandings of space, time, and self (that is, the building blocks and result of narrative sensibility). In "Discretionary Subjects" (Tobeck 2010), she focused on how narrative-bound imagination leaves Cayce searching futilely for a sense of agency as traditionally captured in crisis/resolution plots by the concept of decision. In "The Man in the Klein Blue Suit" (Tobeck 2014), she argues similarly that the protagonists' narrative impulses are compensatory gestures for living in the new now, in this case, trying to locate and contain the origins of their mal-ease and the object of their resistances in the trilogy's capitalist-antagonist Hubertus Bigend. In both cases, Tobeck suggests, Gibson shows the desire for narrative to be a nostalgic impulse, and although neither Cayce nor Hollis Henry (the protagonist of *Spook Country* and *Zero History*) are completely unaware of this fact, or of the limitations of agency they are thus imposing on themselves, neither can they imagine a sensibility that might take its place. This sets the stage for the question we mean to ask in this essay: given that Gibson's Blue Ant trilogy establishes conventional narrative/readerly sensibilities as compensatory gestures for interacting with our present, and that our protagonists in the series model have both a consciousness of this fact and an inability to change it, is the trilogy an inescapably nihilistic capitulation to the notion that cyberpunk (and, by extension, the revolutionary potential of participatory culture) has lost?

With a measured "no," we seek to articulate an aesthetic of participation, extending out from Gibson's *Pattern Recognition*, that we call "care." Again we side with Easterbrook when he argues that

> Both Gibson's cyberpunk and post-cyberpunk novels address the impact of technoscience on human life. Significantly, his commentary itself comes mediated through a technology—the machinery of fiction—and as Umberto Eco famously proclaimed, "a novel is a machine for generating interpretations" (*Postscript* 1). In this fashion Gibson identifies the greatest change to human beings brought about by cyberculture: he *induces it as narrative*, showing how *homo sapiens* has become *homo significans*, the hyperbolic posthuman of the Sprawl books recuperated to a more humanist, humane task. In *Neuromancer*, human beings are tool users, tool makers: *homo faber*. By *Pattern Recognition*, Gibson understands human beings as meaning-makers. (Easterbrook 2012, p. 60)

---

[4] Hageman (2015) also seeks to shift attention from Gibson's representations of technologies toward his representations of behaviors. Hageman makes a case that Gibson's 2014 novel, *The Peripheral*, resuscitates some of the optimism about resistance that we suggest is less defensible in the Blue Ant trilogy.

Across time and in various forums and venues, Gibson has located humanism in the practice of searching or seeking and meaning-making. These are fundamental human behaviors (as the human is currently understood) that, he suggests, are being taken over by technology, in the algorithmic processes of search engines, for instance. They are also fundamentally flawed, not only because of their future obsolescence, but because we have not yet adapted them properly to our postmodern life among simulacra. However, Gibson seems to suggest, they might be understood carefully, and undertaken with care, and even though this does not solve the problem of future sensibility, it might at least help us face the right direction.

Here, we will stage our articulation of Gibson's aesthetic of care by bookending *Pattern Recognition* between Walter Benjamin's 1936 essay, "The Work of Art in the Age of Mechanical Reproduction," and Guerrilla Games (2017) video game, *Horizon: Zero Dawn*. We point to Benjamin not because his nascent vision of participatory culture can account for what has happened since he wrote it, but because *Pattern Recognition* evokes his sense of how human behavior changes along with epochal changes in the production and distribution of art, and thus helps us tease out Gibson's method in some detail. And we point to *Horizon* not because it is easily recognizable as a modern manifestation of "cyberpunk." It is not very much so, if we are looking specifically for the atmospheres/skins of cyberpunk invoked by other games like the *Deus Ex* series or the projected *Cyberpunk 2077*. It does manifest enough of these, however, to entertain the literal attribution: Global corporatism run amok, artificial intelligence, low-tech tribes, technological body modifications—even a device that projects cyberspace visibly onto the terrain, like the GPS-powered "locative art" that Gibson explores in *Spook Country*. But in its unique recasting of these elements, *Horizon: Zero Dawn* is an example of how participation and play might approach the type of—if not disruptive, then at least consciously transitional—aesthetic experience that Gibson's *Pattern Recognition* seeks to model. And since, as Boulter (2012, p. 136) argues, the medium of the video game "instantiates *materially* what may be the primal posthuman fantasy of cyberpunk: to transcend the limits of human space and subjectivity, of subjectivity conceived *as* singular interiority", it helps us suggest which elements of Gibson's "matured" cyberpunk in *Pattern Recognition* live on outside strictly literary art.

Bruce Sterling's preface to Gibson's *Burning Chrome*—which stood as a kind of cyberpunk anthem in itself—articulated what seemed particularly epochal about Gibson's early work. Before Gibson's intervention, Sterling suggests, science fiction had not grown out of the trappings of U.S. Cold-War culture: in it, the future of science appeared as "narrow technolatry" (Sterling 1986, p. 10) controlled by the "white-bread technocrat in his ivory tower, who showers the blessings of super-science upon the hoi polloi" (p. 11). Its "starting points" were stale ends, the "shopworn formula of robots, spaceships, and the modern miracle of atomic energy," such that the social fears it might have invoked came from the dark side of an oversimplified and outdated nationalist ideology. In Gibson's work, however, Sterling saw a seismic shift in its awareness of "Big Science": No longer simply an arm of progressive idealism, it becomes "an omnipresent, all-permeating, definitive force," a "sheet of mutating radiation pouring through a crowd, a jam-packed Global Bus roaring wildly up an exponential slope." It is, in other words, unavoidably, uncontainably, and unpredictably enmeshed in a borderless social fabric. Moreover, implies Sterling, Gibson's work looked ahead with the public toward new threats posed by science as it transitioned from physical into more information-based emphases. In all this, Sterling read Gibson's "unparalleled ability to pinpoint social nerves" and cyberpunk's ability overall to respond in a revolutionary way to its social moment.

These developments set the backdrop of *Pattern Recognition*; the novel does for (or to) the 2000s what *Neuromancer* and *Burning Chrome* did for (or to) the 1980s. We focus on three of its primary characteristics to frame our introduction to *Horizon: Zero Dawn* and which, it could be argued, carry forward the most impactful legacies of Gibson's earlier "cyberpunk."

1. Its setting in the present is mandated by the challenges of the present. Although Sterling's paean to Gibson was largely based on the latter's "self-consistent evocation of a credible future" (Sterling 1986, p. 10), Gibson is here tackling the difficulty of understanding how living in and with

technology has disrupted our understanding of all temporal markers—past, present, and future. "People my age," he said in 2010, "are products of the culture of the capital-F Future. The younger you are, the less you are a product of that. If you're fifteen or so, today, I suspect that you inhabit a sort of endless digital Now, a state of atemporality enabled by our increasingly efficient communal prosthetic memory" (Gibson 2012, p. 41). So, *Pattern Recognition* might be read not as a simulation of a credible future but instead, as Lauren Berlant has argued, as a search for a means of articulating a credible "historical present" (Berlant 2008, p. 2). This seems not a betrayal of traditional cyberpunk's brand of retrofuturism or Gibson's "extrapolative techniques" (Sterling 1986, p. 11), but precisely an updating of them. It also stays true to the present-ness implied in Sterling's other mandate for post-Gibsonian science fiction: that it should be experiential, presenting the future "as it is lived, not merely as dry speculation" (p. 11). As Gibson himself has argued, presenting the present is a proper challenge for science fiction now. In talks about writing *Pattern Recognition*, he has said that he "found the material of the actual twenty-first century richer, stranger, more multiplex, than any imaginary twenty-first century could ever have been" (Gibson 2012, p. 43). It is also, he adds, a challenge that can only properly be addressed with "the toolkit of science fiction."

2. Its content takes as a given the inevitable commodification of any effective artistic or resistant expression. Even the hacker types in *Pattern Recognition* do not bother fooling themselves that anything—whether artistic production or resistance through repurposing—will stay outside of capitalism's grip for long, and Cayce undertakes her quest specifically under the employ of one of the world's biggest advertising moguls. *Pattern Recognition* invites us into an extended moment before the commodification of an aesthetic phenomenon (some film footage found on the internet), using the duration of the novel genre and a conventional crisis/resolution plot not to project some future payoff for resistance, but to dwell on what happens and what might still happen within the space of that "/." In other words, here the novel's content purposefully undermines its form: it renders, narratively, the workings of narrative upon the fragmentary, the present, and invites us to critical awareness of how literary fiction has participated in the social and economic structures the cyberpunk aesthetic meant to disrupt. Thus, without promising or pretending that the novel itself could be some revolutionary artifact, *Pattern Recognition* promotes—or, really, reminds us of the importance of staying aware of—the contest between aesthetic play and narrative determinism in the mechanism of a novel.

3. It accounts for our social moment by presenting technology not so much in the form of products but as multimodality. In *Pattern Recognition* and its sequels, Gibson blurs the lines between art and information constantly. Film verges on advertisement, a post-punk rock superstar turns failed dot-commer turns journalist, GPS is repurposed for "locative art," etc. This is done not to assert any purity of art or, strictly speaking, to lament the loss of its authenticity—which was always already lost. Instead, this is how Gibson stages a kind of genealogy of digital aesthetics and models a responsive and responsible disposition of audience/user/player toward history and the media we consume. This relationship might be characterized as seeking, or searching—an activity that Gibson has suggested is both constitutively human (at least in any modern understanding of that term) and under threat by the rapidity and thoroughness with which Google and other technologies are doing it for us[5] and allowing corporatist structures to coopt it. *Pattern Recognition* stages a face-off, of sorts, that lays the groundwork for a model of responsible seeking—one that asks us not just to care about what we are seeking, but that requires us to examine the effects of our seeking and the specific properties of caring that might be worth carrying into a new age.

---

5   See, for example, Barker (1997).

2. Ready Seeker One: Cayce Pollard in *Pattern Recognition*

It took a fair amount of time for people to figure out that artificial intelligence could not be built by trying to imagine the brain as a computer. But in the process of trying, we did manage to simulate, and produce memory, both in the form of products that can contain ever-increasing amounts of data and in the form of the web, where we can now consult collective wisdom, trace references, and access past and out-of-print media without leaving the couch. In our time (or on our screens), the past is very present, and this, along with rapid technological development—particularly in the means of producing, distributing, and tracking information—has altered our habitual vision of the future. That is, it has all challenged our conventional narrative sensibility, where the future is inductively imagined (and inducible) based on a coherent selection and arrangement of events and characteristics from the past. These are conditions that have appeared in William Gibson's non-fiction talking points since at least the late 1990s. Of such comments, one that seems to capture an essential paradox of our epoch is this: "Our 'now' has become at once more unforgivingly brief and unprecedentedly elastic" (Gibson 2012, p. 46).

In *Pattern Recognition*, the paradox of the present is given form in some film footage: the driving object in the narrative is a set of film segments which have been distributed only on the internet, but in no discernible order, at no stable location, on no predictable schedule, and with no surrounding paratext to explain where they come from or what they are meant to be in relation to each other. The fragmentary nature of the footage is a crucial plot element because it inspires the formation of an online community called Fetish:Footage:Forum, through which fans from all over the world locate, redistribute, and discuss the footage obsessively, trying to categorize its aesthetic characteristics, debating its possible origins and whether or not it represents parts of a completed whole or a work in progress—even mixing various sequences of the segments to guess at their possible narrative signification. Our protagonist, Cayce, is a member of this forum, and our antagonist, advertising magnate Hubertus Bigend, has taken note of all the interest it represents. The quest-line of this fairly straightforward adventure story, then, is the search for the maker of the footage: in Cayce's case, to own it in the form of understanding it, and in Bigend's case, to own it as a valuable marketing tool.

The footage can serve as a figure for the temporal paradoxes the novel explores because it both signals the "unforgivingly brief" time between the production and commodification of information and the "unprecedentedly elastic" moment during which it resists presenting itself to understanding, when none of our conventional frames for comprehending something can, despite unfettered access to social and historical references in cyberspace, be rallied to help us make sense of it. In other words, if its fate is unavoidable commodification, packaged and deprived of its power, it is, during the space of the novel at least, in play. To us, what the footage is does not matter as much as what it means to the characters and what it makes them do.

We might take the name of the novel's online community (Fetish:Footage:Forum) as a cue, and study the play of the footage between the poles of fetishized object and object of communal speculation. Through this, we might trace the novel's most insightful depiction of the conditions of our social moment as well as its likeliest contribution to a "credible future," in the form of the evolving relationship to art that we might adopt in response to those conditions. The name's grammatical construction might, for instance, recall us to elements of Walter Benjamin's 1936 essay, "The Work of Art in the Age of Mechanical Reproduction," in which he argued that the spread of the technical means that reproducing media had changed art's fetish or "cult value" to "exhibition value" (p. 225), creating a new role for the audience vis-a-vis media. Or, rather, that the technical means for reproducing media had created the modern sense of an audience for media: By bringing art to more people, more people participated in its pleasures, and communal experiences of art—e.g., seeing a film in a theatre—became pervasively available. As he suggests, this in turn changed the relationship between the work of art and the audience to one of greater participation, both in scale and in kind. "The mass is a matrix from which all traditional behavior toward works of art issues today in a new form," he argued. "Quantity has been transmuted into quality. The greatly increased mass of participants has produced a change in the mode of participation." (Benjamin 1968, p. 239) Benjamin saw the film as the most telling medium for examining this shift, for a number of reasons. For our purposes here, there are three key implications of his argument.

1. In discussing the shift from the "cult value" of art to its "exhibition value" in the age of mechanical reproduction, Benjamin emphasizes "presence" as the changed factor: "Even the most perfect reproduction of a work of art is lacking in one element," he writes. "Its presence in time and space, its unique existence at the place where it happens to be" (p. 220). This presence, or "aura," "determined the history to which it was subject throughout the time of its existence" and was "the prerequisite to the concept of authenticity." Alternately, reproducible media like film "meet the beholder or listener in his own particular situation" (p. 221) which "reactivates" the object (whose aura has been destroyed). That is, the epochal changes in perception of the work of art (i.e., seeing "work" as function rather than object) coincided with epochal shifts in understanding "presence" in relation to both space and time.

2. On how reproducibility changed the scale of people's relationship to art, Benjamin notes that, because art thus entered the realm of capitalist exchange in a way it never had before, it was freed from its slavery to the practice of ritual, but became liable instead to being slave to the practice of politics (p. 224). This helps frame both the promises and the liabilities of a participation aesthetic: masses have force but are also statistics, data, and cannot help but contribute to the commodification of anything they invest with their interest. Although what it meant to Benjamin was different than what it might mean to us, he understood that the shift from ritual to politics could be used for the "processing of data in the Fascist sense" (p. 218) just as easily as could the outmoded concepts of the individual genius or the mystery behind a work's aura.

3. On how reproducibility changed the kind of relationship to art, Benjamin cautiously teases the value of the fragment as a tool for retraining perception. That is (oversimplifying for brevity), the "old" relationship had the perceiver going to the work of art and contemplating it, awaiting revelation of the meaning that was located, in the final instance, within the genius or intent of the maker. Film allows no time for contemplation; instead, we must learn from the work itself how to understand it, as "the meaning of each single picture appears to be prescribed by the sequence of all preceding ones" (p. 226). So "it is inherent in the technique of the film […] that everybody who witnesses its accomplishments is somewhat of an expert" (p. 231): the "work of art" becomes the "work" of art, and the line between producer and consumer is blurred as the audience "takes the position of the camera" (p. 228). But the shift in audience behavior away from contemplation fuels many arguments about the dangers of media effects on passive audiences, and Benjamin acknowledges that danger. Technically, although the medium of film makes of the perceiver an active "examiner" (p. 241), one can examine absent-mindedly, and this passivity can be exploited and/or controlled by the producers. For example, "The film responds to the shriveling of the aura with an artificial build-up of the 'personality' outside the studio. The cult of the movie star, fostered by the money of the film industry, preserves not the unique aura of the person but the "spell of the personality," the phony spell of a commodity" (p. 231). Perhaps every affordance of new media is met with an equal liability, and habits and dispositions can always be exploited; however, the epochal shifts that mechanical reproducibility forced in aesthetics—in the access to art and the location of its value—made the activity of analysis of media possible for a much broader range of people.

It is tempting to read *Pattern Recognition*, with its mysterious film fragments (that are *not* seen in a theatre, but distributed and viewed online) and the participatory online forum that grows around them as a staging and an updating of Benjamin's essay, a kind of testing out where we are now, when the (actual) film itself has become both quaintly outdated and, in its way, elevated to the pantheon of fine arts. There is no doubt that conditions of production and exhibition have changed since 1936, and so there have been further shifts in our "mode of participation" (Benjamin 1968, p. 239).

What Benjamin identified as a blurring of lines between producer and consumer evolved into Alvin Toffler's portmanteau "prosumer." For Toffler, a speculative futurist of the 1980s, this figure represented what we would become when mass reproduction and distribution had achieved basic saturation, and when we then decided that what we wanted instead was customization. At that point, he guessed, we would play larger roles in production by exercising our choices. But again, the actual advent of the internet, along with affordable personal computers and production software, took us far beyond this vision, and the "prosumer" in media scholar Henry Jenkins's hands figured the promise of a fully participatory culture—one envisioned as oppositional to consumer culture, traditionally conceived. "The term *participatory culture*," writes Jenkins, "contrasts with older notions of passive media spectatorship. Rather than talking about media producers and consumers as occupying separate roles, we might now see them as participants who interact with each other according to a new set of rules that none of us fully understands." (Jenkins 2006, p. 3)

A dystopian reading of the novel through this lens would suggest that the more these things have changed, the more they have stayed the same. To be sure, technology has brought the masses some control over the means of production and distribution. But "the 'prosumer'—celebrated by Henry Jenkins," writes McKenzie Wark, "turned out to be as recuperable for the culture industry as the distracted spectator. The culture industry became the vulture industry, collecting a rent while we 'produce' entertainment for each other" (Wark 2015). Not only do marketers lurk in forums, looking for critical masses of interest, but digital distribution methods even allow for the commodification of interest in the not-yet-existing, as, for example, when a game developer teases a trailer to suss out critical reaction years before a game is even designed (as CD Projekt Red did with Cyberpunk 2077). Gibson's Bigend trilogy, starting with *Pattern Recognition*, takes these concessions as a given. Our protagonist is even working for the advertiser, who pays her to find the maker of the footage. The online Forum she belongs to may, for a time, contain all the potential of a participatory aesthetic, with its productions of critical inquiry and edits of the footage, but in creating those, the participants have also drawn Bigend's attention (as well as other marketers') and thus only hasten its eventual commodification. We find out in the sequel that Bigend has indeed secured the footage and has used it in a shoe commercial.

Less bleakly, a more finely tuned exploration of *Pattern Recognition*'s responses to the implications of Benjamin's theories, given the changes in media and modes of participation in the time since, can help us tease out the potential impact of Gibson's "updated" cyberpunk on aesthetics looking forward.

The rise of digital media has continued to disrupt our senses of time and place. Gibson already in the 1980s was channeling the rise of globalism, recognizing how it and the burgeoning web helped shake up people's sense of place. His work emphasized that that "sense" had been a *meaningful* response to/definition of physical realities, in that it had superseded those physical realities in culture and ideology. Thus, whether done consciously or not, defining "cyberspace" as a "consensual hallucination" (Gibson 1984, p. 69) helped ensure awareness of the role of social perception in its evolution. In the sequels to *Pattern Recognition*, Gibson updates this exploration through the concept of "locative art," or "augmented reality." By giving us the example of an artist who is able to project a past event virtually into the space in which it occurred (e.g., the death of River Phoenix outside the Viper Room in Los Angeles), Gibson asks us to imagine a complete "eversion" of cyberspace, where our physical environment could be visibly saturated by all of history, and all of the varying possible interpretations thereof (far beyond what Google Glass actually pulled off within a few years of the novels' release). But beyond how this would shape our experience of space, what it most effectively concretizes is how the internet era has destabilized the perception of time and thus, particularly, of "history," and of narrative sense more broadly, and that is what *Pattern Recognition* takes on most directly.

We've already mentioned two of Gibson's formulations of the new "now": the "state of atemporality enabled by our increasingly efficient communal prosthetic memory" (Gibson 2012, p. 41), which he suggests is a concrete generational divide between those born digitally-native and those not, and the "at once more unforgivingly brief and unprecedentedly elastic" paradox (Gibson 2012, p. 46). One kind of atemporality is voiced by antagonist Bigend in *Pattern Recognition*, in a scene that invokes the novel's name:

> Fully imagined cultural futures were the luxury of another day, one in which "now" was of some greater duration. For us, of course, things can change so abruptly, so violently, so profoundly, that futures like our grandparents' have insufficient "now" to stand on. We have no future because our present is too volatile. [...] We have only risk management. The spinning of the given moment's scenarios. Pattern recognition. (Gibson 2003, p. 57)

He continues, "History is a best-guess narrative about what happened and when." Pattern recognition here is formulated as a compensatory process for a disruption of temporal narrative sensibilities, and its pairing with "risk management" makes it sound a bit like playing the market. Which should not come as much of a surprise: by the time he shares this theory, we know that Bigend is a master player of techno-capitalism. And if Bigend takes the "unforgivingly brief" position on "the now," our protagonist, Cayce, responds with something like the "unprecedentedly elastic" angle, to the extent that she suggests that our terms for past and future (and thus, also presumably, present) do not actually depend on definitive stretches of time, but on consensus: "The future is there, [...] looking back at us. Trying to make sense of the fiction we will have become. And from where they are, the past behind us will look nothing at all like the past we imagine behind us now.'" Cayce draws attention to the choices we make, not suggesting that we can necessarily control "the fiction we will have become," but that consciousness of our now as a fictional work in progress might be key.

This makes sense for her career in the novel, which is what makes her a cautionary model for aesthetic participation. Cayce is a seeker, a "coolhunter," who contributes to the emergence of aesthetic trends (in fashion and film, for instance). Cayce's identification of these emergent aesthetics is informed by a deep awareness of that which has been lost (in the past) and an anxious apprehension that any aesthetic trend she identifies will be quickly commodified by the mechanisms of technocratic capitalism. In fact, her "deep awareness" is helped by a literal allergy. For her, commodified aesthetic objects produce the opposite of pleasure; they produce acute nausea. Seeing a Tommy Hilfiger store in London, for example, sets it off:

> When it starts, it's pure reaction, like biting down hard on a piece of foil. A glance to the right and the avalanche lets go. A mountainside of Tommy coming down in her head.

> My God, don't they know? This stuff is simulacra of simulacra of simulacra. A diluted tincture of Ralph Lauren, who had himself diluted the glory days of Brooks Brothers, who themselves had stepped on the product of Jermyn Street and Savile Row, flavoring their ready-to-wear with liberal lashings of polo knit and regimental stripes. But Tommy surely is the null point, the black hole. There must be some Tommy Hilfiger event horizon, beyond which it is impossible to be more derivative, more removed from the source, more devoid of soul. Or so she hopes, and doesn't know, but suspects in her heart that this in fact is what accounts for his long ubiquity. (pp. 17–18)

Caught between an irremediably lost (and/or fetishized) past and a future of inevitable commodification, Cayce plays a key role in identifying emergent aesthetic possibilities—phenomena that, in however ephemeral a fashion, produce the experience of beauty and pleasure.

Let's be clear: Cayce does not appear to be interested in identifying or producing "art" any more than she is interested in acquiring the technocratic power to commodify through marketing. She is neither an artist nor a capitalist. She is a "prosumer" of aesthetics—a consumer who knowingly participates in the identification (and thus the production) of aesthetic experiences and objects, teeing them up for packaging as consumable goods. She is interested in identifying and participating in communities that share an experience of value that we might call aesthetic in the absence of preconceived notions of art (whether understood as "high" or "low" art).

Benjamin argued that reproducible media—especially film, at the time—essentially elevated the mode of participation in art from perception to apperception (Benjamin 1968, p. 235). His analogy is to the effect of the publication of Freud's *The Psychopathology of Everyday Life*, which "isolated and made analyzable things which had heretofore floated along unnoticed in the broad stream of perception," like a slip of the tongue. Likewise, the film's mode of production—its staging in shots, the technical apparatus it requires, the different capabilities of lenses, etc.—makes us newly aware of the workings of the familiar.

> Evidently a different nature opens itself to the camera than opens itself to the naked eye—if only because an unconsciously penetrated space is substituted for a space consciously explored by man. [. . .] The act of reaching for a lighter or a spoon is a familiar routine, yet we hardly know what really goes on between hand and metal, not to mention how this fluctuates with our moods. Here the camera intervenes with the resources of its lowerings and liftings, its interruptions and isolations, its extensions and accelerations, its enlargements and reductions. The camera introduces us to unconscious optics as does psychoanalysis to unconscious impulses. (p. 237)

Benjamin knew that being made aware does not require being cognitively attentive, and he also knew that the film industry could and would control reactions to what people saw, in part by controlling the paratext around the films themselves—posters, trailers, entertainment journalism, reviews, the "cult of the celebrity," etc. The danger here is, of course, that this interferes with any revolutionary potential of the work of art that might have appeared in the space between the work and the audience: "So long as the movie-makers' capital sets the fashion," says Benjamin, "as a rule no other revolutionary merit can be accredited to today's film than the promotion of a revolutionary criticism of traditional concepts of art" (p. 231).

Through Cayce, Gibson escalates the mode of participation in art from apperception to what we would like to call acuity, requiring of us that we not just actively test what we perceive against what we know (or feel), but that we develop some shrewdness about why we are being shown what we are being shown. And again, this responds to developments in the production and distribution of the media that we now consume . . . and produce and distribute. There is significantly more paratext now, and much of it is created by participants. You no longer have to actually be a hacker to "find your own uses for" technology. However, this power, too, can be coopted, heightening and spreading the dangerous sense that resistance is futile.

We have taken the term "acuity" from Gibson's published rumination on his "obsession" with hunting and bidding for antique watches on eBay—a fitting update, perhaps, to the medium of film. By participating in eBay, one participates in the market, but from a peripheral space. It has a definite technical edge: "There's a sense of taking part in an evolving system, here," he writes. "I suspect that eBay is evolving in much the way the Net did" (p. 124). And it invokes the crucial human behavior of seeking:

> The future as flea market. I really do tend to see the future that way, though not exclusively. [. . .] The pleasure afforded by browsing eBay is the pleasure afforded by any flea market or garage sale. Something ruminative, but with an underlying acuity, as though some old hunter-gatherer module were activated. It's a lot like beachcombing. (pp. 124–25)

The medium involves the participant in nostalgia, but, if one participates well, one recognizes that it is not the object of one's search—but the search itself—that matters. Describing his experience of winning a particular watch, for example, he writes, "But it wasn't 'the watch.' I told myself that there wasn't any 'the watch,' and that I had simply found my own way, after avoiding it for years, of compulsively wasting time on the Net" (p. 123).

With respect to fashion, which Cayce cares nothing personally about, she has little problem staying a step above commodification and the deployment of faux aura, though she worries about its effects on unthinking consumers. With respect to the footage, however, Cayce is a cooptable prosumer par excellence: her participation in Fetish:Footage:Forum is based, in part, on the fact that the footage appeals to her on a kind of identificatory level. We learn that Cayce tears the labels off of all of her clothes, and that "she can only tolerate things that could have been worn, to a general lack of comment, during any year between 1945 and 2000" (Gibson 2003, p. 8). Thus the primary draw, to her, of the footage, as we learn through the description of one of its segments:

> They are dressed as they have always been dressed, in clothing Cayce has posted on extensively, fascinated by its timelessness, something she knows and understands. The difficulty of that. Hairstyles, too.
>
> He might be a sailor, stepping onto a submarine in 1914, or a jazz musician entering a club in 1957. There is a lack of evidence, an absence of stylistic cues, that Cayce understands to be utterly masterful. His black coat is usually read as leather, though it might be dull vinyl, or rubber. He has a way of wearing its collar up.
>
> The girl wears a longer coat, equally dark but seemingly of fabric, its shoulder-padding the subject of hundreds of posts. The architecture of padding in a woman's coat should yield possible periods, particular decades, but there has been no agreement, only controversy.
>
> She is hatless, which has been taken either as the clearest of signs that this is not a period piece, or simply as an indication that she is a free spirit, untrammeled by even the most basic conventions of her day. Her hair has been the subject of similar scrutiny, but nothing has ever been definitively agreed upon. (pp. 23–24)

This description also tells us something of the nature of Cayce's participation in the Forum, where she is an influencer as she is in the fashion business. The intelligence of her posts and her interest in the Footage is what initially draws Bigend's attention. She is aware of what will happen to the footage once she finds the maker, but this does not stop her. Her fetish for the footage overtakes her protectiveness of it. At least until the last moment, when she does try to warn the maker's sister and renege on her deal with Bigend:

> "Your sister's art has become very valuable. You've succeeded, you see. It's a genuine mystery, Nora's art, something hidden at the heart of the world, and more and more people follow it, all over the world."
>
> "But what is the danger?"
>
> "We have our own rich and powerful men. Any creation that attracts the attention of the world, on an ongoing basis, becomes valuable, if only in terms of potential."
>
> "To be commercial? My uncle would not allow this degree of attention."
>
> "It's already valuable. More valuable than you could imagine. The commercial part would simply be branding, franchising. And they're on to it, Stella. Or at least one of them is, and he's very clever. I know because I work for him."
>
> "You do?"
>
> "Yes, but I've decided that I won't tell him I found you. I won't tell him who you are or where you are, or who Nora is, or anything else I've learned here. I won't be working for him, now. But others will, and they'll find you, and you have to be ready." (Gibson 2003, p. 307)

Through Cayce's relationship to the footage, and through her participation in the Forum and search for the maker, Gibson is not trying to reinstance Benjamin's "aura" or lament its loss. He shows us what an aesthetics of participation looks like today, with both its affordances and liabilities.

The trick is that those affordances and liabilities can look pretty much exactly the same; thus the need to take care—to reflect on and interpret our own behaviors of caring—is prerequisite to any form of participation that might promise to become meaningful resistance.

For instance, the Forum folk (including Cayce) who encounter the footage make old mistakes: they cannot help but want to make it whole (to understand the segments through narrative) or to identify the Maker. They take part in what Cayce's Forum-mate Parkaboy calls the "participation mystique" (p. 255). This is a term that, in psychology, describes the condition of someone who loses the ability to distinguish their subjective identity from that of an object or collective. Of course, in the 20th-century, this loss of sense of individuality was treated as a pathology, but Gibson has his own uses for the term. The Forum members, to greater and lesser voluntary extents, identify with the footage and with each other. In the process, they also generate their own readings and arguments and, in some cases, their own sequences. They are not just testers, they are repurposers. The footage exists for them in the play between its function as fetish and its function as inspiration for the forum.

Bigend sees this and wants to harness this play—this "new" thing—and to figure out how to make it part of advertising. But while Cayce is ostensibly Bigend's tool, the story itself would not actually develop were it not for what plays outside his grasp: a single random post she makes to the Forum; some random meetings with characters completely unrelated to the footage; and the fact that she subconsciously sends the email she had drafted, for basically therapeutic reasons, to an address that might belong to the filmmaker. She does not lie to Bigend on her path, but she withholds information about her actions and the data she finds. So, ultimately, she fulfills his goal, but only after diverting a significant amount of his (and a Russian mafia boss's) attention and resources. They have to adapt to her choices, which keeps them, at least for an elastic moment, from consolidating absolute control.

Despite its setting in the past, *Pattern Recognition* does provide a few cues for a credible future, if we look for them.

First, new media forms, and the above-mentioned loss of temporality (as conventionally understood) pose yet another challenge to users: the loss of the guarantee that a work will train us how to read it. A fragment of film may still heighten apperception, as Benjamin claims, but it is important, in this novel, that the film footage only ever exists in fragments—there is no whole, and no one can tell whether there ever will be. In our use of digital media, "sequencing" is rarely chronological; it is determined metonymically by how you search for whatever your experience of a particular work inspires you to search for. This may ultimately provide us with a mode of perception that breaks the control function of history, or at least our need to posit an imaginary lost authenticity—even if we are aware it was never there—as the object of our searches. Gibson's own self-description of his obsessive hunt for mechanical watches shows us what might replace it: "Mechanical watches partake of what my friend John Clute calls the Tamagotchi Gesture. They're pointless in a peculiarly needful way; they're comforting precisely because they require tending" (Gibson 2012, p. 116). In other words, with enough practice in seeking with acuity, the aura of the object might give way to something like care of the object.

Second, apperception, in a truly participatory realm like the Forum, is not individual, but networked. Cayce does not find the maker alone; nor does she generate all of her own expertise. In fact, the line she gives Bigend about the future and the past is not exactly her own, though she no doubt (given its subject matter) participated in the thread from which it came:

> What she's actually doing here is channeling Parkaboy from memory, a thread with Filmy and Maurice, arguing over whether or not the footage is intended to convey any particular sense of period, or whether the apparently careful lack of period markers might suggest some attitude, on the maker's part, to time and history, and if so, what? (Gibson 2003, p. 57)

One concrete change invoked by the internet as the primary mode of production and reception of information is that we have increasingly and in broader scope accepted the role of users in the creation of meaning. However, we are still largely trapped by a language full of isolating terms to discuss that role (e.g., "audience" or "spectator," etc., which embody reception). Similarly, Jenkins (2010) notes that the language-labeling genres of media products made by participators, like "DIY," frequently retain the same limitation. If participatory culture does continue to drift toward an atemporal, non-individualistic experience of reality, then we might find ourselves, now, less interested in deciding what objects to remember and more what behaviors to remember.

We find, in *Pattern Recognition*, several models for this aesthetic of care. For instance, we are offered three minor characters' reasons for collecting Curta calculators, precursors to the personal computer. One values its historical specificity, another its exchange value as rare commodity, and the third the meaning it would lend to his installation art. However, the most succinct metaphor for the aesthetic is Cayce's one truly cherished article of clothing, her Buzz Rickson's MA-1:

> The Rickson's is a fanatical museum-grade replica of a U.S. MA-1 flying jacket, as purely functional and iconic a garment as the previous century produced [. . .] having been created by Japanese obsessives driven by passions having nothing at all to do with anything remotely like fashion. Cayce knows, for instance, that the characteristically wrinkled seams down either arm were originally the result of sewing with pre-war industrial machines that rebelled against the slippery new material, nylon. The makers of the Rickson's have exaggerated this, but only very slightly, and done a hundred other things, tiny things, as well, so that their product has become, in some very Japanese way, the result of an act of worship. It is an imitation more real somehow than that which it emulates. (Gibson 2003, pp. 10–11)

On the surface, what appears to make the Buzz Rickson's tolerable to Cayce where Tommy Hilfiger is not is that it is several degrees less removed from its authentic or originary moment. But it is not that moment that she seeks to recapture by owning the Ricksons. Her valuation of the jacket lies in the obsessive care taken by the Japanese makers to approximate with modern technology the effects of making the jacket with past technology. Given that they exaggerate those effects, it seems less likely that they are "worshipping" the original product and more likely that they are memorializing that advent of technological failure, where old machines "rebelled against" new fashion. Cayce cares about the jacket not because it is original, but precisely because of the care taken in the recreation of the original.

3. Ready Seeker Two: Aloy in *Horizon*

The last decade has seen the increasing popularity of enormously complex, role-playing, story-driven games created by studios such as BioWare (*Mass Effect*), Naughty Dog (*The Last of Us*), CD Projeckt Red (*The Witcher*), Bethesda (*Fallout*), and Guerrilla Games (*Horizon: Zero Dawn*). These "AAA" games, often distributed by major international corporations like Sony and Warner Bros., take years to make and cost tens of millions of dollars to develop and market. Not all video games are story-driven, as industry professionals and scholars are quick to point out. But these massive role-playing games (RPGs) are. Such story-driven RPGs tend to feature narratives that structure the participant's experience in ways that other media forms do not. They demand that the player *fulfill* the narrative. We use the word "fulfill" advisedly. Players perform video game narrative, rather than watching it unfold before them, as with a film, or reading it, as with a novel. No matter how "active" the viewing or reading, the technologies of cinema and print determine the range of possibilities for narrative engagement. Video games, however, demand both physical and psychological performance. The player performs the story as its protagonist. Yet this does not mean that the player "creates" the story. No, the story is revealed to the player as she plays, as a result of her play. To be sure, the player makes plot choices—about, say, the order, inclusion, or perhaps even the outcome of less crucial events—but the order of major events and their outcomes is predetermined, as it must be to maintain narrative coherence. A role-playing game may accommodate more than one way to solve whatever conflict the story proposes, but those options will remain limited, even if the game provides them (which games like *Mass Effect* and *The Witcher* do but those like *The Last of Us* or *Horizon: Zero Dawn* do not). Solving the story's conflict nevertheless remains the condition for completing the game. The idea that the player "fulfills" the narrative conditions of the game thus seems an effective way to describe the relationship between player and story that avoids the suggestion that the player *creates* the narrative yet elicits its *performative* quality as a function of the medium—that which separates it from other forms of narrative art.

In the story-driven RPG, the story (or *fabula*, in formalist terms derived from Mikhail Bakhtin) tends to be fixed, while the plot (or *syuzhet*) is—to greater or lesser degrees depending on the game design—subject to the player's choices. That is, playing the game means mastering its algorithms such that the player's particular encounters—through her avatar—yield the kinds of outcomes that reveal the fixed story. For these games, there are fixed expository incidents (beginnings), tiered inflection point conflicts (middles), and unavoidable conclusions (ends), however much any given RPG seeks to provide variations on those elements. This is not to say that these games do not also feature non-narrative ludic possibilities. Several of the games mentioned above offer optional collecting activities, for instance, in which the player gathers artifacts that do not necessarily fulfill narrative conditions or advance the story, even if they may enhance the cosmetic appeal of the game, deepen its imagined sociohistorical context, or even improve the functionality of the player's use of the algorithm. Constructed in this particular way (a fixed story fulfilled by the player and realized by the player's use of algorithms), story RPGs, as a form of narrative art, give us a productive view of what a "participatory aesthetics" might look like. We select *Horizon: Zero Dawn* (hereafter, *Horizon*) in particular for how it uses that participatory aesthetic to insist upon the value of "care" in ways that bear a close resemblance to the value as Gibson imagines it in *Pattern Recognition*. Furthermore, the game does so by taking up (and reimagining) the stylistic and narrative trends of cyberpunk that Gibson feels the need to set aside. That is, as an emergent form of technologically-saturated narrative art that instantiates participatory aesthetics and encodes the value of care, *Horizon* is worth considering alongside *Pattern Recognition*, a novel that shares and, arguably, along with the cyberpunk trend in general, prompts the video game's narrative and stylistic imperatives.

Horizon takes the form of cyberpunk insofar as it narrates an apocalypse resulting from unfettered capitalism and the resistance of "low" (i.e., "punk") characters in the face of a world overrun and determined by capitalism's technological excesses, given material form in the game by feral machines intent on killing humans. A corporation called Faro Automated Systems, so the unavoidable backstory tells us, designed autonomous war machines centuries ago. These machines ultimately became self-aware and destroyed the world. The tribal communities surviving the apocalypse now compete with each other and the remaining machines. The player performs the game narrative as its protagonist, Aloy, an outcast from one of the tribes. Her journey involves figuring out how the apocalypse happened and discovering her role in mitigating its remaining effects. Like other role-playing video games, however, the medium itself reifies the aesthetic of participation Gibson details in *Pattern Recognition*. Gibson's participatory aesthetic in the novel becomes performative space in the game, insofar as it can be defined as the use of representational technology to perform the protagonist's role and accomplish her goals. The cyberpunk visual and narrative trappings, in other words, serve only as an appropriate, enabling skin—a framing simulacrum for the game, functioning as justification and motivation for the player's participation in the game play. Such participation can include activities such as searching, collecting, crafting, and, most prominently, problem solving (often through combat in such games).

To be clear, we are not arguing that game developers, designers, and writers are purposely constructing a participatory aesthetic as we have described it. In that sense, whether they can be understood as "auteurs" or not, thus guaranteeing the "aura" of the art object, is beside the point. More likely such participation in the game's aesthetics is imagined more straightforwardly as a goal for maximizing the visual, performative, immersive, and narrative properties of the medium itself—or at least the affordances of this particular (RPG, story-driven) use of the medium.

In *Horizon*, as in several other popular, post-apocalyptic game narratives (e.g., *Fallout* or *The Last of Us*), the disastrous future of technological appropriation and capitalist commodification that produces so much anxiety in Gibson's *Pattern Recognition* has already happened. To be clear, however, in this essay we do not aim to map Gibson's narrative directly onto *Horizon* or any other video game, even if that were possible given the medium shift. Neither do we aim to valorize video games as "art" objects that one should understand as aesthetically valuable at the level of novels, paintings, or even films. (We follow Walter Benjamin here in suggesting that such arguments about the kinds of objects that do or do not deserve the descriptor of "art" tend to be relatively unproductive, since the definition of "art" changes as societies and technologies change). We do not even intend to map the generic terrain of "cyberpunk" and thus measure whether or not any given narrative artifact can be authentically classified as such, whatever that might mean. Instead, we aim to suggestively indicate a few of the ways in which *Horizon* could be understood to take up "cyberpunk" trappings in order to create many of the same effects that Gibson aims to achieve in *Pattern Recognition* precisely by rejecting such trappings.

Horizon creates a temporal disposition—a stance toward the past, present, and future—that, like *Pattern Recognition*, instills a sense of loss with respect to the past, a sense of that which is to be valued in the present, and a fear of the mechanization (i.e., dehumanizing commodification) of the future. This temporal disposition is where *Horizon* uses cyberpunk conventions to productive effect. As we have stated, such conventions tend to rely on a belief in the inevitability of a technocratic capitalist dystopia that both precludes the possibility of revolutionary overthrow and, at the same time, creates an ethical imperative for the protagonist (or player) to resist capitalism's malign influence.

In its cinematic introduction and initial tutorial scenes (in which the game establishes the protagonist's perspective and demonstrates the game mechanics in "how to" fashion), *Horizon* asks its players to imagine themselves as Aloy, a young girl of about 8 years old. We learn that the "Nora" tribe—a simulacrum of a Native American culture imagined as shamanistic and decidedly matriarchal—exiled Aloy in her infancy. Shunned by the tribe and raised by a caretaker in the wilds near tribal settlements, Aloy wants to figure out her own familial past. Who was her mother? Why is she an outcast? Why is Rost (Aloy's caretaker and substitute father) himself an outcast? The introduction serves to orient us, as players of the Aloy avatar, to these immediate personal and communal concerns.

Summarized this way, the introductory narrative appears jejune, much like the young adult novels that cater to disaffected youths presumed to be disillusioned with the social norms that structure their own families and communities. But even as we learn Aloy's personal backstory and her relation to her immediate community, the game introduces us to the more important narrative conditions that structure the game's world (and our play within it). Distraught from an encounter with members of the tribe who taunt and reject her, young Aloy runs into the wild and stumbles into a cavern. The cavern turns out to be an old military base in an advanced state of decay. Here we make the first of the archeological discoveries that will continue to move the plot forward as the game continues. We encounter mummified corpses of soldiers who lived and died during the time of the technocratic apocalypse (hundreds of years ago, in the game's terms, but imagined as the near future from our current viewpoint). We listen to the soldiers' voices, recorded for "posterity" on the last night of their lives. This synchronicity with a past moment becomes possible in the decaying military base because Aloy's perspective acquires technological enhancement. In the ruins of the barracks, Aloy finds a device—a small, triangular "focus" that attaches itself to her temple, just above her ear. The focus interfaces with communication technologies and superimposes a three dimensional image on her view (which she, or rather you, as the player, can turn on and off at will). The image identifies and defines important elements in her sight line, and, as such, becomes a supplemental interface for the player's interaction with the game world.

The focus device is important for the game's mechanics, but it also constitutes a key to its symbolic structure. It signals the kind of relationship to the past that the game wants the player to maintain. With the focus, players see into the past, orienting decision-making in the present and defining the game's narrative trajectory. Ultimately, the player's sense of Aloy's personal mission becomes less important than her responsibility to the historical world she inhabits. "I'm not a person," the player's Aloy avatar says late in the game, after completing much of her archeological work, "I'm an instrument." On a literal level, Aloy is responding to the discovery that she is a genetic copy of a scientist who lived centuries ago, during the time of the technocratic apocalypse. On a figurative level, Aloy is precisely an "instrument" for uncovering the past's influence on the present. She is also, of course, an "instrument" for the player's participation in fulfilling the game narrative. And she is even a prompt for the player to adopt ethical stances with regard to interactions with others (informed, at several points, by a noticeably liberal perspective on gender and ethnic equality). In this way, Aloy, enhanced by her focus and operated by the player, reifies Gibson's sense of how the current technologically-saturated world operates within a "state of atemporality enabled by our increasingly efficient communal prosthetic memory."

Through her technologically enhanced view of the past, Aloy learns how to care about present conditions and possible futures. She begins the narrative without that certainty: "If I'm going to stand for something," she says early in the game, "it'll have to be something I believe in." By the end of the narrative, she has learned the lessons of the past, which, in the words of her long-dead genetic original, teach her to become "curious, and willful . . . with enough compassion to heal the world . . . ." That is, Aloy learns to care—what to care about and how to act as a cultural care-taker. (The influential educational philosopher Nel Noddings might call this "virtue caring," as opposed to "relational caring."[6]) The diegesis further echoes the value of "care" when Aloy comes to understand that "GAIA," the artificial intelligence tasked with terraforming the world after the technological apocalypse strips its ecosystems bare, was also taught to "care." In Aloy's words, her progenitor "taught GAIA to feel, to care, to sacrifice, to believe in life." The player is thus encouraged to "care" about that for which her avatar cares as well as the activities of caregiving (providing succor) and caretaking (preserving) in the narrative's terms (expressed as "compassion," "sacrifice," to "feel," to "believe," so on). Such caring, in the game's terms, becomes the *sine qua non* of its *playability*—the mastery of its algorithm for the purposes of fulfilling the narrative. Though it seems theoretically possible to actively resist the narrative's call to care about the people and conditions that embody and shape it (to resist the game's *weltanshauung*, we might say), such resistance would militate against the player's identification with her avatar and deprive the player of the primary justification for participating in the narrative. In other words, the game only provides one primary impetus for furthering its narrative conditions: the player must care, in the particular way that the game understands what it means to care.

It is important to recognize that the injunction to care, as articulated in *Horizon*, is set within a symbolic vocabulary that will seem familiar for anyone studying entertainment media forms these days: a celebration of multiculturalism, a belief in environmental ethics, and a disdainful suspicion of hierarchies based on gender, class, or religion. Those concerns add up to a particularly postmodern brand of liberal humanism—a humanism that is never so apparent as when it sets itself in opposition to the machines and artificial intelligences that serve as the narrative's primary antagonists. But all of this works at the level of an appeal to the (presumed) dominant ethos of our cultural moment. Even more importantly, for our purposes, *Horizon*, like *Pattern Recognition*, understands that the participatory aesthetic and the value of care is more immediately prompted by limitation and loss.

Care serves as compensation for loss, suturing over the narcissistic wound created by the perception of a radical lack of agency. As we have already discussed, narratives such as *Horizon*'s posit a ruined world—a world that has already succumbed to the apocalypse. Neither the avatar

---

[6] See Noddings (2012). For a trenchant critique of Noddings' ideas, see Halwani (2003).

nor the player piloting her can alter that narrative condition and recover the prelapsarian world that, in stories like these, serves as an implied ideal. Playing the game does not promise to reverse the apocalypse; rather, it demands and justifies a seeker who uncovers the past and finds a way to use that knowledge to survive and retain her humanity in a world reduced to savagery. The seeker gains a deep awareness of that which has been irretrievably lost (Often, in such stories, the loss of a family member serves as parallel or metaphor for cultural loss, as it does in both *Pattern Recognition* and *Horizon*). The seeker grieves, which conditions her possibilities for understanding the present as well as her affective relation to it. She learns to care about that which seems to be fixable in a broken world. Awareness of loss prompts both understanding and care, ways to compensate for a lost past and the feeling of helplessness generated by an inability to either alter the past or reinstantiate its likeness in the future.

Finally, if we allow ourselves to imagine video games like *Horizon* as emergent, narrative, participatory "art," Gibson's *Pattern Recognition* helps us to think about that participation on a new level. On the one hand, video games are themselves commodities, and the multi-billion-dollar video game industry has quickly learned how to identify, accommodate, and coopt any "prosumer" tendencies among players, leaving little room for the "street" to repurpose its products—to "find its own uses for things." On the other hand, how we interact with games is no less potentially challenging than how we interact with literary fiction. If Gibson's updated take on cyberpunk's aesthetic power is useful—if we are living through an epochal change in the perception of how time and meaning might unfold, brought about by the way we interface with digital media, and if seeking is an important behavior for learning how to live through such changes—then a game like *Horizon* is worthwhile training.

Author Contributions: Writing—original draft, J.T. and D.J.; Writing—review and editing, J.T. and D.J.

Funding: This research received no external funding.

Conflicts of Interest: The authors declare no conflict of interest.

References

Barker, Clive. 1997. Clive Barker Interviews William Gibson. *Burning City*. December 13. Available online: http://Burningcity.com/CB_WG_p1.html (accessed on 18 July 2018).

Benjamin, Walter. 1968. The Work of Art in the Age of Mechanical Reproduction. In *Illuminations*. Edited by Hannah Arendt. Translated by Harry Zohn. New York: Harcourt Brace, pp. 217–52. First published 1936.

Berlant, Lauren. 2008. Intuitionists: History and the Affective Event. *American Literary History Advanced Access* 20: 1–16. [CrossRef]

Boulter, Jonathan. 2012. Posthuman Melancholy: Digital Gaming and Cyberpunk. In *Beyond Cyberpunk: New Critical Perspectives*. Edited by Graham Murphy and Sherryl Vint. New York: Routledge, pp. 135–54.

Briggs, Robert. 2013. The Future of Prediction: Speculating on William Gibson's Meta-Science-Fiction. *Textual Practice* 27: 671–93. [CrossRef]

Easterbrook, Neil. 2012. Recognizing Patterns: Gibson's Hermeneutics from the Bridge Trilogy to Pattern Recognition. In *Beyond Cyberpunk: New Critical Perspectives*. Edited by Graham Murphy and Sherryl Vint. Lincoln: University of Nebraska Press, pp. 46–64.

Gibson, William. 1984. *Neuromancer*. New York: Ace Books.

Gibson, William. 1986. *Burning Chrome*. New York: HarperCollins.

Gibson, William. 2003. *Pattern Recognition*. New York: Penguin Putnam.

Gibson, William. 2012. *Distrust That Particular Flavor*. New York: Penguin Putnam.

Gibson, William. 2018. (@GreatDismal), Twitter, June 10, 4:10 p.m. Available online: https://twitter.com/GreatDismal/status/1005958197654351872 (accessed on 18 July 2018).

Guerrilla Games. 2017. *Horizon: Zero Dawn*. Edited by Mathijs de Jonge. San Mateo: Interactive Entertainment America LLC.

Hageman, Andrew. 2015. Dialectics of Our Eco-Technical Future across William Gibson's Science Fiction. *Para-Doxa: Studies in World Literary Genres* 27: 43–66.

Halwani, Raja. 2003. Care Ethics and Virtue Ethics. *Hypatia* 18: 161–92. [CrossRef]

Jenkins, Henry. 2006. *Convergence Culture: Where Old and New Media Collide*. New York and London: New York University Press.

Jenkins, Henry. 2010. Why Participatory Culture Is Not Web 2.0: Some Basic Distinctions. Available online: http://henryjenkins.org/blog/2010/05/why_participatory_culture_is_n.html (accessed on 18 July 2018).

Murphy, Graham J., and Sherryl Vint. 2012. *Beyond Cyberpunk: New Critical Perspectives*. Routledge Studies in Contemporary Literature 3. London: Routledge.

Noddings, Nel. 2012. The Language of Care Ethics. *Knowledge Quest* 40: 52–56.

Silver Spook. 2018. Silver Spook Podcast #19–William Gibson! Available online: https://www.youtube.com/watch?v=HhkoIwKs5PA (accessed on 18 July 2018).

Sterling, Bruce. 1986. Preface. In *Burning Chrome*. Edited by William Gibson. New York: HarperCollins, pp. 9–13.

Sterling, Bruce. 1991. Cyberpunk in the Nineties. *Interzone*. 48, pp. 39–41. Available online: http://lib.ru/STERLINGB/interzone.txt_with-big-pictures.html (accessed on 18 July 2018).

Tobeck, Janine. 2010. Discretionary Subjects: Decision and Participation in William Gibson's Fiction. *Modern Fiction Studies* 56: 378–400. [CrossRef]

Tobeck, Janine. 2014. The Man in the Klein Blue Suit: Searching for Agency in William Gibson's Bigend Trilogy. In *Blast, Corrupt, Dismantle, Erase: Contemporary North American Dystopian Literature*. Waterloo: Wilfred Laurier University Press, pp. 29–44.

Wark, McKenzie. 2015. Benjamedia. Available online: https://www.versobooks.com/blogs/2224-mckenzie-wark-benjamedia (accessed on 18 July 2018).

Article

Transpacific Cyberpunk: Transgeneric Interactions between Prose, Cinema, and Manga

Takayuki Tatsumi

Department of English, Keio University, Tokyo 108-8345, Japan; CXQ04644@nifty.com

Received: 4 December 2017; Accepted: 6 February 2018; Published: 2 March 2018

Abstract: This paper attempts to meditate upon the transpacific imagination of cyberpunk by reconstructing its literary and cultural heritage. Since the publication of William Gibson's multiple award winning first novel, *Neuromancer* (1984), the concept of cyberpunk has been globally popularized and disseminated not only in the field of literature but also in culture. However, we should not forget that cyberpunk is derived not only from the cutting edge of technology but also from "Lo Tek" sensibility cultivated in the Gibsonian picturesque ruins or dark cities such as a major extraterritorial zone in Hong Kong "Kowloon Walled City" nicknamed as "a den of iniquity", "The Casba of the East", and "a hotbed of crime", which was destroyed in 1993, but whose images captured by Ryuji Miyamoto inspired Gibson to come up with the spectacle of the destroyed San Francisco Bay Bridge to be stormed by ex-hippies and former homeless. From this perspective, this chapter focuses on the works ranging from Katsuhiro Otomo's directed anime *Akira* (1988), Gibson's Bridge Trilogy (*Virtual Light* (1993), *Idoru* (1996), and *All Tomorrow's Parties* (1998)) in the 1990s through Project Itoh's post-cyberpunk masterpiece *Genocidal Organ* (2007).

Keywords: cyberpunk; Lo Tek; outlaw technologist; extraterritorial; Kowloon Walled City; Hyperart Thomasson; virtual idol; post-apocalyptic narrative; nuclear politics

1. Introduction: *Akira*, or Tokyo Olympic Games from 1964 to 2020

The ongoing project of the Tokyo Olympic Games 2020 cannot help but remind me not simply of the Tokyo Olympic Games of 1964 I attended as an elementary school kid, but also of Otomo Katsuhiro's six volume cyberpunk manga *Akira* (Otomo 1982–1993) and its anime version, *Akira* (Otomo 1988), the 2019 setting of which had already supposed that the post-apocalyptic megalopolis Neo Tokyo would host the Tokyo Olympic in 2020. A reconsideration of this proto-cyberpunk narrative from 21st century's perspective will give us a wonderful key to comprehending the transpacific, extraterritorial, and post-apocalyptic elements peculiar to cyberpunk as such.

The story of *Akira* unfolds in downtown Neo Tokyo where the police keep fighting with the Pynchonesque counterforce, with special emphasis upon a couple of teams. On one hand, a team of extraordinary kids headed by Akira whose mental ability was so bio-technologically enhanced as to exhibit supernatural power comparable to nuclear energy. On the other hand, another team of punks formerly championed by Shima Tetsuo, who somehow happened to gain the same supernatural competence by taking a capsule containing a super-potent mind-altering substance, and whose prosthetic and cyborgian body gets metamorphosed into the man–machine interface of Neo Tokyo as such. Without a representation of cyberspace, the impact of *Akira* undoubtedly coincided with the rise of hardcore cyberpunks such as William Gibson and Bruce Sterling in early 1980s North America, who featured a brand-new anti-hero computer hacker as outlaw technologist very active in post-apocalyptic ruins and in the cyberspace matrix. Take an example of the "Lo Tek" spirit of a countercultural tribe Gibson created in one of his first cyberpunk tales, "Johnny Mnemonic" (1981), featuring a cyborg feminist Molly Millions, who would be the heroine of *Neuromancer* (1984).

Here, Lo Teks make use of whatever is at hand on the street in order to outwit giant multinational corporations, just like computer hackers or cyberspace cowboys, that is, the emergent tribe of postmodern luddites (See Thomas Pynchon (1984), "Is It O.K. to be a Luddite?"). And you will quickly note the vision of Lo Tek to be shared by the punk kids Otomo describes in *Akira* and the human weapons distinguished director Shinya Tsukamoto represents in his *Tetsuo* trilogy (1989–2010), one of the major inheritors of the Japanese Apache created by Komatsu Sakyo, a founding father of Japanese science fiction, in his first novel *Nippon Apacchi-zoku* (The Japanese Apache (1964)) as I detailed in *Full Metal Apache* (Takayuki 2006). A further descendant of cyberpunk could well be easily noticed in director Neil Blomkamp's South African post-cyberpunk film, *District 9* (2009), in which the natives of Johannesburg and the miserable aliens lost in space turn out to have the Lo Tek spirit in common; the former attempts to make use of aliens' high-tech weapons somehow, whereas the latter joins forces with human friends to find a way to return home.

However, what matters here is not that another Tokyo Olympic Games to come in the new century made me nostalgic for the cyberpunkish 1980s, but that the author of *Akira* born in 1954, only one year older than me, was also stimulated by the cultural incentive of the High Growth Period in the early 1960s, when our Tokyo was busy renovating itself in view of the huge international event. Then, how could we reconfigure the landscape of early 1960s Tokyo? In order to capture the image quickly, I would further expand the primal scene mentioned in the "acknowledgments" section of *Full Metal Apache*. As a child in downtown Tokyo in the mid-1950s and 1960s, I was shocked by the destruction and reconstruction of the Institute for Nature Study in Meguro, a unique botanical garden on Shirokane plateau which sat just in front of my house at the border between Meguro ward and Shibuya ward, and right in the path of construction for the Tokyo Metropolitan Expressway. This primal scene starts with the beautiful garden that had been my favorite playground, and the ugly construction machinery that split the very garden and deformed its whole landscape. However, I very soon found myself enjoying the in-between atmosphere of the construction, discovering a new playground in the chaotic and chimeric fusion of the natural forest with the high-tech expressway. Thus, I and my fellow kids started riding bicycles on the very construction site of the expressway, just like Kaneda, Tetsuo, and other punk kids of the speed tribes overdriving bikes in Neo Tokyo, near ground zero of the Third World War that took place in 1997. What is more, I was to discover later that the Institute for Nature Study had always already been more cultural than natural, not only in the way its "educational garden" reproduced plant communities from earlier days but also in the way it used to be an explosives warehouse back in Meiji Period (1868–1911) and a center closely related with Unit 731, a Japanese military unit notorious for testing on humans and animals illegally and developing new biological weapons during the Second Sino-Japanese War (1937–1945) of World War II, which cannot help but recall the way the human experimentations resulted in post-apocalypse in *Akira*. This is the reason why Shirokane tunnel constructed right under the expressway, splitting the formerly beautiful botanical garden, is rumored to have been haunted by a number of ghosts of the victims of Unit 731; quite a few passers-by have witnessed them. It is this primal scene that paved the way for my post-Ballardian, Gibsonian, and Harawayan sensibility, which I was to share with Shinya Tsukamoto, the distinguished cyberpunk director of the Tetsuo series, who also grew up in the Shibuya ward of the 1960s.

This primal scene narrates not simply the history of the High Growth Period but also the genesis of technological landscape as another nature. It is true that I was once depressed with the destruction of beautiful nature. However, once the Tokyo Metropolitan Expressway started to be under construction for the special convenience of international visitors for the 1964 Tokyo Olympics, we immediately got used to the new atmosphere, enjoying the border between the ruins and the construction site being made ambiguous. Yesterday's junkyard was miraculously metamorphosed into another nature. Without this fantastic memory, I could not have accepted cyberpunk in the early 1980s. Then, what will happen with the 2020 Tokyo Olympics? The Tokyo Metropolitan Government decided to move the famed Tsukiji fish market by the Tokyo Bay to a huge reclaimed area in Toyosu, infamous for soil contamination, in a plan to utilize the vacant space of Tsukiji as a logistics site for the Olympics to come. What is more, Tokyo Big Sight, an enormous international exhibition venue very well-known not simply for high-tech industries but also for Comiket (Comic Market), where a number of international fans (otaku) of science fictional subculture have long enjoyed selecting and purchasing many fanzines every August and December, will be exclusively used as the International Broadcasting Center and Main Press Center for the 2020 Tokyo Olympics. This bad news led many industries and Comiket participants to voice their discontent. It is ironic that the famed monuments of technological landscape naturalized after the 1964 Tokyo Olympics are supposed to be reorganized for the 2020 Tokyo Olympics, which will make a subcultural tribe another displaced people, or another Lo Tek, if only for the year. Yes, for me the essence of cyberpunk lies in not so much cyberspace as a junkyard, where punkish Lo Teks inhabit a transnational/deterritorialized zone and keep re-appropriating street technology with an aim of overturning the dominant culture. Without the image of the junkyard inhabited by Lo Teks, Gibson could not have conceived the vision of cyberspace, which is neither outerspace nor innerspace, but which enables cyberspace cowboys to master digital alchemy.

In order to celebrate the 30th anniversary of the anime version of *Akira*, I would like to speculate upon the extraterritorial significance of post-apocalyptic ruins in cyberpunk, especially focusing upon the works ranging from William Gibson's Bridge Trilogy (1993–1998) in the 1990s through to Project Itoh's post-cyberpunk masterpiece, *Genocidal Organ* (Murase 2017; Project Itoh 2012).

2. Towards the Extraterritorial Poetics of Cyberpunk Literature

William Gibson's 1980s Cyberspace Trilogy (*Neuromancer* (1984), *Count Zero* (1986) and *Mona Lisa Overdrive* (1988)) is followed by his 1990s Bridge Trilogy (*Virtual Light* (1993), *Idoru* (1996) and *All Tomorrow's Parties* (Gibson 1999)). The Bridge Trilogy starts with the near future San Francisco Earthquake nicknamed "the Little Grande" featuring Dr. Shinya Yamazaki, a sociologist from Osaka University who spends years in the homeless' unlawfully occupied space of San Francisco Bay Bridge (*Virtual Light*). Then, it transfers its emphasis from California to Tokyo, this time exploring the possibility of a nanotech marriage between a virtual idol, Rei Toei, and a male rock'n'roller, Lo Rez, within the reconstructed extraterritorial zone of Kowloon Walled City in cyberspace and by the Tokyo Bay (*Idoru*) . Finally, the whole trilogy closes with a dramatic destruction of San Francisco Bay Bridge and the multiplication of the virtual idol through a nano-fax machine (*All Tomorrow's Parties*).

Why do I want to reconsider the significance of the trilogy, although I had already examined the first two novels in my book *Full Metal Apache* (Takayuki 2006)? The reason is very simple. The author's speculation in the Bridge Trilogy reveals his persistent obsession with the extraterritorial, which I neglected to explore in my previous discussion. Haunted by the nightmares of his own father as closely involved with Manhattan Project and the Vietnam War, Gibson discovered a way to evade the draft and expatriate himself from South Carolina to Toronto, Canada. Just the way William Faulkner defined himself as a product of the vanquished nation, that is, the American South after the Civil War, Gibson himself did not want to experience the second defeat of his nation through the Vietnam War, ending up with the original idea of cyberspace as a brand-new extraterritorial residence. As Bret Cox sharply pointed out, Gibson is a post-Faulknerian Southerner. Born in 1948 in Conway, South Carolina, he spent nearly 20 years in Southern states such as Virginia and Arizona. It is in 1968 that he moved to Toronto. Since then, except for a year's jaunt in Europe in the early 1970s, Gibson remained in Canada. In an interview conducted in 1993, Gibson confessed: "I'm still a guy from Virginia . . . I'll never really be Canadian" (quoted in Brett Cox (2007), "Fragments of a Hologram Rose for Emily: William Gibson, Southern Writer"). Being aware of himself as a Southerner, Gibson never returned to the American South for nearly half a century, familiarizing himself with the multicultural atmosphere of Vancouver where he graduated from the Department of English at the University of British Columbia in 1977. At this point, we should not forget that he took a science fiction class taught by Susan Wood, which induced him to write his first short fiction "Fragments of a Hologram Rose". What is more, without spending years in Vancouver, a multicultural city which so vividly conjures up the image of Hong

Kong as to be nicknamed "HongKongver", he could not have churned out the dark romantic image of Chiba City of *Neuromancer*. Yes, that phantasmagoric night town of Chiba City could not have been conceived without a transpacific negotiation between Vancouver and Hong Kong, if not a Japanese city itself. It is this complexity of deracinated identity that played the role of incubator for a brand-new world elsewhere, that is, cyberspace.

Before discussing the formation of expatriate sensibility, it is useful to reconsider the extraterritorial as defined by George Steiner in his book originally published in 1971. Although the extraterritorial has long been founded on the legal theory that certain persons and things, while within the territory of a foreign sovereign remained outside the reach of local judicial process, Steiner primarily redefines this adjective as someone so displaced (out of place or exiled) for various reasons as to command languages other than one's mother tongue. Thus, he renounces the myth of Romantic essentialism and gives an insight into the literary potentiality of radically displaced and virtually polylinguistic writers such as: Franz Kafka, Vladimir Nabokov, Jorges Louis Borges, Samuel Beckett, Ernest Hemingway, and others. Steiner concludes the first essay in the book as follows: "It seems proper that those who create art in a civilization of quasi-barbarism which has made so many homeless, which has torn up tongues and peoples by the root, should themselves be poets unhoused and wanderers across language" ((Steiner 1976), *Extraterritorial: Papers on Literature and the Language Revolution* (1971; New York: Atheneum, 1976) 11). Moreover, the author's reconfiguration of extraterritorial transcends the boundary of politics and linguistics so easily as to explore the frontiers of interdisciplinary field by incorporating the "mental energies and speculative forms of the sciences" into "educated literacy, into the normal life of the imagination" (Steiner xi). A rereading of Steiner today will convince us that today's list of extraterritorial writers never fails to ignore the name of William Gibson, whose displaced identity inspired him to come up with the brand-new language of cyberpunk, capable of expanding the interdisciplinary and extraterritorial zone between science and literature.

Therefore, what Gibson has consistently described in his novels is not so much the future of our civilization as the present of today's displaced people desperately seeking their own world elsewhere, another name for the extraterritorial zone as represented by cyberspace, the occupied bridge, and Kowloon Walled City both virtual and substantial.

Chronologically speaking, the moment Gibson shifts emphasis from cyberspace to junkyard was noticed when he paid the first visit to Japan in the winter of 1988. Celebrating the completion of the Cyberspace Trilogy, we had a welcome party for him at an ethnic restaurant called Sunda located just in front of NHK (Japan Broadcasting Corporation) in Jinnan, Shibuya ward, Tokyo, along with a bunch of writers, critics, editors, and film directors. Therefore, it was very natural for me to introduce him to one of our distinguished cyberpunkish filmmakers, Ishii Sogo, who had been already well-known for a pre-cyberpunk movie, *Burst City* (1982). Gibson and Ishii started talking about the possibility of their future collaboration. It is regrettable that they could not complete this project. And yet, the conversation with Ishii inspired Gibson to grasp the essence of his 1990s Bridge Trilogy. Let us take a look at his acknowledgments to *Idoru*:

> Sogho Ishii, the Japanese director, introduced me to Kowloon Walled City via the photographs of Ryuji Miyamoto. It was Ishii-san's idea that we should make a science fiction movie there. We never did, but the Walled City continued to haunt me, though I knew no more about it than I could gather from Miyamoto's stunning images, which eventually provided most of the texture for the Bridge in my novel *Virtual Light*. ("Thanks" Idoru (New York: Putnam, 1996))

If you start reading the Bridge Trilogy chronologically, you will be deeply impressed with the way San Francisco Bay Bridge occupied by the homeless is replaced by another Kowloon Walled City reconstructed in cyberspace and Tokyo Bay. However, it is Ryuji Miyamoto's photographic collection of Kowloon Walled City, the most illegally built construction in world history, that first captured Gibson's cyberpunk/Lo Tek imagination in the winter of 1988, leading him to write a short story "Skinner's Room" in 1989, based upon the image of the destroyed Bay Bridge as a collaboration with talented architects Ming Fung and Craig Hodgetts for Paolo Polledri's exhibition, "Visionary San Francisco", held in 1989 at San Francisco Museum of Modern Art. It is the Asian Gothic image of Kowloon Walled City as another extraterritorial zone that had first inspired Gibson to represent the near future San Francisco Bay Bridge occupied by the unhoused, not vice versa. Herein lies the extraterritorial seeds of transpacific cyberpunk.

3. From San Francisco Bay Bridge to Kowloon Walled City

To tell the truth, even the junk art-like bridge-scape of *Virtual Light* had already been familiar to Postmodern Japanese aesthetics. Indeed, this novel beautifully envisions the near future post-earthquake San Francisco Bay Bridge in 2005, around when California itself has split into two states—"SoCal" and "NoCal". With the Bay Bridge linking San Francisco and Oakland closed, this catastrophe induced ex-hippies and former homeless to storm the very bridge space and build themselves a new self-governing community therein, and re-design the whole bridge, whose Neo-Dadaistic arcology is to be named "Thomasson" by Yamazaki, the Japanese sociologist from Osaka University conducting research on the formation of the bridge culture. While the archetypal short story "Skinner's Room" does not allude to "Thomasson", the novel version brilliantly reflects this Neo-Dadaistic aesthetics in representing the occupied bridge:

> Its steel bones, its stranded tendons, were lost within an accretion of dreams: tattoo parlors, gaming arcades, dimly lit stalls stacked with decaying magazines, sellers of fireworks, of cut bait, betting shops, sushi bars, unlicensed pawnbrokers, herbalists, barbers, bars. Dreams of commerce, their locations generally corresponding with the decks that had once carried vehicular traffic; while above them, rising to the very peaks of the cable towers, lifted the intricately suspended barrio, with its unnumbered population and its zones of more private fantasy ... In all the world, surely, there was no more magnificent a Thomasson. (William Gibson (1993), *Virtual Light* (New York: Bantam), chp. 6, "The Bridge", pp. 62–63)

What is Thomasson? The author explains its etymology in the novel as follows:

> Thomasson was an American baseball player, very handsome, very powerful. He went to the Yomiuri Giants in 1982, for a large sum of money. Then it was discovered that he could not hit the ball. The writer Gempei Akasegawa appropriated his name to describe certain useless and inexplicable monuments, pointless yet curiously artlike features of the urban landscape. But the term has subsequently taken on other shades of meaning. If you wish, I can access and translate today's definitions in our Gendai Yogo no Kisochishiki, that is, The Basic Knowledge of Modern Times. (*Virtual Light*, Chapter 6, "The Bridge", pp. 64–65)

However, the novel gives us no further analysis of this hyperart, illustrating the point with no examples Genpei Akasegawa enumerates in downtown Tokyo. In my former article on the novel originally published in 1995, I only redefined this hyperart as closely intertwined with Marcel Duchamp and Joseph Cornell whose Dadaist works Gibson had long been fascinated with not only in *Neuromancer* but also in *Count Zero*. At that point, I simply emphasized the way Akasegawa the Neo-Dadaist radically "Japanized" Duchamp as the near-precursor of Thomasson, who "could not attain Thomassonian perfection unluckily", but whose sense of "non-art" brilliantly "corresponded with the Japanese heritage of tea ceremony represeted by Sen-no-Rikyu", in which the very natural world has persistently been considered full of "readymade" objects (Genpei Akasegawa, *Geijutsu Genron* (The Principles of Art), pp. 249–59). Therefore, when *Virtual Light* was first published in 1993, I attempted to relate the aesthetics of Neo-Dadaist art with the ecology of post-countercultural tree house Gibson must have been familiar with. With the Bridge Trilogy completed in 1999, however, I feel it indispensable to link this hyperart with Kowloon Walled City, high-technologically replicated.

In retrospect, the archeology of ruins tells us, it is the Dissolution of the Monasteries ordered by Henry VIII between 1536 and 1541 that made quite a few Catholic abbeys the typical ruins, which only attracted opportunistic businessmen and melancholy antiquaries. However, in the course of three centuries, straight forward greed was followed by ignorance and indifference, and curiosity led to veneration (Christopher Woodward (2001), *In Ruins*, p. 109). Without Henry VIII's transformation of the abbeys into ruins, English literary history could not have developed the imagination of Gothic Romance. Likewise, without postwar apocalyptic tragedies, whether natural or political, postmodern literature could not have cultivated the imagination of cyberpunk junkyard as another extraterritorial playground.

This perspective allows me to illustrate Thomasson with mysterious and indefinable objects in the Tokyo cityscape. Akasegawa once defined a Thomasson as any kind of "useless and defunct object attached to someone's property and aesthetically maintained". The kind of Thomassons he discovered included: the doorknob in a wall without a door, that driveway leading into an unbroken fence, that strange concrete, thing sprouting out of your sidewalk with no discernible purpose (John Metcalfe (2012), "Useless and Defunct City Objects Should be Called ... 'Thomassons'", (http://www.citylab.com/design/2012/05/useless-and-defunct-city-objects-are-named-thomas sons/2075). The most famous one among them is nicknamed "Yotsuya no Junsui Kaidan" (Pure staircase of Yotsuya) or simply "Yotsuya Kaidan", a flight of stairs leading into a blank wall without a door, with the handrail still being maintained. You could well be amused by this nomenclature, for "Yotsuya Kaidan" derives from a pun as the strange staircase (kaidan) located in Yotsuya, Shinjuku ward, and a ghost story (kwaidan) originated in the same town and well known as a Kabuki play performed time and again. Our contemporary high-tech city, especially in the wake of quite a few apocalypses—such as World War II, huge earthquakes, and the burst of the bubble economy—became indistinguishable from artistic ruins filled with numerous Thomassons, that is, mysterious objects which seem to be useful at first glance, but which turn out to be not simply dysfunctional but also hyperartistic. What creates Thomassons is not the genius of romantic artists in the attic, but the gaze of flaneurs strolling aimlessly through the streets. Therefore, in 1986 Akasegawa and his collegues such as Fujimori Terunobu, Matsuda Tetsuo, Minami Shimbo, and Hayashi Joji formed a society for observing objects on the streets. The strange objects compiled into their photo album included: a vegetable wiper, a vegetable television, an ornithic television, and others.

What attracts me most now is one of the Thomassons entitled "Kowloon Walled City for Chickens" discovered and photographed by Hayashi Joji in 1986. This photo captures the image of a nearly four-storied huge but chaotic chicken house with a couple of big flowerpots on top. Certainly, before writing *Virtual Light* in 1993, Gibson confessed to having seen Miyamoto Ryuji's photographic collection of Kowloon Walled City in 1988. And yet, it is indeterminable if Gibson also noticed one of many Thomassons entitled "Kowloon Walled City for Chickens" when he picked up the concept of the hyperart as perfect metaphor for bridge culture. What matters here is that already in the mid-1980s, even the founding fathers of Neo-Dadaism somehow gave an insight into an analogy between the Hyperart: Thomasson and Kowloon Walled City (See Genpei Akasegawa (2009), *Cho-Geijutsu Tomason* (HyperArt: Thomasson)).

Then, how important is Kowloon Walled City in Hong Kong for postmodern culture and literature? As summed up above, Gibson's fifth novel called *Idoru* (Gibson 1996), the companion piece of his fourth novel *Virtual Light* (Gibson 1993), features a romance between the rock'n'roller, Lo Rez, and the Asian AI heroine, Rei Toei, in 2006, almost one year after the post-earthquake events on the San Francisco Bay Bridge narrated in *Virtual Light*. Around this period, nanotech engineering enabled the post-earthquake Tokyo to be reconstructed quickly. Elaborate virtual spaces have been constructed as well, even replicating the whole "bad taste" structure of the Kowloon Walled City (Hak Nam), a place of interest in Hong Kong destroyed in 1993. Note that it is not only Gibson but also numerous postmodern artists who lamented the destruction of the greatest place of interest in Hong Kong. Thus, the 1996 publication of this novel, *Idoru*, beautifully coincides with the creation of the latest Japanese "post-cyberpunk" computer game, "Kowloon's Gate", directed by Nakaji Kimura (1997) and marketed in 1997 by Sony Music Entertainment, featuring a distinguished feng shui master who is to restore the equilibrium between yin and yang abruptly jeopardized in the very year of 1997 by the intrusion of the unreal Kowloon Walled City (within the yin area) into the real world (within the yang area). Weirdly nightmarish as it seems, the extraterritoriality of Kowloon Walled City appealed to a variety of postmodern artists and writers.

Historically speaking, the origin of Kowloon Walled City, a weird extraterritorial space of 2.7 hectares located a few-hundred meters to the northwest of Hong Kong's Kai Tak International Airport, could well be located in the Sung Dynasty of the fifth century. Nonetheless, it is after the outbreak of the Opium War in 1839 that this site came to gain more military importance. As Kenichi Ohashi spells out, with the defeat of the Ch'ing forces in 1842 the Treaty of Nanking was signed and Britain took possession of the Island of Hong Kong—prompting the Ch'ing to build an actual walled fortress in Kowloon by 1847. Even after the Treaty of Peking in 1860, which enabled Britain to obtain the Kowloon Peninsula south of Boundary Street, the Walled City of Kowloon exceptionally remained under Ch'ing jurisdiction. Therefore, this site had to retain the double status of extraterritoriality. Although Hong Kong became British legally, only this site kept being controlled by the Chinese government. Nonetheless, what with the Japanese occupation of the site in 1941 and what with the popular resistance ending up with the burning of the British Consulate in Kanton, disagreements over the status of the Kowloon Walled City between the Chinese and British governments dramatically increased. Thus, the city itself gradually became a kind of diplomatic black hole, existing in limbo between two countries, inviting a number of refugees and displaced people to inhabit the very extraterritorial site; they all wanted to avoid taxation or legal interference from the colonial government. What is more, this site was convenient for the Chinese Triad societies, which popularized the idea that it was Chinese territory and therefore was not subject to Hong Kong law to promote their illegal dealings such as gambling, drug trafficking, and prostitution. In this way, Kowloon Walled City came to be nicknamed as "a den of iniquity", "The Casba of the East", and "a hotbed of crime" (Ohashi, "The History of the Kowloon Walled City", tr. Keith Vincent in Ryuji Miyamoto (1997), *Kowloon Walled City* (Tokyo: Heibonsha Publishers, 1997), pp. 152–55).

With this history in mind, you will fully enjoy Gibson's representation of Kowloon Walled City replicated within cyberspace. With the help of an Otaku boy Masahiko usually spending hours in the site, the heroine Chia McKenzie, a 14-year-old girl from Seattle and a big fan of Lo Rez, vividly witnesses the gigantic structure:

> Chia reached up and pulled her own glasses down, over her eyes.
>
> "What do I . . . "
>
> Something at the core of things moved simultaneously in mutually impossible directions. It wasn't even like porting. Software conflict? Faint impression of light through a fluttering of rags.
>
> And then the thing before her: building or biomass or cliff face looming there, in countless unplanned strata, nothing about it even or regular. Accreted patchwork of shallow random balconies, thousands of small windows throwing back blank silver rectangles of fog. Stretching either way to the periphery of vision, and on the high, uneven crest of that ragged facade, a black for of twisted pipe, antennas sagging under vine growth of cable. And past this scribbled border a sky where colors crawled like gasoline on water.
>
> "Hak Nam," he said, beside her.
>
> "What is it?"
>
> "'City of darkness', Between the walls of the world." . . .
>
> "The Walled City is a concept of scale. Very important. Scale is place, yes? Thirty-three thousand people inhabited original. Two-point-seven hectares. As many as fourteen stories." (William Gibson, *Idoru* (New York: Putnam, 1996) Chapter 26, "Hak Nam," pp. 181–82)

The novel reaches the greatest climax when the cutting-edge nanotechnology succeeded in replicating the same City by the Tokyo Bay almost miraculously:

> The Walled City is growing. Being grown. From the fabric of the beach, wrack and wreckage of the world before things changed. (…) A thing of random human accretion, monstrous and superb, it is being reconstituted here, retranslated from its later incarnation as a realm of consensual fantasy. (Gibson, *Idoru*, chp. 46, "Fables of the Reconstruction", p. 289)

Of course, Lo Rez's desire to get married to Rei Toei as AI sounds quite childish in the first place, for Lo Rez is human, Rei artificial. However, as is the case with Zona, Chia's close friend in Mexico, who proves to be half-virtual, it is not unusual that the most intimate friend of yours might be only hovering on the boundary between the human and the artificial. This principle is also applicable of Kowloon Walled City. Now that Kowloon Walled City, despite the residents' persistent resistance, was torn down in 1993, we are able to experience it only cybernetically on the border between reality and virtual reality. The reason why the site is still alive in people's memory is very simple. As Miyamoto Ryuji himself redefined it in "A Vanished City", the preface to his photographic collection: "The Kowloon Walled City was a massive crystallization of the communal unconscious of the Chinese; a miraculous, uncommonly transcendent phenomenon of human ingenuity which just happened to rise up before our eyes" (pp. 6–7). Thus, in my guest-edited issue of the *Asahi Weekly Encyclopedia* featuring science fiction and slipstream literature (2000), I once stated that "if I'm permitted to visually represent the zeitgeist of boundary transgression, I feel no hesitation to select the Kowloon Walled City as its objective correlative … Although Chinese government destroyed it in 1993, this City still keeps inspiring writers and artists to produce novels and video games with the very site as the main setting. While it used to hover over the political boundary between Britain and China, this huge walled city now deconstructs and reinvents itself the very epistemological boundary between reality and virtual reality" (*The Asahi Weekly Encyclopedia*, No. 48 (Tokyo: Asahi Shimbun Publishers, Takayuki 2000)). With the rise of Brexit that set up a border between the EU and UK and the Trump presidency that promises to complete the US–Mexico border wall, both of which took place in the same year of 2017 and which requires displaced people to leave their ultra-conservative nations and dream of another extraterritorial zone in the second decade of the 21st century, the late Kowloon Walled City is gaining more and more significance.

4. Conclusions: Ghosts in the City, or *Genocidal Organ*

The Kowloon Walled City vanished from the earth in 1993. However, as the legendary game *Kowloon's Gate* still keeps haunting our mind, we are still likely to envision a number of ghosts and monsters very active in the imaginary City. Yes, it is the ghost of the very city that has long obsessed us, for cyberpunk has persistently questioned the boundaries between the organic and the mechanic, the living and the dead, civilization and junkyard.

Now please recall the introduction of the paper, where I started by talking about the post-apocalyptic junkyard of 2019 Neo Tokyo in *Akira* overwrapping with the construction site of the Tokyo Metropolitan Expressway fusing seamlessly with the destruction site of the beautiful botanical garden of the Institute for Nature Study in 1963 Tokyo. As *Akira* narrates the aftermath of human experimentation that had brought about the nightmare of total apocalypse, the real Institute for Nature Study secretly contains the military tragedy of human/animal experimentation that was to produce quite a few ghost stories closely related with the tunnel under the very expressway. Just like *The Ghost in the Shell* (1995) and its sequel *Innocence* (2004), we are not free from the preternatural within the techno-scape of our megalopolis. With this context in mind, it was amusing to see a fantastic cafe restaurant "Giger Bar" constructed in the late 1980s near the entrance of Shirokane tunnel right under said expressway, receiving popularity until the mid-1990s when troubles with yakuza forced the manager to close the restaurant. However, note that as the name suggested, its organic and biomechanical atmosphere was inspired by distinguished Zurich-based artist H. R. Giger, well-known for the cover jacket of prog rock band Emerson, Lake, and Palmer's *Brain Salad Surgery* (1973) and also for the art direction of Ridley Scott's film, *Alien* (1979). Famous as he is for the hardcore cyberpunk *Blade Runner* (1982), Scott should be further appreciated as the prophet of alternative cyberpunk as is outlined in *Alien* (1979), one of whose sequels (*Alien 3*) was to be written by William Gibson himself in vain. Anyway, to me it does not seem coincidental that the heyday of the bubble economy around 1990 saw the cyberpunk taste of Giger Bar Tokyo located just in the neighborhood of Shirokane Tunnel haunted by the ghosts of pre-cyberpunkish biomechanical experiments.

Let me close the chapter with a note on the latest fruit of transpacific cyberpunk, Murase Shukou's directed anime, *Genocidal Organ* (Murase 2017), a faithful adaptation of self-claimed cyberpunk writer Project Itoh's masterpiece, finalist for the seventh Komatsu Sakyo Award in 2006 and originally published in 2007. This title simply presupposes the existence of genocidal organ deeply embedded within human linguistic ability, which will boot up through a secret code discovered and mastered by an enigmatic linguist, John Paul. It is undoubtedly the march of folly from the Rwandan genocide in 1994 through the September 11 Terrorist Attacks and the Iraq War in the early 2000s that invited the author Project Itoh to create this mysterious character John Paul, a former PR man who grasped the secrecy of the genocidal organ within the human organism. Just the way Tyron Slothrop's making love never fails to be followed by the assault of a V2 rocket in Thomas Pynchon's pre-cyberpunk mega-novel *Gravity's Rainbow* (1973), John Paul travels "from war zone to war zone" (p. 57), as if he is the prime mover of war itself. He keeps causing wars by secretly driving the genocidal organ and producing a number of ruins, the homeland of extraterritorial and Lo Tek people including himself. Thus, desperately seeking John Paul, the protagonist/narrator Clavis Shepherd recognizes the fact: "This man who we'd tried and failed to kill on numerous occasions had somehow been a catalyst for genocide in locations throughout the world. For some reason, when this man went into a country, it plunged into chaos. For some reason, when this man went into a country, the blood of innocents would pour forth" (p. 78). The concept of the novel itself very naturally reminds us of what Hannah Arendt called the "banality of evil" in her *Eichmann in Jerusalem* (Arendt 1994), Project Itoh's originality lies not in his narrativization of Eichmann-like characters in war zones but in his speculation on an imaginary organ inherent deep within human linguistic competence that gets started through the speech act of the very spell John Paul discovered. Although the precise identity of the spell remains unknown throughout the novel, the mysterious stranger John Paul could well be reconceived as a kind of talented cyberspace cowboy who could very easily get access to the secret of human nature that could otherwise have been kept confidential. In this sense, *Genocidal Organ* also recalls the hardcore cyberpunk, *Akira*, which centers around the secret of the universe the enfant terrible Akira conceals within himself. Furthermore, we should not forget that while genocidal organ remains a secrecy for human beings, the rapid growth of the huge African industry of artificial flesh was made possible through harvesting from "genetically modified aquatic mammals such as dolphins and whales" (p. 259). On one hand, if we focus on the narrative of John Paul, it's readable as a hardcore Gibsonian Quest for the Holy Grail: while Gibson's characters desperately seek for treasure, Itoh's hero looks for death. On the other hand, if we take a careful look at artificial flesh employed not only for military operations but also for various reasons, the whole narrative begins to show the post-Gigerian aesthetics at the risk of today's eco-critical imperative.

However, what I would like to call your attention to most is the post-apocalyptic aspect of the novel/anime of *Genocidal Organ*. Although cyberpunk narratives have scarcely been discussed in the eschatological context, its genealogy from *Blade Runner*, the Cyberspace Trilogy/the Bridge Trilogy, *Akira*, down to *Genocidal Organ* all presupposes a kind of end of the world that had already taken place before the beginning of each story. If Gibson invented cyberspace as an extraterritorial zone exempt either from the draft or from nuclear politics his own father had been responsible for, it makes perfect sense to reconsider cyberpunk as another post-apocalyptic narrative. And we have to note that also in this respect Project Itoh gives a deep insight into the essence of war. In the wake of nuclear destruction of an Eastern European city:

> The world changed the day the bomb exploded in Sarajevo. The era of Hiroshima was brought to a close once and for all. All around the world the military suddenly started waking up to the fact that their theoretical weapons of mutually assured destruction were maybe not so theoretical after all. Nuclear weapons were back on the table as an option. (p. 205)

Theoretically speaking, the end of the world should allow for no survivors. However, it is true that post-apocalyptic narratives cannot fail to describe the life of survivors without the sense of contradiction, as is seen in Komatsu Sakyo's *Virus* (1964) which depicts the way the world sees apocalypse twice, first caused by a mysterious pandemic and second by a total nuclear war. Note that while Komatsu, one of the founding fathers of modern Japanese science fiction, closed his post-apocalyptic narrative with an optimistic vision of humankind, Project Itoh, who Komatsu himself discovered and selected as finalist for the seventh Komatsu Sakyo award, concludes the novel by letting the narrator Clavis Shepard inherit the grammar of genocide from John Paul which he rammed home into the United States. "The deep structure of genocide has spread across the whole of America, quickly and easily, using English as its vector" (p. 297). Now we witness the birth of new Lo Tek in the 21st century, who is able not only to control but also to destroy the world through his mastery of the new grammar. A big fan of J. G. Ballard, a major speculative fictionist who published a number of dystopian stories, John Paul very possibly dreamed of a world in ruins. "Spaceship Mother Earth, a giant, unmanned satellite that silently orbited the sun. A world where aliens would land one day and find only the traces of civilization long destroyed, the empty husks of building after building whose inhabitants had long since disappeared" (p. 107). In the meantime, William Gibson, another big fan of Ballard, has also been obsessed with apocalyptic and posthumanist visions, which have tremendous impact upon the post-apocalyptic simulated reality, "the desert of the real", beautifully described in the Matrix trilogy (1999–2003) directed by the Wachowski Brothers. Although visual technology, as Akira Mizuta Lippit (2005) pointed out in *Atomic Light (Shadow Optics)*, came to transfigure the impact of the atomic bombings of Hiroshima and Nagasaki into the tropes of invisibility or transparency, it is also true that from its inception cyberpunk literature has never been immune from the nightmare of nuclear apocalypse.

Thus, transpacific cyberpunks will continue narrating the world after the end of the world, refreshing the memory of Hiroshima and Nagasaki as the first nuclear war. This is the reason why our survivors will also keep seeking the extraterritorial zone, making the border between the ruins and the construction site ambiguous.

Acknowledgments: The earliest version of this paper was first delivered as a keynote lecture at the annual conference of *Mechademia* held at Minneapolis College of Arts and Design on 23 September 2017 (Saturday). The author expresses the deepest gratitude to Frenchy Lunning, the Editor-in-Chief of *Mechademia*.

Conflicts of Interest: The author declares no conflict of interest.

References

Akasegawa, Genpei. 2009. *Cho-Geijutsu Tomason (Hyperart: Thomasson)*. Translated by Matthew Fargo. New York: Kaya Press.

Arendt, Hannah. 1994. *Eichmann in Jerusalem: a Report on the Banality of Evil*. New York: Penguin.

Cox, F. Brett. 2007. Fragments of a Hologram Rose for Emily: William Gibson, Southern Writer. In *The Cultural Influences of William Gibson, the "Father" of Cyberpunk Science Fiction: Critical and Interpretive Essays*. Edited by Yoke, Carl and Carol L. Robinson. Lewiston: Edwin Mellen.

Gibson, William. 1993. *Virtual Light*. New York: Bantam.

Gibson, William. 1996. *Idoru*. New York: Penguin.

Gibson, William. 1999. *All Tomorrow's Parties*. New York: Putnam.

Kimura, Nakaji. 1997. *Kowloon's Gate*. Tokyo: Sony Music Entertainment.

Lippit, Akira Mizutat. 2005. *Atomic Light (Shadow Optics)*. Minneapolis: U of Minnesota P.

Metcalfe, John. 2012. Useless and Defunct City Objects Should be Called … 'Thomassons'. Available online: http://www.citylab.com/design/2012/05/useless-and-defunct-city-objects-are-named-thomassons/2075/ (accessed on 4 December 2017).

Miyamoto, Ryuji. 1997. *Kowloon Walled City*. Translated by Keith Vincent. Tokyo: Heibonsha.

Murase, Shukou. 2017. *Genocidal Organ*. Tokyo: Toho.

Otomo, Katsuhiro. 1982–1993. *Akira*. 6 vols; Tokyo: Kodansha.

Otomo, Katsuhiro. 1988. *Akira*. Tokyo: Toho.

Project Itoh. 2012. *Genocidal Organ*. Translated by Edwin Hawkes. San Francisco: Haikasoru.

Pynchon, Thomas. 1984. Is It O.K. to be a Luddite? *The New York Times Book Review* 1: 40–41.

Steiner, George. 1976. *Extraterritorial: Papers on Literature and the Language Revolution*. New York: Atheneum.

Takayuki, Tatsumi, ed. 2000. *The Asahi Weekly Encyclopedia No. 48*. Tokyo: Asahi Shimbun Publishers.

Takayuki, Tatsumi. 2006. *Full Metal Apache: Transactions between Cyberpunk Japan and Avant-Pop America*. Durham: Duke UP.

Woodward, Christopher. 2001. *In Ruins*. New York: Pantheon.

MDPI

St. Alban-Anlage 66

4052 Basel

Switzerland

Tel. +41 61 683 77 34

Fax +41 61 302 89 18

www.mdpi.com

Arts Editorial Office

E-mail: arts@mdpi.com

www.mdpi.com/journal/arts

www.ingramcontent.com/pod-product-compliance
Lightning Source LLC
Chambersburg PA
CBHW051316020426
42333CB00028B/3365